MW01484328

Line of Blood

Other Books By Jana Marcus

*In The Shadow of the Vampire: Reflections from
the World of Anne Rice*

Transfigurations

LINE OF BLOOD

Uncovering a Secret Legacy
of Mobsters, Money, and Murder

Jana Marcus

7 Angels Press

Copyright © 2020 by Jana Marcus. All Rights Reserved.

Thousands of pages of local, state, and federal case documents, including witness statements, autopsy reports, catalogs of evidence, crime scene photos, interrogation transcrip-
tions, news articles, personal correspondences and interviews, as well as other files of
consequence to the Babchick and Reles murders, the Lucky Luciano trial, as well as the
Kovner, Druckman, and Malinski cases, were meticulously researched and studied in
preparation for this book. As no person mentioned in this book has been found, by a
court of law, to be guilty of the Babchick and Reles murders, no guilt should be presumed.
Any views, opinions, or assumptions expressed herein are based solely on the author's
wish to synthesize raw material into a logical narrative and do not reflect the official policy or position of any agency known to the author. Some names of the living have been
changed to respect their privacy.

"Uncle Abe," *Pages From A Scrapbook of Immigrants,* by Morton Marcus. Copyright ©
1988. Coffee House Press, Minneapolis. Reprinted by permission of the Morton Marcus
Trust.

For information about permission to reproduce selections from this book,
write to 7 Angels Press, P.O. Box 467, Aptos, CA 95001 www.7angelspress.com

Library of Congress Catalogue number 2020908048

ISBN 978-0-9833434-3-1

Book cover design © 2019 by Jana Marcus & Eric Sassaman

Text designed and typeset at Side By Side Studios, San Francisco

Author photo © by Jana Marcus

For my nephew, Zachary

Where you come from does not define who you are,
but honoring the past is a prologue to who you can become.

"There are three sides to every story. Mine, yours, and the truth."

—Joe Massino, former boss of the Bonanno crime family

Contents

Line of Blood

BABCZUK FAMILY TREE

Anna Shifra Eizenman & Morris Jacob Babczuk

(1877–1946)   (1873–1930)

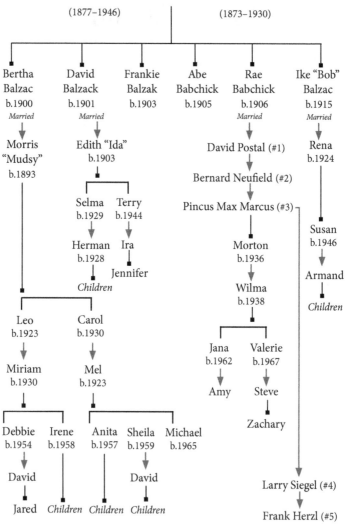

Bertha Balzac b.1900 — *Married* — Morris "Mudsy" b.1893

David Balzack b.1901 — *Married* — Edith "Ida" b.1903

Frankie Balzak b.1903

Abe Babchick b.1905

Rae Babchick b.1906 — *Married* — David Postal (#1); Bernard Neufield (#2); Pincus Max Marcus (#3)

Ike "Bob" Balzac b.1915 — *Married* — Rena b.1924

Selma b.1929 — Herman b.1928

Terry b.1944 — Ira — Jennifer — *Children*

Morton b.1936 — Wilma b.1938

Susan b.1946 — Armand — *Children*

Leo b.1923 — Miriam b.1930

Carol b.1930 — Mel b.1923

Jana b.1962 — Amy

Valerie b.1967 — Steve — Zachary

Debbie b.1954 — David — Jared

Irene b.1958 — *Children*

Anita b.1957 — *Children*

Sheila b.1959 — David — *Children*

Michael b.1965

Larry Siegel (#4)

Frank Herzl (#5)

Introduction

My father was the master of stories—unrivaled when it came to weaving a tale. My sister Valerie and I were mesmerized by his stories as we grew up, drawn into his world, and kept at the edge of our seats as he acted out colorful characters with great enthusiasm—his eyebrows raised and salt-and-pepper beard jutting up and down.

He was poet, writer, and film historian Morton Marcus. A professor by trade—which meant he loved to tell a good story and get your mind working, thinking about things as you never had before. He had a gift for making everything interesting, even the most mundane seemed magical.

Our parents divorced when Valerie and I were small, so weekends with Dad became one of the highlights of my young life growing up in the Northern California coastal town of Santa Cruz. Every Friday night was dinner out and a movie, followed by a Saturday adventure exploring a museum, a Greek street festival, or a road trip in the Bay Area.

As I became a teenager, my father and I would take long walks on the beach or drives through the redwood forest, talking about the mysteries of the universe, the origins of jazz, or the history of American cinema. He was a walking encyclopedia—he knew something about everything.

The stories I loved the most were about our family's early years. Some tales were fantastic and heroic, like the time he was teaching my mother to drive, and the car stalled on railroad tracks in a ravine. As a locomotive came speeding toward them, Dad pushed the vehicle onto the adjacent hill and held it in place as the train passed below. Or, the story about how he stumbled upon a hidden UFO aircraft at Scott Airforce Base when he was in the service in 1956.

Then there were the more romantic tales, such as how our parents met as teenagers at a party on Long Island in the 1950s. Stories of our mother studying dance with Martha Graham and Dad befriending soon-to-be-famous literary figures at the Iowa Writer's Workshop. Or, the story about how beautiful Mom looked in a red sweater when she appeared on the TV game show *Jeopardy* and won enough money for them to "escape New York" and travel across the country in their powder blue VW Bug to start their family in San Francisco.

That was how Dad explained why we were raised in California, although all our relatives lived on the East Coast, 3000 miles away.

I felt very connected to my mother's side of the family in New York. We saw them once a year and had lots of cousins our own age, aunts and uncles who played games with us or just let us run around and be kids. On Dad's side of the family, we only knew his mother, Grandma Rae. She lived in a fancy apartment in New York City that faced Central Park and was very persnickety about manners, appearances, and other things she labeled as "having class." She had once been very wealthy, and Dad had been her only child. We had no grandfather—Dad's father was entirely out of the picture.

"Why did you need to escape New York?" I asked.

"I longed for a place to truly call home, and the redwoods were calling me," my father mused.

That was his take. My mother had another version altogether. For her, the escape from New York was about getting away from her mother-in-law, Grandma Rae, who was constantly criticizing her. I was too young at the time to understand whatever family dynamics were going on. But, our parent's "escape" meant that my sister and I didn't have significant ties with Dad's side of the family—whoever they might be—when we were growing up.

One Saturday afternoon in 1978, when I was 16-years-old, Dad told me the most compelling family story of them all. We were eating corned beef on rye and drinking Dr. Brown's Cream Soda at a deli in Santa Cruz (which he complained wasn't like a *real* East Coast Jewish deli) when he started telling me about his childhood in New York. It wasn't just one story, either. It was several, all interconnecting to make for the most epic tale he had ever told. He gestured wildly with his hands, portraying his aunts and uncles, mimicking their thick Brooklyn accents.

He called his youth an "Oliver Twist childhood with a Jewish accent"—a devilish snicker spread across his lips as he told how Grandma Rae was as glamorous as a movie star, had been married five times, and sent him away to boarding school starting at the age of three. He'd only met his wealthy father once or twice when he was very young. At the dramatic parts, when he attempted to run away from the schools and try to go home, Dad's voice would go up an octave, his blue eyes twinkling. I assumed he was exaggerating. He was known to do that—but always in such an alluring and demonstrative way that I continually wanted more.

There were many colorful characters in his tale: grandparents from the Ukraine who worked in sweatshops after coming to America; Uncle Frankie the Cowboy, who broke horses in the West; Uncle "Jungle Jim," who invented the famous coconut-whip drink; Uncle Ike who failed the bar exam so many times he ended up working as an orderly in a psychiatric hospital; Aunt Bertha who covered her furniture in plastic and barely spoke English; and something about a gambler who was killed.

Then there were his favorite cousins—Aunt Bertha's children, Leo and Carol. With no siblings or father, and a mother who was not around much, Dad credited them for shaping his childhood. Carol babysat young Mort when he was home from school, dragging him on adventures through Brooklyn. Leo, 11-years Mort's senior, became his only male role model, taking him to ball games, teaching him street fighting as he got older, and other "guy" things of that nature.

Dad's stories resembled those old black and white movies he would take us to see every Friday night at the Sash Mill Cinema. The rough edges of his lonely childhood story still succeeded in glamourizing a family that thrived in a New York City that I could only read about, or see glimpses of in those old noir films.

That same summer, Valerie and I traveled to Miami Beach to see our maternal Grandma Jackie, and then flew to New York City to stay with Grandma Rae. In Miami, Grandma Jackie reminisced about her father, who made fur hats and coat collars for the Cossack Army in the Russian Pale Settlement, and the Harris relatives who ran the Broadway theaters in New York. I tried to write down all those Russian-Jewish names as fast as she could spout them off, scribbling names and birthdays until they became a maze of inkblots on paper.

When we visited Grandma Rae in New York, she hosted a family dinner party, serving her famous cabbage soup. Some of Dad's relatives ventured up from Brooklyn to her fancy Manhattan apartment. That's when I first met his two older cousins, Leo and Carol. They were both rousing storytellers, just like Dad. Everyone shouted over each other in loud, broken Yiddish and I remember feeling a bit overwhelmed with culture shock. Still, I loved the tidbits of stories they shared about Uncle Frankie the Cowboy and Dad as a boy. I took their stories at face value—I had no reason to think otherwise. I became increasingly interested in our family's roots, particularly my grandmother's generation and what their lives had been like in the Old Country.

By age 17, understanding who our family was and their place on the timeline of history became all-important to me. My friends were looking to the future and college, while I was looking to the past. I went to the library and found out how to make a family tree. This was long before the personal computer was even a thought. I checked out thick books on genealogy, which I never read, and got the address to the Church of Latter-Day Saints Family Library in Salt Lake City, which I knew I'd probably never visit. I sent letters, with a questionnaire I'd copied from a book, to relatives on both sides of my family. Slowly, I accumulated enough information to construct a family tree.

My maternal tree had shaped up nicely, but on my father's side of the family, I had practically no information. I received a return letter from Dad's Uncle Ike, saying, "Good luck in your search, but I'm sure no one wants to talk about the past." When I would ask Grandma Rae questions during our annual visits, she'd merely shake her head and shush me away. At the time, I lived so far away from the New York clan—and I couldn't fathom how a Mormon organization like the LDS could help me learn about my Russian-Jewish heritage—that I decided to packed-away all my notes and charts for another time.

As it turned out, that "other time" came 10 years later, in the late 1980s, when I was living in New York City. It was then that I stumbled upon the first clue into the real story of my father's family. In what turned out to be a 28-year journey into discovering the truth behind what I thought were my father's exaggerated stories, a series of bizarre coincidences came my way—signs, if you will—that led me on a quest to thread together a history, not only of my family but of New York City itself, with more unbelievable twists-and-turns than my father could ever have fabricated.

This is the story of what happened to me.

PART
I

1

The Secret Drawer

New York City, 1988

Central Park South is a three-block area of 59th Street, between 5th and 8th Avenues, adjacent to the bottom of Central Park. Lined with horse-drawn carriages driven by men in top hats and sprinkled with five-star hotels, it's a ritzy patch of the city that is often congested with tourists and the occasional parade.

But, I didn't think of it as a fancy, upper-class neighborhood, and maybe I didn't really have an appreciation for what it meant to live on this stretch of Manhattan real estate. To me, Central Park South with its dense tree-lined entrances to the park, patinaed statuary, and shining brass banisters of upscale residences, was just where my paternal Grandma Rae had lived for decades.

My parents moved a lot when I was a child, especially after their divorce in 1972, so Grandma's apartment on the park felt like the permanent family home, filled with beautiful furniture, antiques, and wonderful food.

I'd been living in New York City for the past few years, since graduating college and leaving the sandy beaches of Northern California to pursue a career in photography. I was in love with New York. Rich with history at every turn, its crowded and buzzing streets inspired me artistically in a way that the peaceful, open spaces of California never could.

I was busy living the life of a 26-year-old artist in Manhattan—which included working as a photographer, nightclubbing, and spending a lot of time trying to be hip at all costs. I was also spending a lot of time with

Grandma Rae. She was thrilled when I moved to the City. I immediately became her best friend and received up to five phone calls a day regarding whether I was warm enough and eating properly.

It was a cold January day, as I strolled down Broadway from my West End Avenue apartment towards Grandma's house. She was preparing brunch for us, before cooking a family dinner that evening in honor of my father, who was flying in from California.

I rounded Columbus Circle and crossed over to 7th Avenue, passing the New York Athletic Club—the same spot where Cary Grant was whisked away in a taxi in *North by Northwest,* having stumbled into a shadowy world of crime and intrigue. I smiled to myself, remembering when I first saw that film with my father. I may not have missed the beaches, but I did miss my immediate family and was filled with excitement to see Dad. I hadn't seen him in almost a year.

He rarely came to New York, grumbling that it was no longer the city he grew up in. But, after many years, he was returning to see the family and obtain their blessings on a new book of poetry he was writing about their journey to America at the beginning of the 20th century.

As I approached 116 Central Park South, Luis the doorman was already holding the door ajar with one gloved hand and tipping his captain's hat toward me with a wink. He had watched me grow up over the years and no longer bothered to buzz Grandma's intercom to announce I'd arrived.

I crossed the marble-floored lobby and checked myself in the bank of mirrors across from the elevators. I hoped Grandma wouldn't give me a hard time about my appearance, which was often much too "downtown" for her liking. My dark, thick, curly hair fell across the shoulders of a long, vintage overcoat, that hid an oversized sweater and black leggings. Only my silver-tipped cowboy boots were exposed. I had tried to tame my East Village eclectic style for the family gathering. "Whatever," I sighed, looking at my reflection.

My outfit would probably illicit whispers from family members, but I didn't really care. I didn't have a deep connection with this side of the family. My sister and I had been raised in the freethinking, artistic milieu of our Haight-Ashbury era parents, and there didn't appear to be much common thread with the Brooklyn clan. Yet, I adored the rare occasions when we were all together. It was a big family—full of Slavic loudness and a *Fiddler on the Roof* zest for life. When we were all together, it was beautiful chaos.

As the elevator opened on the 7th floor, Grandma Rae was already standing with her apartment door ajar waiting for me.

"Bubelah!" she hollered down the hallway.

Even though I was a grown woman she still grabbed me tightly, slobbered kisses on my cheek as she had since I was a child, then wiped away her spittle with a final pat on my face, snarling, "You!...*shaineh maidel!*" Her greeting was always a dichotomy of calling me a beautiful girl and sneering at the same time. Then her expression would abruptly turn to a boisterous laugh.

"Come, come and eat," she demanded, pulling me into the apartment with a firm grip of her liver-spotted hand that sported a giant yellow topaz ring.

We sat and ate matzoh brei in the small kitchen. She smothered me with questions about the men I was dating, the food crumbling from her lips onto her large chest, staining the stains on the housedress which covered designer clothes.

From across the table Grandma shoved a $50 bill in my hand. "Go see my faygeleh hairdresser and get your hair straightened. Jewish curls don't become you." She stared at me lovingly for a moment, and then crinkled her brow declaring, "What the hell's the matter with you? You'll never get a decent man if you keep wearing those shmattas and boots. Listen to what I tell you—you need a softer look." She sized me up and down again. "Oy, yoy, yoy," she spewed in a pained tone looking at my hands. "Stop with the schlocky black nail polish already!"

She always wanted to teach me a lesson, have me understand that the only way to get ahead in life was to look good, dress well, and end up with a doctor or a lawyer. A typical Jewish grandmother—at least that was what I always thought. Yet often her sapphire blue eyes drifted across the room to contemplate something far-off. I often wondered what she reflected upon in those moments.

Rae Marcus, my grandmother, was 81-years-old at the time. She loved entertaining, and at that point in her life she wouldn't dream of venturing down to Brooklyn to see relatives. They all came to her. The matriarch of the family, she held court at her fancy address, preparing, as usual, to impress them with fine food and wine. She was the one who got out of Brooklyn. She was the one who married several times into money. She was the one they looked to as a symbol of betterment.

Grandma had a strange love-hate relationship with me. She adored me as the daughter she never had and talked about me constantly to others. Yet, she couldn't control me the way she wanted to—couldn't shape my life. That's what she disliked about me.

I was of a generation with different values and ideas then the ones she had at my age. Her dreams of a luxurious life through marriage to a rich man meant nothing to me, yet she kept trying to make me fit into her mold. She couldn't understand how I saw myself in the world and how I wanted to express myself as an artist, be independent, single. Grandma constantly nagged that I didn't know my own worth. But what was her definition of worth? I had no aspirations to be a member of high society or marry a man who would take care of me financially.

We had many good times together—adventures at Carnegie Hall, box seats at the opera and ballet, eating in fancy restaurants, and laughing together hysterically about something silly. She had a sharp wit and could be wildly fun. Those were the times she told me she loved me.

I was also there for the bad times when she would fly into a rage from unmet expectations or bitter disappointments which she claimed were caused by family members—which now included me because I was in close proximity.

I was the only immediate family member who had really tried to have a relationship of any substantial depth with her. My father found her maddening, and most of the relatives stayed at arms-length due to her mood swings and gossipy ways. Yet, they all admired her and counted on her financial help when times were tough. She had isolated almost everyone except for her niece and nephew, Leo and Carol, who were extremely loyal to her.

Grandma could also be very unpredictable. A couple of years earlier, when I had been apartment hunting and briefly staying with her, she suddenly woke me one morning, throwing the covers off me in a single swoop and yelling, "I can't have you here anymore, get out of my house!" Confused, I asked what was going on, but she ignored me, marched to the front door, and proceeded to throw my luggage and clothes out into the hallway, hollering in Yiddish that I was lazy and ungrateful.

As I dashed out of the apartment to retrieve my belongings, she slammed the front door shut and locked it. Only wearing pajamas, I stood in the hallway of the 7th floor, dazed by her actions, until a concerned neighbor opened her door and let me in to change my clothes.

I didn't speak to Grandma for a couple of months after that. Then, one day she called me out of the blue, acted as nothing had ever happened, and wanted to go to the movies. She had a conveniently selective memory. As time went on, and she kept calling, I felt that if I was very old and had isolated everyone in my life, I would want someone to give me another chance. So, I cautiously went back to being present in her life.

Grandma Rae was a very difficult and complicated woman, but I loved her. Because I had been so close to her fire I was sure I knew her better than anyone else did.

"Your cousin Debbie is a real shit-ass!" she suddenly blurted out of nowhere. "Who does she think she is asking me to leave her my mink coat? She can have the stole instead!" She immediately got up from the kitchen table and shuffled in her pink slippers to the living room. I was always shocked when she cursed. In public she had the demeanor of a lady, someone cultured and refined. But she was not bred to it. She had carefully learned to be a sophisticate during her lifetime.

I followed her into the living room where we started to set the mahogany dining table for twelve, rearranging the silver and the Booths' porcelain china for the dinner party.

"Always set your table the night before. It's easier…and don't let cousin Debbie hang her coat in the front closet tonight…if she sees the mink she'll start in on me …oy, gevalt!" She threw her hands in the air, shaking her head.

"…and that Carol with her children, always putting the soda bottles on the table! So classless! She should never get the $4000 crystal vase… you hear me?" Grandma was constantly repeating the monetary value of her personal items to me, and declaring who should get what when she died. Her voice echoed as she quickly scampered between the kitchen and the dining room. I could barely keep up with her.

After she reminded me which fork went where, she no longer wanted my help, and in my usual fashion I exited to her bedroom. Grandma ran a small designer dress business out of her apartment for wealthy women in the neighborhood. Her closets were always bursting with beautiful apparel she bought wholesale in the garment district—the labels were taken out and replaced with designer tags. I looked through her collection of ready-to-wear every time I came to visit.

Her bedroom also housed "the secret drawer." This drawer, at the bottom of her dresser, wasn't really a secret, but it contained ancient treasures my sister and I loved to rummage through. We always found something new and curious, thus the name. It was filled with photographs and papers haphazardly shoved away. They were remnants of another era. Beautiful Rae in diamonds and furs with unknown men at the 21 Club, Rae riding horseback in Central Park, trips to Europe and Florida, handsome men with slicked-back hair in suits and overcoats. It was a glamorous New York of the 1930s and 40s—a New York we'd never know. A Rae we'd never know. Because of her glitzy past, my sister and I had affectionately nicknamed her "Glamour Granny."

With time to waste as I awaited the arrival of my father and the rest of the family, I pulled open the drawer, sat crossed-legged on the floor, and began to explore. I slipped on the rhinestone casts of Grandma's original diamond jewelry, like a little girl playing dress-up, and settled in for venturing through the piles of Rae's memories. I giggled as I found photos of my first birthday party and Dad in the Air Force.

"Grandma, you look so beautiful with these flowers in your hair…," I yelled from the bedroom. She wandered in, shoving a piece of matzoh in her mouth. "Oy, you found the picture of me winning the dance contest at the Stork Club in 1945. I was so gorgeous! Everyone would stop and stare at me wherever I went. Aacchh…," she turned to leave. "You must use your looks while you have them!" she hollered, her hand waving in the air.

Toward the back of the drawer I found a withered envelope, buried under the weight of hundreds of loose photographs. It was yellowed and torn, and inside, neatly folded, was a disintegrating newspaper article. I gingerly opened it and a bold headline read, "Neighbors Ignorant of Babchick's Racket." It was from the *New York Daily Mirror*, dated Friday, September 26, 1941. It read:

> Thick-necked, casaba faced, Abie Babchick was polite to the neighbors in the New Lots section of Brownsville. Maybe he hadn't been to high school and maybe he kept to himself too much, but he was a good boy—for all those neighbors knew, he grew up to be a good man. "Abie must be doing pretty good in that restaurant," they said when they saw him pull up before his mother's house in an expensive car.
>
> And in a very human way they were glad and a little jealous. They were glad for Abie's mother, father, two brothers and a sister, all good people. They were slightly envious of the success achieved by the thick-necked, close-mouthed boy without education.
>
> Abie—who will be buried today, victim of gang guns—was doing well, but not in any way his family or neighbors could know. Abie was making good to the tune of $8,000 a day gross in the policy racket. The man who had been the boy who never talked much but was always polite, was the policy king of large sections of Brooklyn, known as "Jew Murphy." What could the neighbors know of this Abie? They knew he was partial to brown, that he must be rich, that he had few friends. And that is little to know of a boy who was born and raised in the neighborhood. From police sources a clearer picture can be drawn.
>
> His rise into big money gambling hinged on the favoritism shown him by Abe Reles, who lived "just around the corner" in New Lots. To Reles, Babchick long paid regular tribute and was permitted to "bank" a portion of the huge policy receipts. When Reles, enmeshed in operations of Murder Incorporated, had to drop the policy racket, Babchick took over. For some eight years he had been at the top.
>
> Unmarried, with no known girlfriends, he seemed to have an almost frenzied respect for domesticity. He froze employees who asked for a dol-

lar raise, but if he heard one was expecting a baby, or if a wife or child were ill, he would spend thousands to help out.

His mother is desperately ill of a heart ailment. His brothers are hard-working, respectable men. In truth, one way, they've made good. But until the abandoned gang car was found Wednesday with his body in it, Abie was regarded by the neighbors as the quiet, polite boy who had made good.[1]

"Jankaleh, come watch how I make the brisket!" Grandma called from the kitchen.

Who was Abie? What was a policy racket? I tucked everything back into the drawer and went to help Grandma in the kitchen.

I had asked her many times when I was a teenager in family tree building mode, the names of her brothers and sisters. Her simple answer of their names was often followed by a string of Yiddish phrases that came across like voodoo curses as if she were banishing them to Hell. I called it her "Jew-doo." For instance, when mentioning her youngest brother Ike, she would holler, "*Ikh lib gehat zey, naronim on kropeveh vaksen on regen!*" Then break into laughter. I would look at her questioningly and she would respond by shrugging her shoulders and translating: "Fools and weeds both grow without rain."

Back then I thought that was all there was to know. This time I was hoping for a more extended answer as I asked her, once again, the names of her siblings.

"Don't ask, darling, they are all gone now. May their memory be a blessing." She didn't look up from the stove as she replied, then quickly changed the subject to another cousin who annoyed her.

The strange article I'd found in the secret drawer was intriguing. I would ask about it when the family arrived.

By 4 p.m., apartment 7D was abuzz with reunion and conversation. Dad had arrived—his beard now a bit grayer and his head a bit balder, looking like a typical casual Californian in jeans and a velour shirt. He greeted cousins, kissing and hugging, and making sure they placed their coats in the bedroom—not the front closet—according to Grandma's wishes.

Carol arrived with her husband and children. "Mortela, you're so handsome!" she exclaimed, hugging Mort tightly and then affectionately rubbing his bald spot.

Next, Leo arrived, bursting through the front door and striking a pose with his legs bent and arms outstretched toward Mort. "Mottle!" he yelled, "Feel my thighs!" The muscular butcher-turned-summons-server proceeded to plop himself on the delicate damask sofa with his prim English wife, Miriam, who just watched everyone and seldom spoke.

"Mottle, remember the time I took you to see the Dodgers at Ebbet's Field?" Leo bellowed in his rich Brooklyn accent. Mort joined him in the living room and they howled with laughter. Lovable Leo and Carol may have been my father's older cousins, but to everyone they were just Uncle Leo and Aunt Carol.

One by one the cousins arrived. We ate. We drank. The soda bottles were on the table. Grandma Rae rushed around to serve everyone as voices got louder and louder, each person shouting atop the other, until the sound was a legato of white noise.

As dinner ended, cousins retreated to separate corners of the apartment for conversations. Cousin Debbie, Leo's daughter, who never said a word about Grandma's mink coat, chased after her screaming 8-year-old son Jared. Carol's son Michael was assessing Grandma's things for their potential value. Cousins Terry and Selma discussed housing prices in New Jersey, and Grandma was in the kitchen preparing dessert—tasting each serving as she dished it onto the china.

Carol went to rummage through the coats in the bedroom for a hard candy, and I went to join her.

"Hey, Aunt Carol," I asked, "do you know who someone named Abie was?"

She suddenly froze, hunched over the pile of coats. Slowly she turned her round body toward me, peering over the rim of her glasses.

"Whaa? Whaa'd ya'say?"

"Who was Abie?"

"Oy, God rest his soul, go ask your Uncle Leo. And don't talk so loud!"

I returned to the living room making a beeline for my father and Leo, who were still laughing uproariously, this time about some memory of their Uncle Dave, a.k.a. "Jungle Jim."

"Hey," I interrupted them, "do you know who someone named Abie Babchick was?"

"Abie?" Leo looked at me with surprise, then lowered his voice and leant toward me, as if about to reveal a secret of great proportions, and whispered, "Don't let your grandmother hear you say that name."

"He was one of Grandma's brothers," Dad replied.

"Look, we shouldn't talk about this right now," Leo said, shaking his head.

"I found a newspaper clipping in Grandma's secret drawer, and…"

"Not now!" Leo interrupted me, swaying his arms in a hush-hush motion as Grandma Rae entered the living room announcing dessert.

"What did you find?" Dad asked.

"Come look," I turned to go to the bedroom, my father and Leo following, closing the bedroom door behind them. I pulled out the drawer, felt around for the withered envelope, took out the fragile newspaper article, and gingerly handed it to Mort.

"Look what you found!" Leo chuckled with astonishment.

After skimming the article, Dad looked at Leo. "This is OUR Uncle Abe?"

Leo winked, "That's our Abie. It was a terrible thing that went on."

Carol walked in and inspected the weathered newsprint in Dad's hands. Her eyebrows went up. "Oy, here it comes. A lot of yelling for no reason."

Just then, Grandma opened the door. "What's with all the kibitzing? Come, come into the living room for dessert," she insisted. We all looked at her at once, as if guilty of some crime.

When she caught sight of the article in Mort's hand, she frantically reached for it and started screaming, "NO! NO! Give that to me! Don't ever say his name! Don't speak my brother's name!" Then she turned and ran to the kitchen, slamming the door behind her.

Mort let out a gust of nervous laughter at Grandma's reaction. Leo and Carol shook their heads, having expected it. I stood there in amazement, trying to understand why Grandma's reaction had been so volatile.

As Leo, Carol, Dad, and I moved back into the living room, relatives with horrified expressions waited to know what happened. Grandma had locked herself in the kitchen and several cousins were banging on the door to be let in.

In a corner of the living room we gathered around Leo, who told us that Abie was a racketeer and made money—a lot of it—to support the family. He had been Rae's favorite brother and she was devastated when he died.

Who murdered Abe? That was what my father and I wanted to know. What happened to Abe's money? That was what the cousins wanted to know.

Grandma eventually opened the kitchen door, tears streaming down her reddened face, and insisted the evening was over and everyone should go home. She refused any questions about Abe and wanted to be left alone. As she ushered the family out the door, I snuck into the kitchen and slipped the faded newspaper article into my purse for safe keeping—and further investigation.

2

Family Matters

The following day, Dad and I ventured up to the Bronx to visit Carol. I couldn't get over the drama that had ensued upon finding the newspaper article, so during the train ride I asked Dad what he knew about this uncle's murder.

"I knew Abe was a gambler and had been killed, but I had no idea he was a racketeer. I was told as a child he was a restauranteur." From his strained expression I could tell Dad was trying to piece it all together. "It certainly hadn't been part of your stories years ago," I commented.

During our visit with Carol, I was privy to some juicy stories and a deeper understanding of who the family elders were. I learned that Grandma's brothers and sisters all had variations of a similar last name. I also learned that they described each other by comparing their physical attributes to popular movie stars of their day. Aunt Carol's dry sense of humor and boisterous behavior always reminded me of the TV actress Roseanne Barr, but with a Brooklyn accent.

Carol described Grandma Rae's oldest brother Dave as a tall Charles Boyer with soft eyes and thick brows. Along with his wife Ida, he owned several luncheonettes over the years, but he is remembered in Brooklyn lore as "Jungle Jim"—the guy in the grass skirt and pith helmet—at his famous coconut-whip stand at Strauss and Pitkin Avenues. He used the last name of Balzack.

Ike, the youngest brother, resembled Tyrone Power—the swashbuckling, romantic actor—except he was chubby. Ike was the only sibling conceived in America, in 1915, and who graduated high school. Ike was considered the "real" American, and many of the family's dreams were pinned on him when Abe paid his entrance to law school. But, Ike didn't have the drive or smarts to push himself as his brothers had done. Introverted and soft-spoken, he never saw his career in law come to fruition. He married a woman named Rena who insisted Ike change his name to Bob because it sounded more American. They had a daughter and Rena became known in the family as the "tyrannical boss" of Ike's new family. Emasculated and emotionally shut down, he ended up working as an orderly in a psychiatric hospital. He used the last name of Balzac, spelled differently.

Rae's sister Bertha, Carol and Leo's mother, was a square-shaped woman who was fanatical about cleanliness in her home and dished out advice, even when it wasn't asked for. She was considered the backbone of the family. Bertha married Morris "Mudsy" Hecker, who worked at a garment factory with her father. Mudsy was quiet, polite, and half Bertha's size. There was no movie star anyone could think of that resembled Bertha.

Carol had a lot to say about Grandma Rae, whose full name was Rachel. Everyone swore she was a double for the actress Norma Shearer, with her alabaster skin, blue eyes, and glossy black hair. I learned that as a young girl, Rae attended school only through the fourth grade, and then went to work sewing buttonholes in a factory to help support the family. Their father Morris was very strict and known to beat the girls if they bought a stylish hat, or in Rae's case, tried to model, after she had been spotted in a beauty contest in the park.

Great Grandpa Morris' stern ways had Rae running as far away from him as possible by the early 1920s when she married a taxi driver named Dave Postal. "'*He cleans his shoes with a hankie?*'" Carol mimicked how Bertha would describe Rae's first husband with disgust.

"That was the beginning of Rae's string of marriages," Carol continued. "She averaged about five years per husband and then moved on." Dad and I really didn't know much about Grandma's early years. She never spoke of them and strangely enough, we had never seen a single wedding photo from any of her five marriages.

"After a while, Rae was convinced the best way to meet a man with money was by riding horses in Central Park." Carol described how Rae bought a fancy equestrian outfit, took riding lessons, and started trotting through the park regularly.

"It was an unfortunate day for your father, Max," Carol said cynically to Mort, "when he met Rae in the park."

Grandma married Max Marcus in 1935, and they moved into the "swanky" new Century Apartments on 63rd Street and Central Park West. "They also had a magnificent home with horses in Deal, New Jersey," Carol continued. "They traveled, had lavish parties, and Rae paraded around in diamonds and furs." It seemed Max was the "King of the undergarments industry" and he and Rae had everything they had ever wanted in the heart of the Depression.

"Rae would show up at your Great Grandma Anna's house in Brooklyn in a chauffeur-driven Cord…Oy, she had so much money," Carol rolled her eyes. "Then she'd remove her diamonds and furs, and scrub Baba's floors." I had heard that odd story before. Grandma always emphasized how she would get down on her hands and knees and clean her mother's house, which didn't make sense if she had so much money. Despite her riches, I suppose Rae hadn't forgotten where she came from, and taking care of her mother was an act of pride.

My father was born in 1936, and Rae remained married to Max for another seven years—that was a track record for her—but I learned they didn't always live together.

"I was sent away to private schools and never allowed to be at home," Dad said. He never saw his father and Max made no attempt to see his son either. Dad only had small musings of a father he never knew, yet he didn't question Carol further. He displayed great indifference toward Max Marcus, and although I was sure there was more to the story, I knew better than to press the issue at the moment.

"Look," Carol stood up from her Lazy Boy lounge chair and shook her head in disgust. "Rae should have never sent you away. She was not a good mother."

Mort's face reddened and he sucked in his cheeks—a physical cue he was becoming upset. The truth was, Grandma Rae and Dad weren't close—they loved each other, but it seemed Dad loved her out of obligation. They had never had a relationship, as she hadn't raised him—growing up he either had a nanny or was away at private school. When she did inject herself into his life it was often as a meddling troublemaker. Dad described her as an "idyllic, untouchable goddess," and had stayed far away, hosting her once a year in California. The whole situation made me sad. Mort was such a great father—probably because he was making up for what he never had.

Carol immediately changed the subject by showing us some old family photos. We were drawn to a picture in a heart-shaped frame of a jovial, round-faced man in a suit and fedora. Carol told us it was the only photo of Uncle Frankie. This was the Jewish cowboy? I had always imagined him in furry white chaps and a red bandana shouting, "Oy vey, Silver!" as he was thrown from a bucking bronco, his spurs dragging across the red earth of New Mexico or Wyoming. But this photo was of no cowboy. He was a city man, straight out of a Damon Runyon story, his pinstriped suit perfectly pressed and his fedora cocked over one eye.

Carol and Dad were filled with joy as they recalled how, as kids, Frankie would take them for pony rides on Coney Island. Then, in the mid-1940s, Frankie disappeared and was never heard from again. End of story. The legend of the Jewish cowboy was passed down to my generation. I learned that Frankie went by the last name of Balzak (spelled differently than his brothers).

Carol also had copies of the same photos that Grandma had, of a man with slicked-back hair in an overcoat. They had held such romantic fascination for me over the years—it was Abe. He had a slender, short frame and a mass of wavy, dark hair, thick features, an accentuated brow bone, and full lips. He appeared well-dressed and smiling in all of his pictures. Abe went by the last name of Babchick.

"Did Abe have a fortune, as Leo and the news article suggested?" I asked Carol.

"There were oodles of cash," Carol insisted. "And what a fight after his death—Rae and my mother were screaming at each other!" Carol exclaimed. Abe had left money for Rae to disperse among the siblings, but no one had ever received anything. Rae and Bertha argued bitterly about the sum of $50,000, which Carol insisted Rae had kept for herself.

"I was told Abe had won $100,000 gambling the night he was killed," Dad recalled.

"All I know is that they didn't believe in banks back then and hid their money. The night Abie was killed he left his winnings with Rae."

These stories were fascinating to me, and I started to piece together a portrait of Dad's family in a new way. These were larger-than-life characters and I had a million questions. Was Frankie really a cowboy? Why did he never visit the family again? What was Abe involved in? Where was Mort's father Max? What was Grandma doing when Dad was away at boarding school?

I wanted to know more, but for the time being all I had were the informal yarns that relatives chose to tell me.

3

Past is Prologue

My father believed that each of us lives a life that in one way or another was carved out or influenced by those who came before us. The decisions my great grandfathers made, on blustery nights in Bessarabia over 100 years ago, changed the course of their descendants' lives forever, saving us from the pogroms of Russia and the horrors of World War II. They came to the New World with hopes and dreams, like so many other immigrants, of leading a better life. A life of freedom. But what were the tipping points that led them down the paths they chose? What were the moments that shaped how they re-created themselves in this new world of America? I wondered if the journey my great grandparents started in Europe ended with their children, or if their journey continues through me.

Chatter among the cousins for the next few weeks was about where Abe's fortune had gone after his death. Uncle Leo had given a short explanation of who Abe was, but I remained curious about his death and Grandma's explosive response. Grief was one thing, but her reaction had been something else altogether. It seemed no one knew anything more about Abe than what the newspaper article had revealed.

Aunt Carol had provided information about Grandma Rae and her siblings. I had always just accepted, as did my father, that she had been married five times—as if it were normal—but now I was questioning her unions. There were definite mysteries in the family that no one was giving any details about. This included the curious underwear tycoon Max Marcus and the disappearing cowboy, Frankie. Maybe these mysteries were why Glamour Granny stared off into empty space so often, contemplating memories she would never dream of sharing with me.

Once the dinner party fiasco had died down, I asked Grandma carefully chosen questions about her past. She only mentioned Abe when recounting how he, Frankie, and she had landed at Ellis Island in 1914 with their mother Anna from the Ukraine Oblast of Volynia. Their father Morris had come to America three years earlier. He first sent for older siblings Dave and Bertha, who worked in a pants pressing factory with him, to earn enough money for the rest of the family to eventually make the voyage.

Grandma Rae didn't want to revisit her youth and didn't understand why I wanted to know about her life. "Why hold on to the past?" She pressed me. "You must move forward." I wondered if her memories were painful—the familiar immigrant tales of living in cramped tenements, laboring in sweatshops, trying to make a buck so their children could have a different future.

I was drawn to the gaps in the family heritage. Whatever those stories might be, one thing was certain—if I wanted to learn about Great Uncle Abe I would have to seek it out. My curiosity took me to the New York City Public Library a couple weeks after the dinner party, to see what I could find out about this racketeer.

With the date of September 26, 1941, from the newspaper article found in the secret drawer as the first clue, I made my way to the microfilm section and asked the librarian for help. There were more than ten daily papers in New York City in 1941. Overwhelmed by the sheer volume of resources, I asked for *The Daily Mirror,* which had published the article I'd found. Unfortunately, I was told that paper was stored in a warehouse on 12th Avenue and had to be ordered. I was too impatient for that, so I went with *The New York Times* and the *New York World-Telegram.* Those sounded like good choices.

The librarian brought me the microfilm for the *World-Telegram* and settled me in front of an archaic-looking contraption. After the microfilm unraveled several times onto the floor and I resembled something out of a Laurel and Hardy movie, all thumbs and strange comic looks, she threaded the machine for me and wound it to September 1, 1941. I didn't know what I was looking for. Maybe a small paragraph in the back section that might mention his death. Maybe a small obituary. I wound the contraption fast to get to September 26. Nothing in the obits. Nothing in the back section. I moved to the back section of September 27. Nothing.

Then it dawned on me that the article had stated Abe was found dead on a Wednesday. The September 27 paper I was looking at said Saturday. I whizzed back to what would be Wednesday…September 24, 1941. Still, nothing in the back section or obits.

I slowly scanned toward the front section, when it suddenly appeared. A front-page column read, "Find Racketeer Slain In Auto." I scanned through the article quickly. It stated that Uncle Abe was shot after a large gambling win. I moved forward to the next day and found a bold headline stretched across the entire front page of Thursday, September 25, reading, "Gambler Slain To Seal Lips Amen Hints; Paid 20 Cops." I scanned to the front page of Friday, September 26, and there was another headline, "Police to Seize Payoff Agent for Babchick." Saturday, September 27, "Kings' Police 'Take' put at $250,000." It continued on and on and was front-page news for over a week. I feverishly started throwing coins into the contraption's xerox function and copied everything I could find in the *World-Telegram*. More frontpage news in the *New York Times* as well.

I left the library two hours later with a stack of articles about Uncle Abe's murder. As far as I was concerned I had hit the jackpot—mystery solved. I couldn't wait to tell my father, now back in California, during our weekly Sunday phone call. I would read the articles later. I had a date with friends and a bar stool in the East Village in a few hours.

●———●

A pile of black clothing lay in a heap on my closet floor as I hurried to finish dressing to meet up with friends for our usual Saturday night of revelry. I finally pulled my cowboy boots over my fishnet tights, touched up my burgundy lipstick, and grabbed my motorcycle jacket.

Reaching for the front door, I eyed the stack of articles about Abe lying on the foyer table. The headlines captivated me again as I glanced at them. Spellbound, I folded the top copy in fours, shoved it into my upper jacket pocket and zipped it closed. It would be good confab for the evening.

It was 11:00 p.m. when the taxi left me on the corner of 2nd Avenue and St. Mark's Place. The gritty sidewalks were bustling with people as I made my way toward Avenue A, two blocks over. Hardcore kids were lined-up at the street window of Stromboli Pizza, avant-garde art types were buying smokes at Gems, a drug dealer was monopolizing the corner pay phone, and two homeless men were sleeping under the dark awning of the Ukrainian National Home.

Two large bouncers guarded the black door to the Aztec Lounge. They smiled at me—the girl usually with a camera who photographed the club kids—as I entered.

The dark bar smelled of old beer, and thick cigarette smoke clouded my view as I made my way through a sea of art students and rockers, drag queens and Goths, their bodies swaying to the thunderous music.

"Jana!" Someone shouted. I pushed through the wall of people to identify the voice. At the end of the long oak bar were my partners in crime, Man Ray and Myriam. We usually started our nights at the Aztec and then ventured to a club or bar-crawled down Avenue A and back up 1st Avenue to meet with other friends.

"Yo, what's the 4-1-1?" yelled Myriam in her German accent over the music. Man Ray, a Goth musician, was swaying his pale arms in mystical circles like a magician as he sang along to the music and winked at me. They were already in rambunctious moods, several empty bottles of Rolling Rock sat on the bar in front of them.

A handsome, tattooed bartender with a jet-black rockabilly coif caught our glances and dodged the mass of people waiting for libations to come our way. "How ya' doin' tonight?" he asked, leaning over the bar and kissing my cheek. Mark, the bartender, was one of the main reasons we came to the Aztec. He and I had dated a few times but we had found a special connection as friends, and that had endured.

"What can I get you?" he asked with a roguish smile. The question made everyone burst into laughter. For all the time I spent in bars and clubs with my friends, I didn't drink. I always ordered water and it drove the bartenders crazy—often they just plopped a pitcher of water in front of me. However, Mark made the best Kamikaze in the East Village, and tonight I was feeling differently. "Yeah, yeah," I retorted, trying to stop their teasing. "Tonight I need one of your specialties."

"Alright!" Mark responded with a glint in his eye. "What's the occasion?"

"I've just found out I'm related to a gangster…and he was murdered."

"Whoa! Jana has Mafia blood, don't cross her!" Man Ray shouted with laughter.

"Really?" Mark asked, shaking the neon green liquor and pouring it into a V-shaped glass.

I pulled the newspaper article from my jacket pocket and flattened it on the wooden bar, placing my drink on top of it. Earlier, at the library, I had been distracted thinking about going out, but now that I was here all I could think about were the articles. I didn't know what a policy ring or grafting were all about. These were foreign words to me. Suddenly I realized Mark was looking at the article as well, though upside down from his vantage point.

"Is this about your relative?" he asked. I nodded in response. "Yeah, I'm trying to figure out this puzzling story." We scanned the article together. "This is interesting. I love a good mob story," he said. "Leave it for me? I'd like to read it later."

I handed Mark the article as my friends pulled at me to leave. It was time to venture to our next locale and put the mystery away till later.

●———●

The next day I studied the articles I'd found at the library.

"Gangster Found Shot Near Brooklyn Police Station." The *New York Times* said his name was Abe "Jew Murphy" Babchick. The *World-*

Telegram said his name was Abe Schwartz. Both papers reported he had been taken for a "one-way ride" after a big gambling win in Chinatown. Abe's sedan was later found with his body inside, shot execution style with two bullets to the back of his head, just blocks from the 71st precinct on Empire Boulevard in Brooklyn. As I skimmed through the articles, the two papers each reported different details.

I called Dad. I was hoping to talk through the articles, but he was filled with excitement about his own news. A long conversation with Uncle Leo revealed that Leo's father, "Mudsy," had been one of Abe's key men in his numbers-running operation. When Abe was murdered, everyone involved at the racket headquarters was arrested, including Mudsy. Leo distinctly remembered their photographs, and Abe's body, appearing on the cover of a newspaper. Leo also mentioned how he had tried to save his father from a jail term by pleading with the court. The big news was that Leo said the notorious hitman of Murder Incorporated, Abe "Kid Twist" Reles, came to the family house in the Brownsville section of Brooklyn for dinner on Sunday nights.

I didn't know what Murder Incorporated was, or who "Kid Twist" Reles was for that matter. Dad didn't stop to tell me, he was to elated about recollections from his childhood—piecing together the mystery of Uncle Abe that resonated with his own memories.

He reminisced about a time when he was a young boy and thought he had dreamt of a man in a dark suit crawling through his bedroom window from the fire escape late at night, his gold-framed spectacles glinting from the streetlight. When he asked his Aunt Bertha if she knew who that man with the gold-rimmed glasses was, she screamed, beating her chest and running from the room. Sixteen-year-old Uncle Leo was recruited by his mother Bertha and Grandma Rae to explain who the man was, and to ensure that young Mort wouldn't mention it again. It hadn't been a dream. It had been Uncle Abe, sneaking into the house, after an evening of God-knows-what.

My father also had memories of Abe living with Rae at her apartment on Eastern Parkway in Brooklyn when she was separated from Max. When five-year-old Mort was home from school he would stand on a chair watching Abe shave, mimicking his motions. Dad remembered

Abe as a quiet ghost, coming and going, drifting down the hallway of Grandma Rae's apartment, then disappearing into the night.

Mort's memories, along with the newspaper articles, prompted rewrites on his poetry book about the family. Although I remained fascinated with all these characters, I was too preoccupied with my own life to question the details that didn't make sense to me. I was satisfied Dad was writing something about all this and sent the newspaper clippings his way. I'd let me him figure it out.

4

The Glamour Girl
& The California Kid

My tumultuous relationship with Glamour Granny Rae continued to decline over the years. The strain of being the main attraction in her life was taking its toll.

My friends adored her elegant and delightful ways—she had the amazing ability to charm anyone, especially men. But they never saw her other side, never understood when I would tell them she was driving me crazy. She loved my costume designer friend Tommy, and they talked fashion together, schmoozing over cocktails. But when the evening was over she would mumble "faygeleh" under her breath with a sneer. She always appeared endearing to my boyfriends, wining and dining them, but afterward, she would grab my arm and tell me to never see them again, that I was wasting my youthful looks on "nobodies."

When not directed at me, I continued to witness this flip side of Rae's lady-like façade during her weekly two-hour-long conversations with Aunt Carol. During those marathon phone calls, Rae would lounge on her bed in a pink negligée with a thick layer of cold cream slathered on her face, and one-by-one go down the list of family members, mixing praises and curses without taking a breath.

"Morton is an artist for God's sake!…what does he know of the real world?…the children know nothing of what it means to have good credit …Carol!…Carol! …listen to me…we sacrifice so much…and for what?…*Azoy vert dos kichel tzekrochen*—but look, that's how the cookie crumbles…you hear me?…and that new wife of his, such a princess expecting to be waited on...Carol!...*Di kats hot lib fish, nor zi vil di fis nit einnetsen*—the cat likes fish but she doesn't want to wet her paws!" Then would come Grandma's cackle of hysterical laughter that could shake the windows. "I don't know what the fuck you are talking about! ...Carol! ... Carol!" And the conversation would continue at ear screeching decibels as she shouted her Jew-doo.

What I learned over the years was that Grandma always needed to be mad at someone. Focusing her anger toward someone—anyone—allowed her to feel righteous and in control. In turn, she was able to be generous and charming to others who were not on her "hit list" of the day.

My father had extended an olive branch to Grandma and suggested they take a trip to Europe together. This was a big deal, as Dad often could not be around her for more than a day without losing his mind. Grandma meditated on taking this journey, gathered all her internal resources, and found new victims to release her unexplained anger upon— Valerie and me—so she could have a pleasant trip with Dad.

The incident happened during one of my sister's weeklong visits to Grandma's house. Valerie hadn't experienced the nasty side of Grandma and didn't understand why she was summoning us for a meeting. Rae sat us down on the overstuffed ivory sofa and appeared very distant as she poured seltzer water into crystal tumblers and carefully place the drinks on cocktail napkins. Valerie had no idea what was coming, but I sensed the brewing storm and squeezed her hand as we huddled together on the sofa.

Across from us in a high back chair, Grandma crossed her legs and rested her elbow gracefully on the chair's handle, staring at us with a glossy-painted fingernail between her teeth. After several moments she leaned forward and announced in a calm tone, "I'm extremely disappointed in the both of you and no longer want to be your grandmother." She explained that her reasoning was to "preserve" herself for the trip with Dad. She needed to extract herself from our lives in order to do that. Valerie was completely bewildered.

"I know you don't mean this," I retorted. "Take it back."

"Oh no, bubelah, I'm dead serious. I can't stand the sight of either of you." That was it. I'd had enough. Valerie was in tears as I led her to the bedroom to pack her bags and immediately take her to my apartment for the duration of her visit. I hated that she had to see this side of our grandmother.

That summer, Rae and Mort had a "spectacular" trip abroad together. Obviously, her venom-flushing had worked. Upon her return, she started calling me daily and expected us to pick up our relationship as it had been previously as if nothing had happened. I wrote her a long letter and stated I needed some space and wouldn't see her for a while, reminding her of the declaration that Valerie and I were not the kind of grandchildren she wanted in her life. She acted surprised and complained to Dad how ungrateful and rude I was.

I had a notion of what a grandmother should be—someone loving and caring that I could talk with who didn't have the same expectations of me that my parents probably did. I wanted Rae to love me for who I was. But she didn't love in any of the ways I had hoped for. She could be financially generous, but it came at a price, and no one could live up to her unrealistic expectations—not family, friends, and certainly not her grandchildren. I needed time away from her to work through my hurt and disappointment.

●————●

By the early 1990s I decided to take a break from the craziness of New York City—which included my grandmother and the ulcer I had developed—and returned to the land of fresh air and open spaces on the Left Coast to focus on my photography career.

When I was finally starting to feel settled, Grandma Rae announced she was moving to California for her golden years. After more than 80 years in New York she was breaking with her past, with the blaring car horns and garbage-cluttered streets of her once-new world, to be near my father, in yet another new world. The two of them were having a renaissance relationship since their European trip together. Grandma Rae was now 89-years-old and they were finally enjoying each other's company.

Shortly after her move to California, my desire to stay away from her solidified at a family dinner when she picked a fight with me. She was prodding me about where some of the furniture from my New York apartment was now located. It seemed odd, as she had never mentioned this before, but she often focused on something mundane when she wanted to start a fight. Grandma was obsessed about a small gate-leg table she insisted was my father's first writing desk as a young man. I had left some furniture pieces with my friend Anne, and the table Grandma was referring to was among them. She became irate that I had left it behind, saying I didn't appreciate anything, which then led into a full-scale Glamour Granny attack that climaxed with her statement, "You only love me for the things I give you. You will get nothing when I die! *Ir di eyer viln zayn kliger fun di hiner!*" Jew-doo translation: The eggs think they're smarter than the chickens.

I grabbed my current boyfriend by the arm and walked out of the restaurant. Grandma was so distrusting and hurtful. She thought everyone was manipulative and out to cheat her. The truth was she was the one who was manipulative, often pitting people against each other.

After that I convinced myself I didn't have to love her just because she was my blood relative and took another hiatus from spending time with her. Dad was confused and rather upset by my decision, even though he'd felt the same way for much of his life. He asked me to remain open to visiting with her and I conceded.

Grandma had demanded to live in an "upper class" retirement community in Monterey. The distance only allowed for weekly visits at most. "I don't want to be a burden on my children," she insisted. But being that far away was a burden on Dad, who made the two-hour drive twice a week. Since I hadn't learned to drive, having lived my adult life in New York City, I chose to see her only occasionally or on holidays.

One Christmas, the family gathered for our traditional lox and bagel breakfast while opening presents, and then ventured to the movies to see the film *Bugsy* about the Jewish mobster Bugsy Siegel, starring Warren Beatty. As we left the theater, critiquing the film and talking over each other in our usual fashion, Grandma Rae remained quiet. On the drive home we asked if she enjoyed the film. She simply responded, "Bugsy wasn't anything like that." Everyone in the car became silent with shock. Then, as if counting a beat, we all started asking her a million questions at the same time. But Rae was finished talking and stared out the window at the cloudy December sky.

Her flippant statement was like a bomb going off. My mind was flying in every direction with questions about her—about things that I had just taken at face value or assumed were normal. She was a conundrum, not only for her unknown past, but also for her irrational behavior. She was always talking about herself—but never her past experiences—only about how beautiful she had been and the extravagant lifestyle she had when married to Max. Yet, she never actually said anything about Max. She was very good at side-stepping the details of her life. Who was she? Who were the husbands? Grandma's choppy stories, filled with Yiddish curse words, were often all we had to hold on to for a family history.

I started plying her with questions when I would see her. She never mentioned Bugsy Siegel again, but I did manage to extract some small musings here and there. Still sharp at age 92, she briefly mentioned Abe. Of all the older siblings, he had received the most education, attending Public School #109 in Brooklyn through the eighth grade. The family called him the "Little Professor" because he had a "brilliant mind."

Unfortunately, most of our conversations quickly turned to her usual statements of self-importance. "I'm really an artist, you know, I have a very keen eye when it comes to fashion…I was so beautiful everyone would stare at me wherever I went…Jankaleh, pull your hair back for a softer look so people can see your *shaina punim*…"

As she continued talking, I found myself being pulled, as if through a vortex, to a time when Abe was young, wearing knickers and playing stickball on the streets of Brownsville, unaware of who his neighborhood pal, Abe "Kid Twist" Reles, would become, or for that matter, what his own destiny would be many years later in 1941.

I was again enticed by Abe's mystique and started reading books about Jewish gangsters and Murder Incorporated in order to grasp the context of the hints that had been dropped over the years. I went back and read all those articles I had collected, but there were so many clippings I only got through a few and had to put them away. There were too many versions of what happened the night Abe was killed. It was overwhelming—I couldn't process it all. However, I wanted to put together the pieces that might connect the mystery of my grandmother with the mystery of Uncle Abe. It was time to do some research.

Dad had given me a copy of Rich Cohen's book *Tough Jews* and I stuffed it in my flight bag as I boarded a plane for New York. It was his good luck gift to me, as I was planning to do some digging about Uncle Abe's case.

I was returning to the City to get ready for the launch my first documentary photography book *In The Shadow of the Vampire* about vampire culture in America and the fans of Anne Rice. And, of course, whenever I returned to New York I would get together with old friends. My closest pal was Mark, the bartender from the Aztec Lounge during my club days. We had stayed in touch over the years and he was now married with a baby boy. He had made the jump from mixology to criminology— currently working in law enforcement. He had started as an undercover narcotics cop in Brooklyn and was now a detective.

Mark picked me up at the airport and we headed down to the Village for a meal. This was our tradition. We would catch-up on our lives and recall the old days when we had been cool cats in the underground scene of the Lower East Side. The places we had haunted on a Saturday night for cocktails or to dance the night away were the same places where my ancestors probably peddled their goods or crowded into tenements some ninety years earlier. I imagined the spirits from that time rising with the steam from the manhole covers to greet me as I walked up 1st Avenue with Mark. The streets were paved with the stories of Jewish immigrants. But I longed to find the story of my ancestors—and of Great Uncle Abe.

Mark had always reminded me of a young Al Pacino—compact, muscular, and bursting with energy. His dark eyes always had a mischievous glint to them. He was street savvy, but also book smart, having graduated from NYU with a degree in philosophy. He had a giant sense of humor and loved to tease me, especially because I always blushed, and then would somehow come back at him with a one-liner.

"You've become a soft Californian," he jabbed at me, as we strolled down East 9th Street past our old hangout whose doors were now boarded-up. "You've lost your New York edge!" Mark laughed.

"That edge was too sharp!" I laughed back, butting my shoulder against his.

I figured my old New York attitude was better left behind. But I found remnants of it as we turned onto Avenue A, reminiscing and joking about the characters we knew. Looking back, I thought those carefree nights in the shadowy seduction of the East Village would be the defining moments of my life. How wonderfully naïve I was.

I mentioned that I was going to the library to do further research into the mystery of my great uncle's death. Mark loved New York history and was intrigued by Abe's story, just as he had been years ago when I first mentioned it to him.

The next evening, I returned to his home in Rockaway, excited about the stack of new articles I had found about Abe. For over a week the murder and its fallout were the headlines in every major New York paper: the *Brooklyn Daily Eagle*, the *New York Journal American*, the *New York Herald Tribune*, and over ten dailies. The *Daily News* was still in library storage on 12th Avenue and had to be ordered. I didn't have time to see it on this short trip.

Mark and I spread the articles I had found on the living room floor and read them, while his toddler, Mark Jr., crawled around us. We were trying to piece together the aftermath of the murder into a cohesive picture. Abe's death had sparked a huge investigation involving the gambling racket in Brooklyn. I questioned why Abe wasn't mentioned in any of the history books about Jewish gangsters that I had been reading.

He was first described as a gambler, playing for big money, but not considered very important in the larger scheme of things. The papers said he had won between $20,000 to $75,000 that night at a crap game in Mulberry Bend in Manhattan, and was later seen outside DuBrow's Cafeteria Restaurant on Eastern Parkway in Brooklyn around 2 a.m. A spot where he often did "business."

Four hours later, a delivery driver found Abe's body on the passenger seat of his sedan parked on Empire Boulevard, just 3 blocks from the police station. Detective Frank Sarcona was the first on the scene and recognized Abe. He had booked him on policy charges several years back.

The Brooklyn District Attorney called the murder a robbery-gone-wrong and Abe a "cheap punk"[1] of little importance. A Special Prosecutor for the State Attorney General had another scenario which immediately blasted into the headlines stating Abe *was* important, and he had proof that Abe was making as much as $10,000 a week in the huge policy ring he controlled.

"Jew Murphy" or "The Boss," as Abe was known, was wanted by the Special Prosecutor for questioning about protection money he may have been paying to authorities to keep his policy racket thriving.

Mark explained that when police take money dishonestly it is known as "grafting." A "policy racket" was an illegal lottery or numbers game played in poor neighborhoods across the United States before the lottery became legal in 1964. Players would place their bets with a bookie at a semi-private location that acted as a betting parlor. A runner would then carry the money and the betting slips between the parlor and the headquarters, which was known as a "policy bank." The name "policy" came from its similarity to insurance—both seen as a gamble on the future.

"Do you think there are any police records we could look at?" I asked Mark eagerly.

Mark thought they should be public record at this point and would inquire at work. I was thrilled to have a cohort interested in this. I felt like Nancy Drew with a Hardy Boy.

The following day Mark reported that the records were public, but non-computerized files (anything before the 1970s) were housed in a warehouse in Queens. Civilians couldn't go there without a police escort, even though it was public information. The warehouse was only open during normal weekday business hours. That meant Mark had to plan a day off to go there, which he couldn't do during my visit.

"What should I look for?" he asked me.

"Crime scene photos!"

Three weeks after my return to California, I got a call from Mark.

"You can't believe the mess it is up there in that warehouse. Nothing is organized, files are thrown everywhere. It's a disaster area. I couldn't find anything. It will take weeks to look through that place, because nothing is in date order."

I let out a sigh.

"And, if it's something fishy, the records are probably gone. Conveniently lost. Every cop has had access to that place for decades. Even if I spent a few more days looking around, I don't think I'd find anything."

We had run into a brick wall. No records. No book references. Only newspaper stories to piece it all together. I returned to reading *Tough Jews*. When I opened the cover I found a sticky note, secretly placed by Mark on the opening page: "When are we going to Vegas…gangster style?" Despite his good humor I was disheartened. I realized I needed to spend more time with Glamour Granny before all her stories were gone forever.

5

The Hunter

It was clear that I was staying in California, so it was time to finally learn how to drive. I got my license and my first car at age 38. Becoming a driver suddenly meant I had added responsibilities, including visiting Grandma, some 40 miles away, and picking up some of the slack for Dad. I was rather a nervous adult driver, having to know exactly how to get to my destination. At first I got lost a lot because I had never paid attention as a passenger, but eventually I found my way to Grandma's retirement home in Monterey.

Now in her mid-90s, Rae was fragile and less aggressive. I took her to lunch and to the doctor several times, and although she would still nag me about my appearance, her sense of humor was more dominant than her criticism. "Jankaleh...Bubelah...I may not like the way you wear your hair, but if anyone else says something to you, tell them they can kiss your ass in Macy's window!"

During our visits I continued to push for details on the broken record of family stories. She wouldn't talk further about Abe, so I zeroed in on my grandfather, Max Marcus. I wanted to know who the Marcuses were. It was always the same, seemingly exaggerated story: Max was a millionaire who abandoned his son.

On one of our excursions, Grandma elaborated that Max had a wife before her, and a son named Walter. She also rattled off the names of Max's parents and siblings. This was more than she had ever said about him before. As we drove back to her apartment from the doctor's office I got lost—a good reason to keep the conversation going. When I asked her why Max never wanted to have a relationship with Dad, she waved her hand back and forth exclaiming, "He was a gambler! That was his whole life. *Hok mir nit kayn chainik*...stop nagging me already!"

After a brief silence, her tone softened. "Of all those husbands, Siegel was the love of my life." Her eyes became glassy and she turned back toward the window so I couldn't see her tears as she mentioned her fourth husband, Larry Siegel.

"...and I loved Abe," She added. With that, she was done talking for the afternoon.

By 2001 Grandma had developed anemia and some kind of stomach ailment. On one of her weekly doctor visits for a blood transfusion, she patted her protruding, bloated belly and sheepishly looked at Dad and me. "Morteleh, do you want a baby brother?" As tough as she was, I can't deny what a marvelous sense of humor she had.

A few months later she worsened and had gone into hospice care with seemingly no will to live, and decided not to eat anymore. After several days of no food, she suddenly looked at Dad and me, with eyes full of wonder, and declared, "Let's get the hell out of here!" Dad always joked that it was "her natural venom" that had preserved her. But the humor only lasted so long. Six months later, in January of 2002, Grandma Rae died at the age of 96.

At the funeral, family and close friends gathered around her plot in the shade of a large tree at the Oakwood Memorial Park in Santa Cruz. A cantor was singing and I was sobbing uncontrollably. It might have been the guilt I felt for not having spent enough quality time with her in the last few years, or the fact that her secret life would remain unknown. Dad tried to comfort me with the reminder that we never really knew which Rae we were going to get from visit to visit. But that didn't help the extreme loss I felt, or the deepening mystery of who she and her siblings had been.

When I step back and look at the arc of her life, I can see she was always in survival mode. Her priority was taking care of Number One.

She had five husbands that we knew of—from Max-the-Millionaire to Frank Herzl (a relative of Theodore Herzl, who founded Zionism). There was rumor that there may have been a couple of others, such as matches made by her parents when she was very young. According to her, the only one she truly loved was Larry Siegel, a swarthy man with beady eyes and a pencil moustache who, according to Dad, beat her and stole all her money. It was one of the mysteries that died with her. There are literally dozens of photos of Grandma at famous nightclubs in the 1930s, '40s and '50s, dining and dancing with unknown men. And, there were those missing wedding photos.

Most of all, I questioned her selfishness. My father basically had no parents. With her grandchildren she had tried to be financially generous, but she really didn't know how to give…or love.

There are so many adjectives that describe her: proud, elegant, generous, charming, humorous, inquisitive, narcissistic, abrasive, invasive, penny-pinching, street-wise, busybody, angry, and at times, just plain mean.

Regardless, I will always remember her in a full-length mink coat and bright pink lipstick, eating a fresh steaming bagel from a brown paper bag at H&H after a night at the Metropolitan Opera House. That memory sums it all up for me—she may have traversed the slums of Brownsville to the wealth of mid-Manhattan, but she still ate her bagel from a bag. Her life, full of allure and obscurity, had gone into the earth; her stories, struggles, and joys buried with her. I loved her, and I realized I hadn't known her at all.

●————●

Cleaning out Grandma's California apartment, bundling up the papers and photographs of her life, new items that once resided in the secret drawer were now in my possession. I discovered telegrams from the 1930s from Mort's father Max, lists of furniture bought when they moved into the Century Apartments in 1935, stationery with Max's company name imprinted in bold ink—Marcus & Thomas, Inc.—and love notes to Rae signed "Maxi." Upon Mort's birth Max wrote, "Darling, may our love and happiness continue to be with us in our new home and with our wonderful new child, and remain everlasting." Once upon a time Max loved her and Mort.

Other treasures included documents with the family's original last name from the old country—Babczuk—and Rae's application for naturalization, which listed all of her husbands and the years they were married. We also found a book on sexual pleasure that Rae had kept for over 75 years, with certain areas deeply underlined. We found it so funny that we added it to the "keep" pile.

I unearthed pastel colored birthday cards embossed with deco cartoons signed to Dad upon his birth from Great Grandma Anna, his father Max, Uncle Frankie the Cowboy, and numerous friends and relatives. There were also several cards signed, "Lovingly, your Uncle Abe." Abe seemed to be winking at me from behind those old birthday cards, trying to get my attention.

One evening, Dad and I were sitting around sharing stories in our usual fashion. I showed him the faded birthday cards from Max and Abe. He acted like he didn't care about anything regarding his father. As he explained it, "He never wanted to know me, why should I care about him?" Nothing seemed to penetrate the protective shell that my father had built around himself from a childhood of abandonment.

I pondered aloud whether Rae drove Max away with her crazy ways, keeping Dad from seeing his father out of her own sense of vanity. Somewhere he had a half-brother and I had an uncle—I wanted to find him. Dad was enamored with my tenaciousness, and even gave me an official nickname—"the hunter"—but he didn't want to investigate his family. He was more interested in the narrative he had spun around why his mother sent him away. It was a saga based in fact: A three-year-old boy was in tears, too young to understand what was happening, except that his mother was leaving him in a far-off land called "upstate" or "Connecticut," with sadistic schoolmasters and kids who teased him. Mort attended over 13 schools between the ages of 3 and 18. At each one he attempted to run away, back to New York City, where he hoped his mother would welcome him home with open arms. But each time, glamorous Rae sent him back. During the holidays she was gone, so Mort stayed behind at the schools when the other children went home to be with their families. In summer, a time for family vacations, Mort was sent to camp.

"What was Grandma Rae doing with her time? Why weren't you ever allowed to be home for any length of time?" I asked for the umpteenth time.

"I have a theory," Dad said in low whisper. He stretched his arm out to draw me in closer to him on the sofa. "I believe I was sent away to those schools because of a phone call."

I looked at him, bewildered.

"Uncle Leo told me that after Abe's murder the family received a phone call that has haunted them ever since. A male voice said, '*If anyone tries to find out what happened to Abe, we'll kill the whole family, starting with the children.*'"

6

The Little Professor, Kid Twist, & The War for Brownsville

The revelation of the death threat to the family was bone chilling. This had been a situation of great magnitude and I had to know what it was all about—to understand who Abe had been and how he had become part of a dark underworld that led to his ultimate demise.

A local librarian helped me find an article about Abe that had appeared in the *Alexandria Gazette*. There was no new information, but it was interesting that Abe's death was recorded in a Virginia newspaper. More digging at the library revealed that his murder had been national news.

I retrieved one of the handwritten birthday cards to Mort from Abe and stared at it for a long time. Running my fingers across his signature, I thought of how my fingerprints were now covering his. I imagined him writing the greeting and sealing the envelope. The cards were the only items I had that were connected to him. He was a real person—not just another headline.

I read through several more books about gangsters, and used one of Abe's greeting cards as a bookmark, hoping somehow it would bring him to life, conjure his spirit. But I could find nothing written about him despite that fact his death had been frontpage news. Abe's story seemed to be buried—and I wanted to unearth it.

My first logical step was to understand the New York in which Uncle Abe had been raised. I knew Abe "Kid Twist" Reles had been his childhood friend and frequently came to dinner at Great Grandma Anna's house in Brooklyn. Learning the history of Murder Incorporated could possibly help me understand the circumstances of Abe's life.

In Rich Cohen's book about Jewish gangsters, *Tough Jews*, he talks about them as a lost breed of people, a product of their situation, where ordinary men were pushed to do extraordinary things. I like to think that "Kid Twist" would not have turned out to be the ruthless killer of a murder-for-money gang had it not been for the circumstances he stumbled upon. We all have defining moments in our lives, moments when the path before us opens and we must make decisions about our lives.

I pondered what might have been Uncle Abe's defining moments. Did he just fall into the wrong crowd, having befriended Reles at a young age? Or, did he consciously decide there was no other way to better his life and the life of our family? As I put together all the pieces of family stories collected thus far, combined them with U.S. census and immigration records, and written histories of Jewish gangs, I started to form a sense of who he was and that long-ago time in New York.

Uncle Abie, as Carol and Leo called him, was nine-years-old when he came to America in 1914. The family originally rented a house on Sackman Street, in the East New York section of Brooklyn, where Abie saw his father stagger home after a 14-hour workday from a pants-pressing factory and his sisters stitched buttonholes for pennies. Yet, Abie must have seen the well-dressed, pinkie-ringed men of the neighborhood collecting money on the corner. They were the mobsters—the Jews who would not be victimized any longer. They would make it out of the ghetto at any cost. Cohen described them as heroes for the young kids of Brooklyn. As they ducked into their convertible Cabriolets or Buicks, they were role models for the kids who looked to them as achievers who could lead the way out of grinding poverty. They were tough Jews, willing to fight back and grab their piece of the American dream.

Abie heard his father grumble about how he refused to work for anyone any longer. Great Grandpa Morris saved his money and started to buy up small lots around Brownsville, marking his territories in the New World. On three of those parcels Great Grandpa eventually built the family home at 9214 Avenue B at East 92nd Street. The lessons for young Abie were fraught with gaining independence—work for yourself, get what you can, support the family.

Around the corner from the Avenue B home, at 649 East 91st Street, lived Abe Reles. The two Abes grew up together and were close pals. The son of Austrian-Jewish immigrants, Reles looked like the Babchick boys—thick black curly hair, exaggerated facial features and a short, stocky build. According to Leo, Great Grandma Anna thought Reles "was such a nice boy."

Upon graduating from the eighth grade together, around 1920, Uncle Abe was given the title "The Little Professor," as he had gone further in school than any of his Babchick siblings thus far. Soon after leaving school he took a job for a short time selling pretzels at Ebbets Field during the ball games. Reles was arrested for stealing $2 worth of gum from a vending machine. In the days of penny candy, that's a lot of gum—imagine him running away with 200 gumballs! Reles was caught and sent to a children's reform school for five months in Dobbs Ferry, New York.

I discovered that the lives of the two Abes remained intertwined. The Brownsville neighborhood was cramped and congested, and home life felt unbearable with parents stuck in the old ways, which lead to more and more kids hanging out on the streets and ultimately filling the halls of the houses of refuge (detention centers for juveniles). Many of the Jewish youth formed gangs that leaned toward thievery, rather than violent acts, and many of these gang-kids grew up to become "masters of their craft."[1]

Reles took a job as a printer's assistant, but found himself unemployed when the business folded. With much leisure time on their hands, Abe and Reles haunted pool halls and candy stores, the local stomping grounds and social clubs for young Brooklyn boys.

In this "back room" culture, social success was everything. It equaled power. The right relationships on the streets added to one's clout. It was all about doing favors for those more powerful, and that meant the Shapiro Brothers—Irving, Meyer, and Willie—a group of Jewish-American hoods who controlled the Brooklyn rackets in the mid-1920s. If you wanted any part of the street action it started with doing favors for them.

Along with his other close childhood friend Martin "Buggsy" Goldstein and new pal Harry "Pittsburgh Phil" Strauss, Reles started committing petty crimes for the Shapiros—such as minor theft and breaking and entering. Reles was arrested on one of his missions and sent to the Elmira Reformatory upstate. He was angry that the Shapiros didn't step in to help, so during his two-year sentence he started plotting how he could work for himself.

The plan was simple at first—do some numbers-running on the side. When Reles was released, he and his chums jumped right in to making some money for themselves, keeping their side business out of sight of the Shapiros.

It was at this time, when Uncle Abe was about 23-years-old, that the first newspaper reports about him appeared. He started as a policy collector for Reles and worked his way up, being promoted to investigator or the "thumbs-up man" because of his wide acquaintance within the neighborhood. Abe was known as the "walking Dun & Bradstreet"[2] of the Brownsville rackets. Whenever Reles talked with a new prospect, Abe would give the thumbs up gesture if the stranger's rating was okay.

As they became more successful, Reles and his gang got cocky, adding to their list of enterprises the beer racket, loan sharking—demanding that local loan sharks place them on their payroll as added protection—and muscling in on the Shapiro's slot machine business. They installed machines in the back rooms of local candy stores and pool halls, charging a fee for rental and maintenance, and also receiving a cut of the earnings.

By the late 1920s, the prosperity of Reles' group and their encroachment on the Shapiro territories angered the brothers Irving and Meyer to no end. Realizing they needed to stamp-out Reles and his gang, Meyer decided to send an undeniable message by kidnapping and viciously assaulting Reles' girlfriend before releasing her.

This was Reles' tipping point, taking him from slot machine king to murderer. Revenge was imminent, and necessary for what the Shapiro's had done. Reles would no longer hide his rackets in the shadows—it was time to take over. But he needed to build his alliances in order to wipe out the Shapiros' monopoly of Brownsville.

That's when Reles and his chums started frequenting a pasticceria off of Pacific Street, owned by mafioso Louis Capone in the neighboring Ocean Hill area of Brooklyn. It was a popular hangout for young hoods, where Capone (not related to Al from Chicago) would give them free food and entice them into doing criminal deeds for him and Mafia boss Albert "The Lord High Executioner" Anastasia. Being the elders or "advisors" at the café, they represented power for the neighborhood thugs. Capone had loansharking rackets in New York, ties with the Purple Gang in Detroit, involvement in the labor rackets, and was close with mobsters Anastasia and Joey Adonis.

It was at the pasticceria that Reles met, and soon joined up with, an Italian gang led by Harry "Happy" Maione and Frank "The Dasher" Abbandando. Their alliance was approved by Anastasia and mediated by Capone, strengthening their position against the Shapiro brothers. Another Maione associate, George Defeo, had a brother who was connected with the Bugs-Meyer Gang led by Ben "Bugsy" Siegel and Meyer Lansky. This group was the most feared and affluent underworld organization working on the East Side of Manhattan. The Defeo association allowed Reles to receive "a credit line on pinball machines"[3] and an inroad with "Louis the Wop," who was reportedly "the person in charge of the pinball department of the underworld."[4] Under the "watchful eye of the mafia,"[5] this new combination was in business and Reles had the troops he needed. The war with the Shapiros was on.

June 4, 1930, Reles made the first attempt at revenge on Meyer Shapiro. His newly formed gang combination, known as the Brownsville Boys, shot Meyer in the stomach while he was standing in front of the Globe Cafeteria on Sutter Avenue. Meyer survived, and his brother Irving Shapiro retaliated with a plan to exterminate Reles and his men the following week. Around midnight on June 10, Reles, Maione, Defeo and Louis Asperti were exiting a restaurant at Linwood and Glenmore streets where they were collecting slot machine receipts. Only Defeo noticed their automobile had a flat tire and as he bent down to look closer, a spray of .45 caliber bullets rained down on them. Reles was shot in the back,

Maione had the tip of his nose blown off, Asperti and a passerby were wounded, but Defeo was killed. "The slot machine wars," as the papers called them, quieted down as Reles and Maione recovered from their wounds. But a year later, in early July of 1931, they resumed.

It was quiet on Blake Avenue at 3 a.m., when the Brownsville Boys parked in the shadows near New Jersey Avenue. At 3:25 a.m., Irving Shapiro drove up to his home at 691 Blake with Sam "Smoky" Epstein. Irving was going to change his clothes so they could meet up with his brother Meyer at a Turkish bath house. Irving went to open the front door that led to the outside vestibule of the house. As he reached for his house keys the silence was broken by ten rounds of bullets. Irving died instantly.

Meyer swore he would avenge his brother's murder. Sawed-off shot guns, spattering bullets and screeching car tires became the norm all that summer between the two rival mobs. Meyer prided himself on being invincible, having survived being shot several times over the years. But luck was no longer his lady when two months later, on the night of September 16, he was found dead inside the unlocked basement doorway of 7 Manhattan Street, on the lower East Side.

"That's too bad,"[6] responded Reles sarcastically in regard to Meyer's death. He, "Buggsy" Goldstein, "Pittsburg Phil" Strauss, and "Happy" Maione were arrested for the murder but released due to lack of evidence.

Three years later, in July of 1934, Willie Shapiro, the last brother, was found dead—beaten and buried alive, tied inside a sack in the Canarsie sand dunes.

With Reles's revenge complete, he and his cronies were free to run the rackets in East New York. They made their home base a candy store, located at the corner of Saratoga and Livonia Avenues in Brownsville. Upstairs, on the second floor they plotted and planned their various endeavors. The candy store proprietor was an elderly woman named Rose Gold. She and her son, Sam "the Dapper" Siegel, ran a bail bond racket and managed Reles' loan shark intake. Often known to keep a light burning till the wee hours so The Boys could find their way "home," the infamous candy store was nicknamed Midnight Rose's.

How much of this mayhem 25-year-old Uncle Abe was involved in we don't know, but he did grow up in the Relcs gang and this was the world he lived in. According to the papers, his first arrest for policy charges came on August 1, 1930, and he received a suspended sentence. His second arrest occurred on April 2, 1932, for disorderly conduct and violation of the Sullivan Law. Despite what action may have taken place that night, all charges were dropped.

At this same time, the bloody battle between the two Italian-American mafiosi—Masseria versus Maranzano, also known as the Castellammarese Wars—was coming to an end. The underlying tone of the war was a generational divide between the Old World ways of the Mustache Pete's from Sicily, and a younger, more forward-thinking group called The Young Turks, who embraced multi-ethnicity as the future of organized crime. The group included Lucky Luciano, Albert Anastasia, Vito Genovese, Joey Adonis, and Frank Costello.

Luciano merged with Ben "Bugsy" Siegel and Meyer Lansky's gang, known for bootlegging and handling various murder contracts during prohibition, to take out the last faction of the old Sicilians. Siegel, assisted by Anastasia, Genovese, and Adonis, murdered Joe Masseria. However, they soon realized that if they didn't take out Maranzano, he would be coming for them. This was bad news for Jewish gangsters. They were invested in Luciano and the Young Turks to "keep a community of interests between the like-minded gangs."[7] It was in everyone's interest to get rid of those who refused to work with non-Italians. Siegel and Lansky, having gained Luciano's confidence and being great believers in the new multi-ethnic thinking, conceived a meticulous plan to assassinate Maranzano—the genius of which was that neither of them would be suspected because they were Jewish.

With the success of the second assassination, the way was paved for Lucky Luciano's rise to the top of the U.S. Mafia and his structuring of modern organized crime—The National Syndicate. Luciano, aided by Lansky, created The Commission, a board of directors, to oversee all mafia activities in the U.S. and mediate disputes between New York's five families as well as Al Capone's Chicago Outfit and Magaddino's Buffalo family. During the Commission's first gathering on November 11, 1931, Jewish and Italian mobsters came together. A new chapter in American crime had begun.

Siegel and Lansky disbanded their Bugs-Meyer Mob and with Luciano created the concept of a network of assassins that would do the Commission's bidding to keep things in order and also to keep the bosses out of the fray. This network was assigned to Louis "Lepke" Buchalter, who ran the garment industry unions, and Anastasia, who was also the leader and controller of the International Longshoremen's Association and its unions. Both men were feared and had ruthless reputations. Anastasia, assisted by Lepke's longtime associate Jacob "Gurrah" Shapiro, would relay a murder request from the Syndicate to Buchalter, who in turn would assign the job either to his group of labor sluggers or the Brownsville Boys, whom Anastasia admired, especially Reles. This network of contracted killers, who were committing hundreds of mob murders across the country, had no name—but ten years later the press would label them "Murder Incorporated."

By 1933, Abe "Kid Twist" Reles moved further away from the rackets and became more absorbed in the workings of the murder-for-hire mob. Uncle Abe went into business for himself, "inheriting" Reles and Maione's policy racket as well as buying out the policy bank of Red Hilderbrandt, another well-known Brownsville policy racketeer at the time. Together, these takeovers made Abe "Jew Murphy" Babchick one of the top policy kings in the borough. It was noted that "except for a few cracked skulls," Abe's "ascension to power was marked by an absence of violence."[8]

Abe gave himself the nickname "Jew Murphy," honoring a gangster from a generation earlier. In 1912, a Jewish gang led by "Dopey" Benny Fein in the East Village was in the protection business for laborers. His chief lieutenant was Isidore Cohen, who didn't mind working with the Irish, and demonstrated his freedom from racial prejudice by naming himself "Jew Murphy." Uncle Abe employed several African-American men in his operation, which was practically unheard of in the 1930s. Abe chose his name for the same reason as his predecessor.

Uncle Leo reported that Great Grandma Anna didn't see much of Uncle Abe around the house anymore. Often he was gone for weeks at a time. She was told that he was doing well in the restaurant business, and from what we know, he did own a couple of delicatessens.

Uncle Abe is remembered as being quiet and serious, yet generous to a fault. During the height of the depression a reported 750,000 people were unemployed in the metropolitan area and that especially devastated Brownsville where many of the residents had lost their jobs in the garment industry. Abe took care of those he could. He hired all his childhood friends from the neighborhood, set-up his brother-in-law Mudsy with a delicatessen, and put his younger brother Ike through law school. Carol remembered that he always paid for the housing of family members where he could ultimately have floating meetings with his crew. He refused to marry, as he felt no woman should have to live the life he had chosen.

Grandma Rae and Abe were only a year apart in age and close companions. There are photographs of them in the Catskills with friends—laughing and vacationing in golf attire. Abe stayed with Rae and young Mort the last year of his life, when Rae was divorcing Max and living in a fashionable luxury apartment at 95 Eastern Parkway. There were dinner parties and affectionate times spent with Mort when he was home from school.

Jewish gangsters never saw their "profession" as something to be passed down to the next generation. They wanted in, make the money, and get out—unlike the Italians who saw their underworld businesses as a legacy to stay within the family. This immigrant generation of Jewish gangsters wanted a life free of crime for their children, nieces, and nephews.

Yet, there were still lessons to be taught. Dad and Leo remembered Uncle Abe repeating the mantra, "If you want something from someone, kiss his ass. When he wants something from you, he'll kiss yours."

Abe saw his third arrest on June 6, 1937, for vagrancy in Queens. This had me picturing him drunk and begging for money on a street corner, but in the 1930s, vagrancy meant you were "consorting with other known criminals." Again, the charge against him was dismissed. Uncle Abe had managed to stay out of jail for his illegal policy racket and gambling ring, but that all came to an end the following year, on August 4, 1938, when he was convicted on two counts of conspiracy to conduct a lottery, fined $500, and sent to the workhouse for nine months.

Meanwhile, Reles became known as Brooklyn's "No. 1 Bad Man."[9] By the late 1930s he had been arrested 43 times and was often mentioned in the newspapers. The cops were well aware of Reles and The Boys, often stopping them for simply driving around, or leaving their regular hangouts like Midnight Rose's or Louis Capone's restaurant, Oriental Danceland, on Stillwell Avenue in Coney Island. They were picked up for anything from vagrancy to suspicion of murder, but most of the time the charges didn't stick. Reles had served several small jail terms, and had been charged with homicide five times, but was never convicted. "I guess I'll have to walk around with a bail bondsman all the time," he scoffed at police in his usual sarcastic manner during one of his many arrests.[10]

By the spring of 1939, Uncle Abe was released from the workhouse and back to business as usual—just a few short months before everything started to unravel for the Brownsville Boys.

After a massive two-year manhunt, Murder Incorporated CEO "Lepke" Buchalter finally surrendered to authorities on August 24, 1939, for the murder of candy store owner Joseph Rosen. This meant The Brownsville Boys had lost one of their biggest allies. It would be important to keep "The Lord High Executioner" Anastasia happy, so when Reles was ordered to get rid of a petty crook named Irving "Puggy" Feinstein in September of 1939, he did just that. The Boys would later testify that they were just taking orders from the bosses. "I don't ask questions; I just obey. It would be much healthier," said murder-mob member Sholem Bernstein.[11] Reles was soon arrested for suspicion of the Feinstein murder, and this time there was no easy way to wiggle out of the allegations.

"Kid Twist" Reles has been portrayed in the history books as "a ruthless, cold-blooded killer" and a "sociopath with dangling arms and body odor."[12] Juxtapose that with his family members, who remember him affectionately as a generous, "well-mannered mensch with a quick-witted sense of humor."[13] Both descriptions are probably true. Most notably, he deeply loved his children. So much so that the Brooklyn District Attorney's office and its detectives were willing to bank on it when Rele's wife, pregnant with their second child, begged him to talk to DA William O'Dwyer to avoid the electric chair.

Reles decided to turn state's evidence in order to save himself and his family, and was quickly whisked into protective custody. As he started to sing, his combination cronies were arrested or put into protective custody.

Uncle Abe, now the Czar of the Brooklyn rackets, remained untouched—at least for the time being.

PART
II

7

The Man Who Would Be King

As the years passed the mystery of Uncle Abe's murder took a back seat to living life. Although that chirping sparrow continued to peck at my window, there had been few resources to access further information on his murder. Instead, I had focused my attention on attending graduate school and completing a documentary photography project that was gaining public attention.

Dad was writing his literary memoirs, and I soon began assisting him by editing and scanning old photos, as well as the articles about Uncle Abe I'd found years ago. That re-ignited our interest in the family stories and the questions that were still unanswered. We were haunted by the voices of our ancestors, in the Old World and the New. Dad yearned for connection after his lonely youth and I craved a sense of history.

It was around this time that I began having dreams about Uncle Abe on a regular basis. The dreams were always the same. Shadowy and silent, he would stand at the edge of my bed, simply watching me sleep. His silhouette traced the contours of his overcoat and darkened face. I always woke with a start, my heart racing.

As 2007 began, my research was re-awakened. It seemed as if I was being guided down a path, each doorway leading to yet another, until I was standing directly in front of one of the great family mysteries with some hope of an answer.

It was a phone call to my maternal Auntie Helen that started it. Helen was a fast-talking, joke-cracking New Jerseyite, who was the keeper of the family tree on my mother's side. I adored her. We had bonded over family history when I was young and when I became savvy enough, took over for her.

We spoke on a Friday afternoon. I was trying to convince her to attend my Manhattan art opening in two weeks, but as invincible as Helen seemed, she had a crippling fear of heights, which would not allow her to attend the reception slated for a 4th-floor gallery. Changing the subject, she was beside herself that she'd lost all her family archives in a recent move. Hoping to sway her to take the gallery elevator to my opening, I promised to bring her copies when I arrived in New York.

After the call, I descended into the dark recesses of my garage to retrieve the needed information and rummaged through crates filled with photographs, tchotchkes, and paperwork I'd saved from both my maternal and paternal grandmothers. I had forgotten how many treasures I possessed—their full value still unknown to me.

I sorted the two sides of my lineage into piles. Babchicks to the left; the Kantrowichs, my mother's side, to the right. I was motivated to give Auntie Helen some good stuff, so I decided to reorganize everything into a new family tree as a gift, and before I knew it the whole evening was gone. I didn't have a lot of spare time. But in my usual fashion, when I got started on a documenting project, I was committed.

When I finally sat back and admired my handy computer work, my maternal side of the tree was full, going back five generations. On my paternal side, the Babchicks stopped at Grandma Rae's parents. The Marcus side was completely blank. *Who the hell were the Marcuses?* For years I had pondered both their existence and the truth behind why Mort never knew his father Max. Dad's lack of interest and my lack of clues had kept me from doing research. But with Mort currently writing his memoirs, it seemed timely to find some answers. Mort deserved that, regardless of his lackadaisical attitude. There had to be information just waiting to be found—but where?

I had photographs of Max from Grandma Rae's secret drawer. I cropped his round, beaming face in Photoshop—his broad smile staring back at me—and added it to the tree chart. I stared at it for a long time, trying to see my father's features in his. *Why didn't we ever know you?*

I had a photograph of Max's parents. Nameless and regal, they looked off thoughtfully in different directions, as was the tradition in those old turn-of-the-century portraits. The woman's dark hair was braided and swept across her head. Her black lace dress was adorned with a long gold-linked chain that wrapped around her neck and found its way to a waist-length pocket that housed the rim of a watch. Her right arm was gently propped on her husband's shoulder. He, in a three-piece suit, stared boldly into a future that had long since passed. His thick, black mustache hid any expression on his lips.

Grandma Rae mentioned their names to me once. *What were they... Mae? Jacob?* The photo was mounted on a thick, disintegrating board and I flipped it over. Black print read "Flaschner Co. 1368 Third Ave. New York." Illegible pencil script was scrolled across the back, faded with time.

It was close to midnight when I went back to the garage and dug through the crates again, this time looking for my old papers—notes I had scribbled some ten years earlier. I had recorded that Max had a brother named Jack, and I had a creepy wedding photo of him, looking like the Phantom of the Opera with a midget bride. Max also had sisters named Minnie and Sophie. The latter had owned a dance hall on 2nd Avenue. No other clues. There had to be something I could discover with this information.

It had been years since I tried the genealogy sites online. I hadn't had much luck in the past, but I decided to give it another shot. To my delight there was currently so much information available on the computer that my mind was reeling.

For the next 48 hours—from Saturday morning till Monday morning—I barely spoke to anyone, didn't answer the phone, never left my computer, and was in a frenzy to locate pieces of the Marcus puzzle and fit them together. Ancestry.com's databases led me to the 1920 U.S. Census where I eventually found Max Marcus. I knew it was the correct Max because his siblings were listed with the same names Grandma Rae had told me years ago. The reason I had never been able to find information on Max before was that I had his middle and first names reversed. He was actually Pincus Max Marcus. The census listed his parents as William and Esther Marcus. They were no longer just faces.

Next, I went to the 1930 Census. It took hours of digging and inputting several name combinations, mostly because the sisters were married by then with different last names. But I finally found Sophie Marcus. In 1930, Sophie was married to Jack Rothstein and her mother, Esther Marcus, was living with them in Brooklyn. Most importantly, the census recorded that Sophie had a 7-month-old baby named Stanley.

I was in an altered state. In the last two days I had found copious amounts of information about the Marcuses. By Monday afternoon I could think of nothing else but getting back on my computer to find Max's nephew, Stanley Rothstein. He was the only possible, traceable, link to the unknown Marcus family I could find. I wondered if he could still be alive.

I had committed to spending the afternoon with Dad, so I took a break from my hunt and helped him finish some details on his memoirs before it was to be sent off to the book designer. I excitedly recounted for him how I'd found his grandparents William and Esther Marcus in the U.S. Census, and his first cousin, Stanley Rothstein.

Mort's eyes became wet with tears and he started sniffling. These were not tears of joy at discovering his grandparent's names, but from the dander of Max-the-Cat, who was purring furiously and nuzzling his leg.

"The only notable time I ever saw my father was outside a courtroom," Dad said to me. "He'd come as a character witness for Grandma Rae, who was being sued for divorce by Larry Siegel (husband #4). I was twelve then, and Max strode up to my mother and me, dapper in a dark gray business suit, and without extending his hand, looked me in the eye, and said, 'So you're my son.' It wasn't a statement of affection, but of verification, and after he said it, he turned on his heel and sauntered away before I could reply, 'And you're my father.'"[1]

These stories broke my heart. As our afternoon together gave way to early evening, I walked him to his car. "If it's the last thing I do, I will find Stanley Rothstein," I promised.

Dad smiled at my eagerness. "Why don't you just Google his name?"

"If only it were that easy. You're the generation that left New York. Stanley could be anywhere."

As Mort drove off, I darted back to my computer. I found Stanley Rothstein, estate planning in New Jersey; Stanley Rothstein, campaign contributions; Stanley Rothstein, welfare officer for the military order of the Purple Heart. He could be any one of these guys.

Two more clicks into my search I found a professor and writer named Stanley Rothstein who was retired emeritus faculty at UC Irvine in Orange County, California. His bio stated that he wrote under the pen name "William Marcus." I stopped breathing, staring at the screen in shock. That was Dad and Stanley's grandfather's name—It had to be him.

I easily found his phone number and address via an online search and immediately called Dad, rattling off my new information so fast he could barely keep up with me. "So, do I call him or do you?" I asked breathlessly, unsure how interested he really was in finding his long-lost family.

"Well, why don't you come over to the house and we'll call him together."

Thank goodness Dad only lived about two miles away, because I wasn't paying attention to street signs as I raced to his house. The implications were staggering. If this was *the* Stanley we were looking for, we were about to touch ground zero with the unknown Marcus clan and find out if all those wild stories of the "millionaire underwear king" were true.

●———●

"Do you know what tonight is?" Dad asked as I entered his house. A yahrzeit candle was flickering on the kitchen counter. "It's the fifth anniversary of Grandma Rae's death." I stared into the flame. "Maybe Grandma is finally ready for us to know the truth," I whispered.

I was positioned at a phone extension in the living room as Dad dialed Stanley Rothstein's phone number on a cordless phone, and then joined me on the sofa.

A woman with a New York accent answered the phone and inquired who was calling. Gingerly, Dad replied, "My name is Morton Marcus. We've been doing genealogical research on the Marcus family, and I believe Stanley is my first cousin."

The woman didn't answer. The silence seemed to linger forever until it was finally broken by her loud yell. "Stanley! Stop brushing your teeth… there's a Morton Marcus on the phone!"

After another long silence—looking at each other anxiously from our phone extensions—the soft, inquisitive voice of a man came on the line.

"Are you Rae's son?"

Dad was completely caught off guard by the immediate recognition. "Ah,…yes,…I'm Morton Marcus."

"Well…I've been looking for you for years, Morton!" Stanley declared joyously.

That was the beginning of a lively two-hour conversation. Stanley remembered Rae fondly, as she had taken him horseback riding in Central Park when he was a boy. "She was beautiful and very sweet. As for your father, Max,…well, he was a remarkable bastard…legendary!" Stanley cried out. "That son-of-bitch could win anyone over, he was the world's greatest salesman, always starting his pitch with, 'Your worries are over…' and that's when you knew you were in trouble!"

Stanley enjoyed telling family stories. Once he started, there was no stopping him. He lovingly described William and Esther as charismatic and cultured, escaping Kishinev during the infamous pogroms in the Bessarabian Governorate of the Russian Empire in 1903, and eventually coming to America. He told tales of Max and his brother Jack joining the British Royal Fusiliers' volunteer Jewish Legion, fighting against the Ottoman Empire for a free Israel during World War I, and returning to New York as decorated war heroes.

After the war, Max followed in his father's tailoring trade and had a meteoric rise as a multi-millionaire, becoming known as the "King of the Intimate Apparel Industry." But, Stanley told us that Max gambled away his fortune, not once, but twice!

It had been an incredible evening on the telephone. Two lone Marcus descendants, adrift in the west, had found each other. Making that family connection had meant more to Dad than I could have ever imagined. We quickly planned a trip to Orange County to meet the Rothsteins.

When I crawled into bed later that night, I felt a great sense of satisfaction. It had been a major goal for me to find Dad's family. I had wanted answers, for myself as well as for him, to fill in the emptiness of his childhood.

I had been moved by Stanley's stories of the great grandparents coming to America. As I closed my eyes, I pictured them wrapped in natty wool scarves and heavy coats boarding a large ship that would take them to a new world—their choices affecting what I would become.

That night my dreams were a jumble of images. I saw Max and Uncle Abe together, hooting and hollering at a crap game. A pair of dice came crashing down in a fiery explosion, about to reveal who the ultimate winner of my hunt would be, when suddenly I awoke. In the darkness I tried to focus my eyes and felt the air in the room seem to shift—as if someone were there, watching me—and then it was gone.

During our visit to Orange County to meet Stanley and his wife Sue, we had a wonderful day filled with colorful tales about Max's exploits.

Toward the end of the afternoon, Stanley's animated tone became serious as he directed his attention to Mort. "I'm not surprised you didn't know your father, but I'm not sure that we can judge him," Stanley paused thoughtfully. "Max created amazing wealth and because of that people treated him differently; they all wanted something from him. His freedom was never restricted by money—although he was an avid gambler who lost everything only to then build it up again. But this is the curse of America—we are desperate for wealth, but it dehumanizes us."

I asked if he knew of Max's other son, Walter. "Max completely ignored his son Walter, who died recently. The daughter he didn't see either."

"Daughter?" *There was a daughter?*

"Yes!" Stanley shouted back excitedly. "Both children were from his first marriage. These children suffered greatly from not having their father around." Stanley continued talking, but I was stuck on the part about the daughter.

"I never saw my parents either," Stanley revealed. "They weren't around, so I buried myself in books. When Grandma Esther became deathly ill, Max made sure she had the best doctors and supplied the money, but no one wanted to take her in. I was mortified! These people were shit!" Stanley shouted. "Finally, my mother Sophie gave in. Esther recovered for a couple of years and I spent much of my time with her. She was very affectionate and would tell me all her stories."

"I remember her. I used to call her the 'tall grandma,'" recalled Mort. "My mother took me to see Esther once in Brooklyn. Everyone at the house was sitting around playing cards, and Rae said, '*See that, that's the Marcuses. They gamble and play cards day and night. You are never to gamble.*'" Dad had never told *that* story before. It was curious to me that Max had been a heavy gambler—just like Abe.

"Look, these were emotionally impaired people!" declared Stanley. "They went from one culture to another in a single lifetime. They were larger-than-life characters, but they lacked emotion. Esther had old world values and believed in working hard to keep the family together, educated, and interested in things like music. But Esther's children were Americanizing themselves, and they weren't interested in family or culture. My mother badly wanted to be American and became a flapper, smoking and drinking all night. When Grandma Esther died, my parents divorced. I was only 13, and was left alone most of the time."

Stanley paused, shaking his head in deep-rooted disappointment. "I loved my mother, but I didn't like her. I suffered for her mistakes. I was dependent on her, but she wasn't around, even when I was 7-years-old."

Stanley looked at Dad. "Morton, you would have never been alone all those years in those schools if I'd known where you were. I would have come and got you. Then neither of us would have been alone any longer." Their eyes filled with tears as they acknowledged each other's abandoned childhoods. A deep understanding and admiration for each other was sealed, and they embraced.

●━━━━━●

With the names and clues I'd received from Stanley, I set out to find the rest of the Marcuses. Not only was this a significant discovery for Mort, but it was also when I was learning to hone my detective skills using online resources, cold-calling strangers for information, and tracing missing documentation.

I managed to speak with many Marcuses, but of them all, Willy Marcus was *the* man. He was Max's nephew, son of Max's brother Jack (yes, that Phantom of the Opera picture I possessed), and named after Great Grandpa William. At 82, Willy was the eldest living member of the Marcus clan and resided in Florida with his wife, Sherry. When I telephoned they were both delightful, possessing a wonderful sense of humor. Willy was happy to tell me stories—and he certainly did. Willy knew firsthand about Max and his character. His perspective was different from Stanley's, and how could it not be? Willy had been Max's favorite nephew and he had set him on his career path in the garment industry.

"When I got out of the service, during World War II, and was looking for a job, I went to Uncle Max's office to have lunch with him," Willy told me during our phone call. "I was told to wait for him in a room full of desks. I waited forever, so being bored, I started fishing around and opened the desk drawers to find they were stuffed with cash! This was my introduction to my rich uncle!" Willy let out a loud belly laugh at the memory.

Willy verified that Max had built his first $10 million fortune by the mid-1920s, but when the stock market crashed in October of 1929, so did Max. "He lost everything, but he had a lot of moxie about the industry which allowed him to flourish again very quickly."

By 1933, Max had rebuilt his empire and was living the high life again. "Max was a genius in his field," recalled Willy. "He was the greatest cutter in the industry. He could take a bolt of cloth and get the maximum number of garments from it. His company, PM Undergarments, was *the* company, the one people would remember. He designed lace underwear and lingerie as well as the famous days-of-the-week panties."

Though Max was tremendously wealthy, he was also a big gambler. "And not that smart of a gambler, either!" declared Willy. "He owned horses, had a trainer at the NY track, and he frequented a club in Manhattan where he played cards—Gin Rummy—for money. His stakes were so high that they had to get a group together that would chip-in to play against Max." While playing cards, Max would also be listening to the ball game on the radio, on which he bet immense amounts of money.

"Max always claimed he had a system for gambling," Willy continued. "In Max's office there were scoreboards of all the horse races across the country, and he bet constantly, telling Frank Erickson, the biggest bookie in America at the time, to put down money on all his favorite horses from coast to coast. It was amazing!" Willy chuckled. "He also gambled a lot with your grandmother's brother."

"What?!?" I cried out in shock, then lowered my excited pitch to sound composed.

"I believe he was a bookie or something like that," continued Willy. "They played a lot of craps together, and he booked some of Max's pari-mutuel horse racing bets. It seemed Rae's brother was a more successful gambler than Max," Willy snorted. "Max had to borrow money from him when he was on one of his many losing streaks."

I was stunned. Forget about Aunt Carol's story of Rae riding horses in Central Park to meet a wealthy man. I was willing to bet that Rae had actually met Max through Abe!

"Your grandmother was a gorgeous woman. I never knew she gave birth though, never knew your father was even born," Willy continued. Despite my silence, my mind was racing at 100 MPH to fit the pieces of this new puzzle together.

"Truthfully, Max didn't do everything above board," said Willy. It seemed Max had gambled away his second fortune by 1944, which was the year Rae officially divorced him. But riches came Max's way for a third time via black market deals he ran through his dummy corporation Esther Undergarments. When a few of his jealous peers caught wind of the "Industry King's" scam, they saw an opportunity to put a stop to Max's success and had him arrested. He spent the next eleven months feeding the pigs at a medium security workhouse for non-violent criminals in Connecticut.

Upon release, Max started gambling heavily again and losing big. By the dawn of the 1950s, he was desperate to make money and started to drain off all his funds to get credit for his business. When he issued false statements in the mail, the government quickly caught up with him and sent him to a prison upstate, where he resided for a couple of years. When Max was released on parole, he went to work as a cutter/stitcher for a garment competitor for $1000 week.

"That's how good he was—he was always in demand." Willy continued, "I picked him up from prison, and as we are driving back to the city he says to me, *'I have something that's bigger than the atom bomb—I developed a system in jail that can beat the crap tables in Vegas.'* I knew this was impossible and told him I didn't want to know because if it was true, his life wouldn't be worth a nickel—he'd kill a trillion dollar business! To this day I regret not listening to his system." Willy's voice dissolved into laughter.

"By the 1970s Max had fallen on bad times. He was broke and driving a taxicab. Is that humiliating, or what? He was Pincus Max Marcus, the millionaire!" Willy recalled with fervor. "He would drive that taxi and tell people, *'I was the king of the underwear industry once.'*"

Willy let out a long sigh into the telephone. "Max had everything and then had nothing. In the end, I think he was very depressed. Some people say it was an accident, and others say that he did it on purpose."

"*What* was an accident?" I probed.

"Max stuck his head in the gas oven of his apartment, and it blew up. He survived, but he was burned so badly they had to put the bedsheets on poles so they wouldn't touch his scorched skin. He lay in the hospital for several weeks before he died." Willy paused briefly, taking on a serious tone. "I know he was depressed."

We were both silent for a long moment. I couldn't take any more shocking surprises from him.

"So...that was Max," Willy summed up, regaining his cheerfulness. "He was a legend, especially to the people in the garment industry. People loved and hated him—he could be a real son-of-a-bitch at times." Then Willy added, "I've sure have had fun talking with you. I'd be super delighted to hear from your dad, but how do I tell him the truth about Max? Should I glorify it?"

I assured Willy there was no need to color Max any differently than the stories he had shared with me. When we finally said goodnight, his wife Sherry got on the phone and invited us to Florida for an official visit.

Willy had painted a very disarming portrait of Max. His life had encompassed more dramatic moments than a Shakespearian tragedy. He was an immigrant, a war hero, a business tycoon, a pianist, a criminal, a survivor, and an addict. I wish I had known my grandfather first-hand. He may have been a bastard, but he was also an extraordinary and remarkable man.

I was blown away by Max's connection to Uncle Abe. And his connection to Frank Erikson, the biggest Mob bookie in the country, who was associated with Frank Costello and Joey Adonis, who ran the Eastern axis of the syndicate. Everyone I was attempting to hunt down seemed to be inexplicitly linked. Their stories, like a cosmic web, contained filaments that were weaving together into a mysterious architecture.

8

Trail of Blood, Part 1

Uncle Abe and his story were resurfacing in my life again. A few years back I had pieced together a snapshot of his young life and entanglement with "Kid Twist" Reles, but I was still deeply curious about the circumstances surrounding his murder. I had never clearly understood all those varying news articles I'd collected over the years, and back in the day I was simply too preoccupied with matters of being young to really seek out the answers. But now, having found my father's family, I had the confidence and determination to again look at the facts of Abe's case.

There was still no online information to access about Abe in the late 2000s. I ordered his death certificate from the NYC Department of Records and I did most of my research at the library, obtaining interlibrary loans of microfilm. Every time I went through the articles I had collected, I was overwhelmed by the number of differing names and information that were reported. This prompted me to put together a chart. I started with the day of the murder and tracked what every different newspaper reported on that day, and the following days of the investigation. Studying the information chronologically, I was able to sort through the varying details and see clearly the order of events, including where family stories fit on the timeline. Piecing it all together, it became a trail of blood, weaving through the convoluted mystery of Abe's demise.

Wednesday, September 24, 1941, Brooklyn, 8:00 a.m.

When the dailies hit the stands early Wednesday morning, the murder of Abe "Jew Murphy" Babchick, only a few hours earlier, was frontpage news. "Racketeer Slain In Auto." "Gangster Found Shot Near Brooklyn

Police Station." The articles were a jagged tapestry of facts and sordid details.

The *World-Telegram* reported that Uncle Abe's name was really Abe Schwartz. He had been abducted after a large win at "Fats" Feldman's Chinatown crap game in Mulberry Bend. He later was found on the passenger seat of his sedan with two bullets to the back of his head, just blocks from the 71st precinct on Empire Boulevard in Brooklyn. Abe's sedan had been bought from, and registered to, an African-American named Theodore Fenner, who was brought in for questioning.

The *Journal-American* reported that Abe's name was really Abe Heckler, who was disliked by the remnants of Brooklyn's murder-for-hire gang because he was a good friend of Abe "Kid Twist" Reles, who had sent several of his former Murder, Inc. associates to the electric chair. They reported that Abe's pockets were turned inside out, a $20 and $10 bill, along with a nickel on the seat next to him, said to be an underworld sign of a squealer.

The *Brooklyn Eagle* said his name was Abe Bebchick, based on the driver's license in his wallet, but claimed his real name was Schwartz, and listed his previous arrest records.

What was more interesting than the fact that no one knew his real name was that three groups stepped forward as players in a drama that would unfold for the next week in the press: the Brooklyn police department, the Brooklyn District Attorney's office, and Special Prosecutor for the State Attorney General, John Harlan Amen. Each had a theory about the man and the murder.

The police immediately had a scenario. They learned Abe had broken the bank at "Fats" Feldman's, then hid his winnings. They suggested the game's losers took him for a ride to find the money, and when it wasn't found, killed him.

Brooklyn District Attorney, William O'Dwyer, who was credited for taking down Murder Inc. with the help of his concealed pointman, "Kid Twist" Reles, was quick to state that Abe was a "nobody," a small-time policy runner who was trying to muscle into the Brooklyn rackets. O'Dwyer said he would personally take charge of the murder investigation. "It's a simple case of a hold-up or crime of vengeance."[1]

O'Dwyer's statements didn't sit well with John Harlan Amen, who had been appointed by New York Governor Herbert Lehman in 1938 to launch an investigation into official corruption in Brooklyn. Amen's four-year exploration was to become one of the most far-reaching of its kind in the city's history to date, leading to ramifications for police, judicial, medical, business and gambling circles. Amen was suspicious that Abe's murder was a cover-up to quiet his potential witness.

Thursday, September 25, 1941, Brooklyn

Four men were picked-up when the police broke down the door and raided Abe's headquarters the night before—Mudsy Hecker (Leo's father), Meyer Rabinowitz, Jack Meyer, and Phillip Gross. They were questioned for hours at the Empire Boulevard Precinct, where they made statements to DA O'Dwyer that 626 Lincoln Place in Brooklyn was the "nerve center" for their pari-mutuel horse racing policy. Their names and addresses hit the newsstands in the early morning editions, while they were shoved into a line-up. When the police felt convinced the men knew nothing of Abe's murder, they were charged with violating lottery laws and then returned to O'Dwyer's office for further interrogation.

O'Dwyer was holding tight to his robbery concept, now calling Abe a "cheap punk," trying to muscle in on a dice game combine. "He was a welcher," O'Dwyer declared. "He didn't amount to much as a racketeer. He dabbled in policy but concentrated on dice for his income. Last week he left a game owing several thousand dollars and didn't pay until ordered to 'get it up or else.'"[2] O'Dwyer promised that an arrest was imminent.

Special Prosecutor John Harlan Amen, on the other hand, had discovered that Abe was the largest of the well-known policy bankers in Brooklyn, calling him a "millionaire policy king," bringing in an estimated $8,000 to $10,000 a day and employing hundreds of policy bank lieutenants, comptrollers, pick-up men, and runners.

After hearing Amen's public announcement of how large Abe's racket really was, the police issued a new statement, now calling Abe "The Policy King of Brownsville." They claimed that his operation was still new and they believed he had been exterminated by rivals.

Amen countered the police and DA's statements, firing back in a press conference that Abe had *not* been murdered for his gambling winnings or by rivals, but possibly to halt the policy racket investigation his office was conducting, stating, "He possessed invaluable information."[3]

Three months earlier, in June, Amen had been contacted by a lawyer who represented Abe and was negotiating on his behalf to come in and testify before Amen's Grand Jury about the police on his payroll. The conditions asked by Abe's attorney were supposedly "too extreme" to finalize a deal, so Amen was given four detectives for his staff—their sole mission to bring Abe in for questioning. The detectives, who had been looking for Abe all summer, were now being called on the carpet for failing to bring "Jew Murphy" in before his murder. The news journalists questioned why the detectives hadn't picked him up. They stated Abe wasn't in hiding. He could have easily been found on his daily routine from Brownsville to Manhattan and back.

Amen went on to publicly compare Abe's death to the murder of Herman Rosenthal back in 1912. Twenty-nine years earlier that case had rocked the New York underworld. Rosenthal was the gambling king of his day. When a sweeping investigation into gambling was launched, Rosenthal was pressured to talk. He decided to spill about how gambling was permitted by paying off conniving police officers. Police lieutenant Charles Becker knew that if Rosenthal talked, his jig would be up, so he hired four killers—Gyp the Blood, Lefty Louis, Dago Frank, and Whitey Lewis—to close Rosenthal's mouth permanently. They did, shooting him down on a Manhattan street. The scandal shook the city and later the four gunmen, along with Lieutenant Becker, were sent to the electric chair.

Pointing out the Rosenthal similarities to Uncle Abe's case, reporters asked Amen if there was a war of extermination against witnesses in his police corruption investigation.

"A program of intimidation against my potential witnesses in this investigation has been in operation for some time," replied Amen. "It is more than likely, according to our information, that this is another move in the same direction."[4] It was later revealed that during Amen's investigation, the life of another prominent policy banker had been threatened as well.

Although Amen was responsible for pursuing all phases of official corruption, he had to make sure his work was not sabotaged. He continued to vigorously pursue his investigation into the alleged Babchick-police tie-up, promising to give supporting information to DA O'Dwyer in his efforts to apprehend the killers. Amen was confident that Abe was the key to nabbing the authorities protecting the policy rings, and had been put out of the way, directly or indirectly, to hinder his investigation. It was mandatory, Amen now felt, to follow every angle in clearing up the circumstances surrounding Abe's murder.

Still other angles on the murder were surfacing. It was revealed that Abe had extended his policy racket operations from Brooklyn into Manhattan, North Jersey, and West Philadelphia. Homicide Chief John J. McGowan stated that Abe might have incurred the enmity of a rival policy mob in West Philadelphia.

10:30 a.m.

The quartet picked up at Abe's headquarters—Mudsy, Meyer, Jack, and Phillip—after being questioned by police all night, arrived in Felony Court for their arraignment.

Uncle Leo had told the following story: As the judge heard the case, a rustle in the back of the courtroom made all heads turn. Standing at the entrance to the courtroom was seventeen-year old Leo. He was breathless, having run all the way to the courthouse, beads of sweat glistening on his forehead.

"Please, your honor!" shouted the Leo, everyone in the courtroom followed his approach to the bench, shifting in their seats. "Please be lenient on my father, Morris Hecker. He has a family to support. Please don't put my father in jail. Please!" Leo stood motionless before the magistrate. The silence was finally broken by the thud of the judge's hammer. "$2000 bail each. Get them out of here!" The hearing date was set for October 10.

Abe's youngest brother Ike posted Mudsy's bail, after identifying Abe's body at the morgue. Mudsy scolded Leo in the lobby of the courthouse, shaking his finger in his face to never show up at there again.

Next came Aunt Carol's story of the argument between Rae and Bertha about where Abe's money was. Carol insisted that Rae had taken $50,000 that was supposed to be dispersed to the siblings. No one had received anything. One cousin rumored that Abe and Rae kept money in overseas accounts, but Carol insisted they hid money and didn't believe in banks.

I believe the $50,000 Carol referred to was the gambling win from the night of the murder, even though the police reported to the press the gambling win was only $20,000. Supposedly Abe broke the bank with his win, but $20,000, even in 1941, would not have broken a high-stakes crap game. Mort had been told that Abe won $100,000 that night. The win had to be at least that much. Besides, how would anyone know the amount of Abe's win unless it was told by a witness at the crap game?

Let's say it was $50,000. Why were they fighting about $50,000? It didn't seem like that much once divided. But, according to the U.S. Inflation calculator it would be valued at over $700,000 in today's market. That would have been worth about $150,000 for each of the five siblings in that era. Their anger at Rae seemed justified. Yet, it was reported that Abe was taking in over $250,000 a month after paying for police protection. Where was that money?

Friday, September 26, 1941, Brooklyn, 10:00 a.m.

Abe's funeral took place at Temple Petach Tikvah in the Jewish Memorial Chapel at 1406 Pitkin Avenue. The neighborhood was laced with police detectives stationed at various points, hoping to pick up leads for their investigation. The family gathered in the chapel with Rabbi Abraham P. Block and mourned the loss of their brother, son, provider. They were overcome with grief as well as fear, with so many police present.

Later, joined by a handful of friends, the family gathered on the green lawn of Montefiore Cemetery in Springfield, Queens, as Rabbi Block read the Kaddish. One by one they said their goodbyes, filling their hands with the freshly unearthed dirt and tossing it onto the coffin. Abe's final resting place was grave 13, row 10, block 84 at section 7, gate 90S. Now he was just a string of numbers.

The newspapers said Abe was 38 years old when he died. Montefiore recorded his age as 36. The headstone stated he was 35. Like his many aliases, and all the theories of his murder, the truth was unknown.

1:00 p.m.

Two days had passed since the murder and Special Prosecutor Amen had two unique witnesses in his custody who were being guarded under heavy police protection. They had some very important information to spill.

One witness, who would only go by the name of "Zoo," said he was with Abe until 1:30 a.m. at Dubrow's Cafeteria Restaurant on Eastern Parkway the night he died. The *Journal-American* described "Zoo" as a flashy dresser who acted as Abe's bodyguard and chauffeur. "Zoo" told the police that he drove to the restaurant in his own car. Abe drove up in his convertible sedan, in which his body was later found, and parked across the street from the restaurant, in front of the New York Savings Bank.

"From 12:45 a.m. to about 1:30 a.m. we were in the restaurant having a bite to eat. Then the Boss got up and we walked out arm-in-arm. He told me, '*You can go home. I won't need you anymore tonight*,'" remembered "Zoo." "This was a surprise to me. I looked him over. He seemed okay. Just about that time I noticed two young guys loitering in the darkness near the restaurant. I didn't get much of a chance to see what they looked like. But they suddenly flanked the Boss, one on either side, as he stood there, and all three of them got into the convertible. They drove off. I went on home, not thinking much more of it, but that was the last time I saw the Boss alive."[5]

This left me wondering who "Zoo" was. Described as both a chauffeur and bodyguard to Abe, it didn't make sense that he would leave him on a street corner "flanked" by two men who came out of the shadows. The two men were now being sought by police as the killers. This fit DA O'Dwyer's declaration that the murder was a robbery—slain for his dice winnings earlier that evening.

Amen, on the other hand, was speedy to insist that he now had evidence that would expose a police corruption case totaling over $500,000 a year in pay-offs, twice the amount he had originally suspected. These new details had "shaken the police department as never before,"[6] reported the papers.

Amen's second witness, known as "Cappy" or "The Scientist," described as coming from a "good Brooklyn family," was Abe's payoff agent, dispersing a shocking $5000 a week to the authorities. "The Scientist" was now giving details, and his testimony would break Amen's case wide open.

Amen and his staff held to the belief that Abe was silenced to protect the police on his payroll. "If Babchick was killed to stall my investigation of the police department," said Amen, "the murder was in vain."[7]

It appeared that Uncle Abe's death may actually have hastened charges against members of the department. During the previous three years of Amen's investigation he had collected statements from more than 120 people who worked for Abe in his various gambling enterprises, and from these sources evidence was obtained against a number of patrolmen and high-ranking officers. It also produced evidence linking police to the larger crime syndicate. Although "Kid Twist" Reles dominated the concession, the larger syndicate, which embraced policy, gambling, bookmaking, prostitution, and vice, was currently under the greater control of Cosa Nostra boss Joey Adonis.

Adonis, a major criminal power in Brooklyn, had many politicians and high-ranking police officers on his payroll, and used his political influence to assist the criminal rackets of the Luciano crime family and associates such as Louis "Lepke" Buchalter, the head of Murder, Inc., who was currently on trial for murder.

Amen's information was verified by a raid on the gambling headquarters of "Fats" Feldman and Frankie Shields, who were members of the syndicate and operators of the largest games in New York—the very one where Abe had gambled on the night he was killed. After scores of well-known businessmen who frequented the gambling joint had been questioned by Amen, he felt he had enough evidence of police graft to warrant the coming shakedown of the department. Amen's evidence showed that gambling protection was so complete, that "big businessmen and gangsters mingled together openly around the dice tables, secure in the knowledge that police would not harass them."[8]

The newspaper quote left no doubt in my mind that Max Marcus and Abe were definitely gambling buddies.

Saturday, September 27, 1941, Brooklyn, NY

Police detectives were mingling with baseball fans at Ebbet's Field, looking for the two men responsible for Abe's slaying described by the witness "Zoo." Deputy Chief Inspector William T. Reynolds and Captain Howard O'Leary stationed thirty of their men at the gates among Dodger fans, but if their suspects were there, they were lost in the crowd.

The police appeared very busy trying to find suspects for their robbery theory of the murder. But the papers also reported the other side of this mystery—"intimates of Babchick had vanished from the Brownsville scene. This action was assumed to be ordered by 'higher-ups' who are trying to block every path to their door and bar every possible proof of their identity or connection with the lush policy racket."[9]

I wondered who these "higher-ups" were—the syndicate or the police authorities on the take?

Monday, September 29, 1941, Brooklyn, NY

At a press conference, John Harlan Amen put out a plea to the authors of over 100 anonymous letters who claimed to know about Abe's murder and about the police who took bribes. Amen urged the tipsters to come forward. "I hope the writers of these letters will communicate with my assistant, Harold Cohan. He will arrange appointments in the strictest confidence in places outside this office so that spotters and mobmen will not be able to identify anyone who gives information. These letters came on the heels of newspaper reports showing that my office has been investigating payments by Babchick's policy organization to police officers and many appear to contain important information that bears the stamp of real knowledge."[10]

Amen went on to promise full protection for anyone who came forward. "The people who have written me can get in touch with me either by telephone or by writing, safe in the knowledge that their identities will be protected, and they will be furnished police guards if necessary."[11]

Who would feel safe with a police guard if you thought maybe the police were behind all this?

Amen and his team continued to race through leads as fast as the horses at Belmont Park. Before his two Extraordinary Grand Juries, Amen questioned six police, two captains, one sergeant and three detectives to add to the testimonies of over twenty officers and an inspector on bribery charges. All were asked to explain how they made lavish expenditures and amassed fat bank accounts in amounts over $30,000 on their official police salaries of only $4000 a year.

In the five days following Abe's death, over 50 police officers had either disappeared or immediately retired. Simultaneously, a stampede of police and other persons charged into Amen's office in an effort to trade information for protection against prosecution.

Amen planned to question nine more detectives who appeared on Abe's previous four arrest records in the coming days, but he was careful to specify, "This is no reflection on them."[12] He also continued to question every member of the police department who had worked in Brooklyn within the last five years, regardless of where they were currently stationed.

If all that wasn't enough for one day, Amen also uncovered a staff of lawyers with a central assignment office for the crime syndicate. If someone from the syndicate found himself in trouble, despite police protection, an attorney would be sent immediately to his aid, as well as bondsmen, all provided by the syndicate. These lawyers were retained on a monthly fee, which they received whether called upon or not. This legal staff would be summoned before Amen's Grand Jury for testimony and charges would be filed against them with the Kings County Bar Association.

•————————•

John Harlan Amen would go down in history as the "Racket-Buster" of New York's largest investigation into corruption by a municipal body.

From its inception in 1938, Amen's inquiry was making headline news. Mayor La Guardia had started an investigation some six months prior to Amen's appointment, in regard to the theft of over 7200 pages of police records taken from the Brooklyn Bergen police station to cover up evidence of police involvement in the bail bond racket. Magistrate David Hirshfield wrote a strong letter of response to Governor Lehman suggesting he widen his inquiry to include the mayor and his office. Everyone was pointing fingers to bring everyone else down. It was a circus, with a theatrical run slated for the next four years.

One of Amen's earliest moves was to take possession of the court calendars for six magistrates overseeing criminal cases in Brooklyn. This was an historic act, as no court files had ever been under scrutiny before, but Amen stated that every criminal case originated from the magistrates' courts. Brooklyn DA William Geoghan attacked the investigation, calling it "a campaign to smear Brooklyn by persons with political ambitions,"[13] and went on to complain that the Mayor never gave his department funding that came close to what Amen's staff was given.

Amen had all his investigators fingerprinted and scrutinized prior to hire, then sent the information off to Washington. He was confident his staff was "clean" before working on the investigations, and his diligence was also to protect them.

By early 1939, the Governor allowed Amen to create a second Grand Jury to hear the wealth of information he had uncovered in regard to official corruption and graft. Amen already had evidence of thirty cases of such importance that they warranted immediate presentation before a Grand Jury. The Governor's approval had the "effect of partly lifting the lid of secrecy and revealing the extent of Amen's scrutiny of the much-criticized administration of justice in Kings County."[14] Amen's investigation quickly included the criminal courts, the District Attorney's office, the Department of Corrections, and the office of the Commissioner of Jurors.

By 1940, Amen was appointed Assistant State Attorney General to widen the scope of his investigation, but it was fraught with difficulties over the years. Witnesses voiced fears of potential bodily harm if they talked to Amen, and some actually went missing while under police surveillance. Officers were suspended. Police lieutenants who were called into question immediately retired in order to avoid testifying or disappeared from the area altogether. Some committed suicide.

Gambling and the policy rackets were just a part of Amen's investigation, but a big one. By early 1941, Amen requested the appearance of 120 Brooklyn plainclothes patrolmen and their commanding officers before his two Grand Juries, investigating charges that more than $40,000 a month was paid to members of the police department for the systematic protection of organized gambling rings in Brooklyn.

Amen and his staff interviewed many people working for Abe, who detailed key aspects of how Abe ran his organization.

As for the murder, Amen was only allowed to investigate the graft aspect of it. The murder investigation was led by DA O'Dwyer and Homicide Chief John J. McGowan. Amen was not allowed to cross the line and had to work with O'Dwyer's team if he wanted to know the truth behind Abe's slaying.

9

Mystery Road

February 2007

When I arrived in New York for the opening of my photography exhibit it was icy cold. Mark-the-Cop, as I liked to call him these days, picked me up at the airport and we headed for dinner in the Village. He was eager to know if I had learned anything more about the Uncle Abe mystery. I was still hoping to find a crime scene photo, even though Mark could not find a file on Abe's murder. I told him about a clue I had received from Uncle Leo many years ago, that there was a crime scene photograph of Abe's murder on the front page of one of the newspapers, as well as a photo of Leo's father Mudsy, being arrested at Abe's headquarters. That was what I would be hunting for on this trip, during my small amount of spare time.

I was also trying to locate any reports or notes that may have accompanied Special Prosecutor Amen's investigation into Abe and racketeering, which was mentioned in the newspapers. I had no idea where those would be located, but I was sure they held important information and I was determined to find them.

The next day it started to snow and the white flakes were quickly turning to slick ice. I fought the elements to the New York State Office that housed vital records and old photographs downtown on Worth Street. They had nothing about Abe. Shivering, and not wanting to walk around, I returned to the Public Library. I hadn't been there in nine years—maybe those 12th Avenue warehouse files were now in-house.

The afternoon quickly passed as I sped through new articles about the murder. To my surprise, I discovered information about Uncle Frankie, the cowboy. He had resurfaced after the murder, according to the *Brooklyn Daily Eagle's* October 8, 1941 headline: "Abe Bebchick's Brother Faces Lottery Charges—Slain Racketeer's Kin Seized with 4 in O'Dwyer, Amen Raid."

Adrenalized, I met up with Mark and we read the articles together.

Frank Balzak, brother of Abe Bebchick, Brownsville racketeer, whose body was found on the morning of September 24, slumped in the front seat of an automobile on Empire Boulevard with bullet wounds in the back of the head, was one of five men under arrest today charged with contriving a lottery.

The men were taken into custody last night in a raid on a four-story brick house at 287 Hancock Street, by detectives of District Attorney O'Dwyer's staff, agents of Special Assistant Attorney General Amen, and detectives and plainclothesmen of the 13th Detective District...

...Those arrested with Balzak, who said he was 38 and a restaurant proprietor but gave no address, described themselves as Morris [Mudsy] Hecker, 46, Sidney Lewow, 27, Warren Sauer, 23, and Nicholas Sililo, 46,...

The *New York Herald Tribune* reported that Uncle Frankie, Mudsy, and the other men were in the basement of the Hancock Street building counting 35,000 slips, when it was raided at 6:30 p.m. on October 7, 1941. They were locked up at Brooklyn's Gates Street Station and were arraigned in Felony Court the next morning.

According to Edward Heffernan, Assistant District Attorney, the numbers game for which the Hancock Street Basement was the bank, with Balzak supposedly the chief banker, used to be served by over twenty-six drop stations where slips were deposited, but, after Babchick's murder the number dropped to twelve.[1]

The articles stated that Uncle Frankie had been arrested several times, including contriving to run a lottery in 1932, and as far back as 1924 for violation of the Sullivan Law.

"Do you know what that is?" I asked Mark.

"That means he was in possession of a gun."

"What the hell was he doing with a gun in 1924?" I shook my head in amazement.

"Well, cowboys have guns too," Mark snickered. "It makes sense that he may have worked with his brother Abe. Seems to me he was probably always in the business—it was a family business. Let's see if we can find an old arrest sheet for him."

"This is the first real information about Uncle Frankie," I said excitedly. Carol and Dad had said he disappeared in the mid-1940s. I was eager to find out what had really happened to him. It seemed I now had a double mystery on my hands.

●————●

I followed a lead that the *Daily News* had an archive of photos which weren't available at the library. I had yet to find that mythic crime scene photo of Uncle Abe's murder. I called the *Daily News* directly the next morning. They promised to look into the dates and get back to me shortly.

A week later, back in California, I received their reply. They had found the front page of the September 25, 1941 late edition and sent me a high-resolution copy via email.

As I clicked open the file, a bold headline read, "Bullets for Breakfast: The Mobster Died at Dawn."

There it was…the crime scene photograph. The image was a side view of Abe's convertible sedan with the passenger door open, police peering inside from several angles at his lifeless body, which sat upright. Hands in his lap, Abe's head leaned onto his right shoulder. His fedora covered the top portion of his face, and blood ran from his nose down across his cheek.

In an odd sense I found something disarmingly peaceful about the photo. All the complicated political implications and underworld backstabbing that surrounded the murder fell away. There was just Abe, not smiling from a Catskill's vacation photo, but silent and bloody. Whatev-

er violent struggle had taken place that night, Abe was finally at peace—
or was he?

My father often talked about voices when he wrote. "Listen to the voices that speak through you, and then shape those words to have meaning
for others." Abe was continually coming to me in dreams, but they had
morphed slightly. Now he would sit at the edge of my bed, watching me
sleep, as if waiting for me to wake. He didn't say anything. He was like a
dark angel, waiting for the day his voice would flow through mine.

Lost in thought, I went into the kitchen to prepare supper and clicked
on the TV for companionship. Suddenly, I heard my father's voice fill
the room. As I turned back to look at the television screen, it was filled
with an image of Abe. The moment I had turned on the TV, Dad's biography was airing on the local station—and it was the part where he
talked about Uncle Abe. This may have been a random coincidence, be it
appeared to be a sign—Abe *was* trying to speak to me!

10

Trail of Blood, Part 2
Everyone Is Going Down

New York, Autumn 1941

To understand Uncle Abe's murder, and now Frankie's involvement, I had to understand the New York they lived in. I continued researching and adding to my sequential chart of news reports after the murder. The autumn of 1941 was a very busy time for Brooklyn cops and crooks.

During the late September hoopla surrounding Abe's death, a low-level thug named George Gunther was picked up and questioned by Police Captain Frank Bals of DA O'Dwyer's office about the Brownsville rackets. Gunther had a fractured jaw. He spilled that Nathan Katz, an associate of the murder-mob, had caused the injury. They had gotten into a tussle about discrediting Reles and the other Brownsville Boys who would soon be testifying against Murder, Inc. commander "Lepke" Buchalter at his upcoming murder trial. Gunther informed police that Katz was trying to take over as head of the Brownsville rackets now that both "Jew Murphy" Babchick and "Kid Twist" Reles were out of the way. Supposedly Katz had extorted $300 from Uncle Abe before his murder.

So, who *was* running Uncle Abe's policy turf?

Abe Frosch was a round-faced, dopey-looking guy who had started his life of crime by working for his parents in the bail bond racket. He would make bail for the likes of Reles and others by putting forward a property as collateral that was not his. He and his parents were eventually caught, and 28-year-old Frosch turned State's evidence in 1939 to be a witness for Special Prosecutor Amen's Grand Jury presentment against Lieutenant Cuthbert Behan.

Behan had stolen 7200 pages of police records from the Brooklyn Police Department to cover-up his involvement in the large bail bond racket.

While Frosch was in Amen's custody he was allowed to meet privately with Reles, who was sequestered under heavy police guard by the DA's office at the Half Moon Hotel on Coney Island. Criminologist Alan Block wrote that this curious meeting was "supposedly only concerned with an attempt by Reles to bribe his way out of trouble, and Frosch was his liaison."[1] Amen was embarrassed that Frosch was party to this ploy while under his jurisdiction and the incident never appears in Amen's final grand jury report. What Block writes as "startling" is that it appears Frosch took over part of Reles's gambling operation as well as Uncle Abe's policy ring following his murder. Several years later, the new Brooklyn DA, Miles McDonald, broke Frosch's gambling ring and sent him to Sing Sing.

According to all the reports I had collected, Uncle Frankie had taken over Uncle Abe's policy racket, but he was arrested two weeks later. This had me wondering when Frosch had his meeting with Reles and took over the racket—before, during, or after Frankie?

On October 7, Judge Peter Brancato, of Kings County Felony Court, slapped Frankie into jail for his six previous arrests to await trial. Mudsy was held on $5000 bail on top of the $2000 bail he already had pending for his arrest the day of Abe's murder at the Lincoln Place headquarters.

Other than Uncle Frankie and Mudsy's arrest, everything regarding Abe's murder quieted down in the press. There were no new clues from the police who supposedly had 50 officers working on the slaying under the direction of Homicide Captain John J. McGowan and acting Deputy Chief Inspector William T. Reynolds, just a week earlier. They had nothing.

Suddenly, on October 29th, over a month after the murder, the police were hot on the trail of three thugs known for sticking-up card games and robbing gamblers.

Sam Kovner, Abe "The Killer" Beitler, and Sam Kablonsky were spotted creeping around Times Square looking for victims. The police and

District Attorney's office still held to their belief that Uncle Abe's murder was a robbery-gone-wrong and the three thugs became their prime suspects, based on the eyewitness testimony of "Zoo."

According to news reports, Detective Robert Bowe of the Brooklyn Homicide Squad spied Sam Kovner on 47th street and cornered him in a doorway where Kovner immediately put his hands in the air and gave up. Accompanied by Empire Precinct officer Edward McGowan and Manhattan Detective Hyman Levine, Bowe took Kovner back to the Hotel Abbey on 51st and 7th Avenue, where "The Killer" Beitler's gang had been hiding out in room 949. They handcuffed Sam Kovner and waited, hoping Beitler would return. Several hours transpired when finally, at 2:30 a.m., there was a secret knock at the door.

"Get it," demanded Detective Bowe of Kovner.

Shaking his head back and forth, Kovner refused. "Not me. When the door opens the Killer'll start shooting!"[2]

Bowe threw Kovner to the floor and made for the door. It was Beitler, and he started shooting away like a regular Jesse James. He wasn't alone. Kablonsky was behind him and the two ran down the hall in opposite directions—the chase was on. Officer McGowan ran after Kablonsky to the left while Detective Bowe volleyed shots with Beitler all the way down the corridor to the right.

Beitler made for the elevator and ended up on the 22nd floor, fleeing into a dark ballroom. The police told reporters that when Beitler entered the ballroom, he saw a man through the far window. He thought it was a cop and fired twice. What Beitler didn't realize was that the Hotel Victoria was smack-dab against the Hotel Abbey, having once been a single hotel. The man in the window was a songwriter from Detroit, in town for his first successful Broadway show, who had gone to the window to see what all the commotion was about. He died, shot in the heart and the head by "The Killer" Beitler.

By the time Detective Bowe got to the ballroom, he said Beitler had turned the gun on himself and lay dead on the floor.

Kovner and Kablonsky were taken into custody and questioned for 24 hours by DA O'Dwyer and Brooklyn Homicide Chief John J. McGowan. Interestingly, McGowan was now reporting that Beitler had extorted

$500 from Uncle Abe a few weeks before his September 24th murder. He suggested the thugs either saw Uncle Abe's murder, knew about it, or assisted Beitler in committing the crime.

Kablonsky had been released from Sing Sing prison only a few weeks before the Times Square shoot out. He had no information about Uncle Abe's case and was immediately sent back to prison for parole violation.

Kovner was held on suspicion of a robbery committed several months earlier and was indicted before Judge Samuel Leibowitz on charges of first-degree robbery, grand larceny, and second-degree assault charges. Kovner pleaded not guilty and waited in the Raymond Street jail for his court date.

On November 12, exactly seven weeks after Uncle Abe's murder, "Kid Twist" Reles mysteriously fell to his death from a window at the Half Moon Hotel on Coney Island where he had been a protected witness for almost 14 months by the Brooklyn District Attorney's office. The police bantered that he was "the canary that could sing, but couldn't fly."[3]

Reles had turned state's evidence in 1940, naming seven of his pals in Murder, Inc., including Martin "Buggsy" Goldstein, and saw them eventually sent to the electric chair. Reles claimed he was afraid of no one except mob boss Albert "The Lord High Executioner" Anastasia, whom he would soon be testifying against.

Considered one of the great mysteries in crime history, it has never been resolved if Reles jumped from the hotel room window on the 6th floor, where he was under heavy police guard, or if he was pushed. In the last 75 years there have been many theories about his death, but according to renowned crime writers, there are holes in all the theories.

From the moment Reles' body was found on the extension roof of the Half Moon Hotel, a 40-foot plunge from his hotel room window, the investigation was plagued by incompetence. Captain Bals, feeling overwhelmed, called his friend Chief McGowan to help him sort through the mess. Neither of them had the crime scene preserved or recorded according to standards. Reles' body had not fallen at the correct trajectory to assume he had jumped, but McGowan and Bals never accurately measured the distance. Statements from hotel employees were never taken. Reles' clothes were never collected from the medical examiner. Testimonies by the five police who were watching the oceanfront suite of rooms on the 6th floor, changed from the morning of the event to the official hearing, and again during the reopening of the case ten years later in 1951.

Reles had become Special Prosecutor Amen's second potential witness to die violently before testifying about Brooklyn police being paid to protect gambling in the borough. Amen had an agreement with DA O'Dwyer that Reles would be turned over to him for questioning about his relationship with politicians and police after the DA's office was through with him as a witness against Murder, Inc.

Amen had only spoken to Reles once, ten months earlier in January of 1941, when Reles was under O'Dwyer's custody. Amen was not alone with Reles during this questioning and felt Reles was uncomfortable divulging details about the bribes being given to officials. Amen admitted to the press that Reles' death "has cut off an important source of information in so far as my office is concerned."[4] Reles' death may have been an even greater blow to Amen than to O'Dwyer's prosecution of the murder-mob.

Two weeks after Reles death, on November 30, Louis "Lepke" Buchalter, the head of Murder, Inc., was found guilty of first-degree murder along with his cohorts Emanuel "Mendy" Weiss and Louis Capone for ordering the hit on candy store owner Joseph Rosen. Although Reles died before he could testify, murder-mob member Allie "Tick Tock" Tannenbaum's testimony sealed the deal. On December 2, 1941 Buchalter, Weiss, and Capone were sentenced to death in the electric chair.

It had been an extraordinary three months of crime activity—but the year ended with "a date which will live in infamy."[5] On December 7, the Japanese attacked Pearl Harbor and President Roosevelt swiftly declared war. The cops-and-robbers stories in the news took a backseat to America's focus on the war.

11

L.A. Confidential

Santa Cruz, August 2007

I searched through Grandma Rae's papers for clues. As I sifted through the old photos I discovered one of Rae with another woman, whose hair was neatly rolled in a 1940s up-do. Their clothes reminded me of The Andrew Sisters and I started humming *Boogie Woogie Bugle Boy* as I turned the photograph to its reverse side. The caption read "Rae and Birdie."

Birdie Sunkin had been Grandma Rae's best friend. They grew-up together in Brownsville, and although Grandma had spoken of her often, Birdie had moved with her husband and children to Los Angeles in the early 1940s. I telephoned Dad and asked about Birdie. He immediately responded, "Don't you remember?" reminding me that I'd met her in 1974.

I was 12 years old and Grandma Rae was visiting California. Birdie drove up from Los Angeles with her brother to rendezvous with Rae one afternoon at our home. Birdie was blonde and faceless in my memories, but I vividly recalled her brother. He was a tall, boisterous gent in a brown suit who became very taken with Valerie and me. He tossed us up in the air, chased us around the living room, and finally dared us to a game of Gin Rummy. We giggled and drank soda pop while Rae and Birdie stirred their coffee and kibitzed at the kitchen table.

I can remember standing on the curb of the street, waving goodbye to the nice man and his sister when the afternoon ended. I could still feel the imprint of his big hands where he lifted me up for a good-bye hug.

He seemed so massive, like a jolly green giant. He insisted my father come to L.A. for a visit—they would take us kids out for a good time at Disneyland.

Once back in the house, a distressed Rae confronted Mort. "Did you like him? Are you going to L.A. to visit them?"

"Well, Mom, you know I can't stand L.A., but it was very nice to…"

"Promise me," Rae interrupted. "SWEAR to me you will never see him again…SWEAR!!" Rae's bellow immediately turned to a hysterical sob, and she threw herself on the sofa, burying her face in the pillows.

"Mom, what is this?" Mort went to her side.

"Mortelah, he was your Uncle Abe's driver that night…you see?" she sobbed. "After the murder he disappeared. He's never worked a day in his life since and has a new Cadillac every year. SWEAR to me you will never see him again…*a finstere cholem auf dein kopf!*" Rae pushed her face back into the pillows and moaned. Jew-doo translation: A nightmare upon his head.

Mort had never seen his mother like this before. He was stunned. Of course the discovery of the news article at the 1988 family dinner was 14 years in the future, when she would again become hysterical at the mention of Uncle Abe.

Grandma Rae was accusing the fun-loving giant of being the point-man on the night of Abe's murder. She insisted he was involved and knew the truth about what happened that night—something we all wanted to know.

Dad concluded his story by adding that Birdie's son, Burt, called him several times in the last years of Rae's life to make sure his "Aunt Rae" was being well taken care of.

I was astonished to learn Birdie's brother had been Abe's chauffeur. Could he be the mysterious "Zoo" who gave the eyewitness testimony? After an hour-long conversation on the phone with Dad, which dove-tailed into rehashing Abe theories, I asked for Burt's phone number. He gave it to me and we said good night.

Two minutes later Dad rang me back. "Why do you want to call Burt? You can't just call people up and start asking them questions. You don't know if these people know anything or not. Why drum up family secrets they may not know anything about. They may not be able to handle it!"

"Dad, what if he *does* know something? Trust me—I'm pretty good at cold calling people these days."

"You're just fortunate the Marcuses opened up to you. Most people aren't like that. If someone like you called, asking questions, I'd hang-up on you."

"That's great, Dad." I rolled my eyes and sighed. I was surprised at his unwillingness to make connections that might lead to answers. "Look, I'm not going to come straight out and ask, *'was your uncle involved in my uncle's murder?'*"

"You better not. Wait and see what he tells you," Dad instructed me.

"Yes, but what if he doesn't say anything because he thinks I don't know?"

Burt Sunkin was more than willing to speak with me. He swooned over his love for "Aunt Rae," and how she and Birdie had an exceptional friendship that lasted for decades. I told him that I was interested in stories about Rae, Birdie, and the old neighborhood in Brooklyn.

"Well, my mother was Birdie Rabinowitz back then. It was long before she married my father, Harry Sunkin."

"Rabinowitz?" My mind immediately flashed back to the newspaper articles. "Are you related to a Meyer Rabinowitz?"

"Yes,…that's my uncle. How did you know his name?"

"Ahh…well…umm…I had it written down someplace. I think he worked with Rae's brother." I was struggling to keep my answer simple.

"I don't really know anything about the old Brooklyn days, I was just a small child when we left New York. You should really talk to my older brother Mickey. He's 80 now, and knows everything. He's the keeper of the family stories."

Unbeknownst to Burt, he had just given me a *huge* piece of the puzzle. I knew his uncle Meyer's name because he was one of the four men arrested at Abe's headquarters the day of the murder. Meyer Rabinowitz had been Birdie's brother! The papers had announced his name, address, and bail amount. Would the police really have given him the protective name of "Zoo" just three days later? Meyer's address in the papers had been listed in Gutenburg, New Jersey. How did a Brooklyn guy end up in Jersey?

●————●

The next evening, I called Mickey Sunkin, introducing myself as Rae's granddaughter.

"Oh my god! Oh my god!" he crooned ecstatically in a thick Brooklyn accent.

He asked about Mort and we exchanged pleasantries about our current families—Mickey always responded with an exuberant, "I'm thrilled ta hear…that's wunda-ful. Wunda-ful!" I explained that I had spoken with his brother, who suggested I call him for the old Brooklyn stories.

"He wouldn't know anything. He was only three years old. I was 13!" he boasted. "I remember Rae as clearly as if she were my own mother!"

"I understand they were friends since they were small children in Brownsville?" Mickey disregarded my question and immediately started his delightful stories.

"Rae was from Europe. My mother was born in Harlem. Rae lived in a tenement, I think. There was a guy who lived in the building, a fighter named Slapsie Maxie Rosenbloom. He ran around with them. He was a famous punch-drunk fighter. I knew Slapsie!" Mickey gushed with pride, then lowered his voice to a whisper. "Rae had a couple of marriages, ya know…"

"I do know," I answered, and we both laughed.

"The last night we were in New York, before we got on a train to move to California, my mother, Burt, and I stayed in Rae's apartment on Eastern Parkway. Rae and Birdie grew up in Crown Heights, next to Brownsville. Do ya know Brooklyn? The end of Eastern Parkway is Brownsville, from Eastern Parkway up is Crown Heights. That's where the Lubavitches came from. You wouldn't know what that is, right?"

"Sure, that's the Hassidic Jews…," but Mickey was so excited to tell stories that he had already moved on to the next subject.

"And I knew your Great Uncle Goggie. The one that was shot!" He bellowed into the phone. "We called him Goggie because he had glasses as thick as coke bottles. That was his nickname."

"How funny!" I exclaimed at this new piece of information.

"It was not funny!" He blurted back in a serious tone. "We came to California in '41 before the war, and we heard on Walter Winchell's radio show that Goggie was shot. What else do you want to know? You can ask me anything you want."

"I'd like to know about Uncle Abe."

"You mean Goggie!" Mickey shouted again. "He was a bookmaker, a professional gambler. I think he died in late September '41. I remember cause my birthday is September 26."

"What was he like?" I asked eagerly.

"He was a good guy. He loved crap games, prize fights, and all the action. He was never a tough guy, he wasn't like with the Murder Incorporated fellas. He was a bookmaker, numbers guy—always played the odds and stuff like that. He was doing that during the depression. I can still picture him in my mind. We all loved him."

"Did any of your uncles work for him?"

"My mother Birdie worked for him!" he shouted again. "It was very bad times in Brooklyn during the depression. My father was a taxi driver and it was very difficult to make a living. My mother used to stand in front of the building where we lived in Brooklyn and Goggie's guys, who would collect money for the numbers, would come and give her paper bags filled with cash. Then she would wait for Goggie to come at the end of the day and give him all the bags. I knew it was for the numbers racket. He gave her a few bucks every day, so it helped us. This was around 1938."

"What did your family think when he was killed?"

"Aww, we were all I very upset over it," his voice got serious. "My mother was crying. We loved him. He and Rae were family."

"Your uncle, Meyer…" I began to ask.

"Meyer is gone. They are all gone. He was my mother's younger brother. He lived with us when he was single. It was tough times and he drove the taxi at night after my father drove it during the day. Meyer was into some shady things. Goggie may have done some stuff with Meyer, but I wouldn't know about that. The depression was bad in New York. You couldn't get work. A taxi drop was a nickel or a dime and another nickel every half mile. It was very tough. We had nothing. Rae, thank god, was married to the guy Marcus. After that she got another guy. Rae was a good-hearted person."

"She did get married a lot!" I giggled.

"Yeah, well listen, if you didn't know anything you had to marry well to have money. The circles she and my mother hung around in…they didn't know any doctors or lawyers, you know what I'm saying?" Mickey chuckled. "They ran around with just average guys, and my mother didn't marry my father until he proved himself."

"Did you ever hear a story that one of Birdie's relatives was a driver for Abe?"

"Well it must have been Meyer, because he was a taxi driver. He drove at night and Goggie…well…I don't think he could see so good with those thick glasses. It's very possible."

"Meyer never talked about the old days when he was out in California?"

"Nah, Meyer finally got married to a woman with a kid from New Jersey…in Bergen county somewhere."

"I read in the papers that Meyer was one of four guys arrested at Abe's headquarters."

"You mean Goggie!" he bellowed into the phone to correct me. "I was told they had a crap game that night and there was a big argument. Someone said something, and someone said something else, and boom, Goggie got shot. That's all I knew. The strange part is that Meyer came to California very quickly after that. As you are talking to me I am putting two and two together. But Meyer never carried a gun or anything. He was into small-time petty things…he didn't rob anyone, he just enjoyed a little swindle here and there."

"Did he ever go by the nickname 'Zoo?'"

"I only knew him as Meyer. But he changed his last name to Rabin when he came out to California. He got a job working in a junkyard and then short-changed the owner," Mickey chuckled heartily. "All I know is we got the story about Goggie from Walter Winchell on the radio that night. My mother and father ran about three blocks to the drugstore, cause we didn't have a phone, and called Rae. She was in shock, like. And I heard about it when my parents came home. Meyer came out to California a couple months later. I'll tell you one thing though—Meyer never had a nickel. He knew some people in Los Angeles who gave him a job."

We continued to talk for over an hour. Mickey was an overflowing fountain of bubbling stories. Everything was "Wunda-ful!" Family: Wunda-ful! Grandchildren: Wunda-ful! I love old Jewish men—no one else can tell an animated story, filled with so much character and love, the way they can. "If you need any more *bobbemyseh*—you know what that means? 'Grandmother's tales,'—you call me. I'm the character in the family, I know it all," laughed Mickey.

This had been a very revealing conversation—Birdie had worked for Abe, and Meyer had quickly started a new life in L.A. What really moved me was that I had just spoken to one of the few people still alive who had known Abe, and it was touching to hear how he was so loved.

Goggie—what a name. Dad remembered Abe wearing glasses. Obviously he needed them. Yet Abe is not wearing glasses in any of the photos I have of him. Perhaps he was self-conscious. But, in the crime scene photos of that dreadful night, Abe is not wearing glasses either. He wouldn't have gone gambling without them. He wouldn't have attempted to drive himself home without them.

I was sure Meyer had to be the police witness known as "Zoo," but I didn't understand why Grandma had been so fearful of him. It was looking like her best friend's brother may have orchestrated events the night of the murder.

12

Trail of Blood, Part 3
The Fall Guys

Brooklyn, February 1942

Five months after Abe's murder, John Harlan Amen was wrapping up his second Grand Jury investigation into Brooklyn corruption. He named over 49 lieutenants, sergeants, chief inspectors, detectives, and patrolmen who had been extorting from Uncle Abe. Fourteen of them sought immediate retirement rather than being forced to testify. Even if some of the officers did not receive punishment, their names and photographs splashed across the frontpage of newspapers succeeded in humiliating them for the rest of their lives.

Mudsy, Jack, and Phillip, picked up at Abe's headquarters, were each sentenced to one year in prison. It didn't appear that Meyer had served a jail term, and according to Mickey Sunkin, he immediately moved to Los Angeles. He may have cut a deal with the DA for his witness testimony as "Zoo," which would explain his quick departure while the other men went to jail.

On February 10, 1942, Uncle Frankie faced the court on charges of violating lottery laws. The *Daily News* reported that Frankie told the judge that Balzak was the real family name—insisting that Babchick was an alias used by both he and Abe to protect the family, who were scared by threats and trying to distance themselves from the murder.

Uncle Frankie swore to the court that he was out of the numbers game, but had been lured back in, determined to flush-out his brother's killers. Judge Peter Brancato didn't believe him. The Magistrate felt the rich receipts from Abe's racket were his real motive, and he demanded Frankie receive the maximum 36-month sentence.

At the same time, Sam Kovner, arrested the previous fall in the Times Square shoot-out for potentially being involved in, or knowing about Uncle Abe's murder, was facing the Supreme Court for an early robbery charge. His trial started—and ended—on February 11.

I found several curious news articles which reported that Judge Samuel Leibowitz threatened Kovner at the end of his trial to tell what he knew about Uncle Abe's murder. This seemed oddly out of context, so I ordered the court transcript to review Kovner's case. I discovered that his story was a vital piece of the Uncle Abe mystery—and a complicated one.

Sam Kovner was a tall guy with an unruly bush of hair who worked as a shoe salesman in Brooklyn. The 28-year-old had several previous robbery arrests and was known to bet on the pari-mutuel horse races and other gambling games. The case against Kovner stated that he had robbed 30-year-old bookmaker, Lawrence Armocida, in December of 1940 at a candy store on Church Avenue in Brooklyn.

Armocida claimed that he was sitting at the soda fountain when Kovner appeared in the doorway and asked him to come outside to talk. Armocida refused and claimed Kovner used force to take him down the block, where a short man in dark clothes was waiting for them. When cross-examined, the bookie changed his story, saying that Kovner had not forced him, and he had been able to easily release himself from Kovner's grasp, went back to the candy store, took the cash out of his pocket and hid it. The bookie stated that Kovner then came back into the store followed by the short man in black, whom Armocida identified as "The Killer" Beitler—Kovner's cohort during the October Times Square shoot-out.

Armocida finished his account, saying that Beitler pointed a revolver at him and the candy store owner demanding their money. "[Kovner] put his hand in my pocket and removed a $15 check, He tried to punch me, then crumpled the check into a ball and threw it over the counter. He walked out. Beitler followed him."[1]

When Kovner took the stand, he said he placed horse bets with Armocida and they often drank together at Bucky's Bar on Utica Avenue. Kovner's version was that he had gone to the candy store to retrieve his gambling winnings in the amount of $140 that Armocida owed him but refused to pay. Kovner said Beitler was not there, nor had he seen any strangers hanging around on the street.

When asked if he knew Beitler, Kovner replied yes, but wanted to explain. The Court would not allow him to speak in his own defense or explain his relationship with Beitler. Judge Samuel Leibowitz would not grant Kovner's lawyer an extension for witnesses or answer the jury's questions about the charges. the Judge was in a hurry—he wanted the case closed by the end of the day.

The verdict was guilty of first-degree robbery and Kovner was facing a 15- to 30-year sentence for stealing the $15 check—but Kovner hadn't stolen anything (at least in this case). Even the bookie testified that Kovner threw the crumpled check back over the counter as he left the candy store. Kovner insisted he had been framed, and that "The Killer" Beitler was not there. Even though Kovner was vigorously cross-examined about his relationship with Beitler, he continually insisted he'd only met him a few months earlier and was unaware of what Beitler "was all about."[2]

The DA's team seemed determined to tie Kovner to Beitler during the robbery, and even had Homicide Chief John J. McGowan testify against Kovner for his involvement in the Times Square shootout, which should have been thrown out of court.

Before Judge Leibowitz sent Kovner back to his cell to await sentencing, he shook a stern finger at him. "You know the killers of Abe Babchick, and take it from me, you'll talk to the District Attorney about it if you know what's good for you."[3] The Judge's threat asserted that Kovner would be sent to Sing Sing for the full sentence if he didn't.

At no time during the trial had Uncle Abe's name ever come up, even when Kovner was asked about bookmakers he knew or was associated with. It was bizarre that Judge Leibowitz mentioned Uncle Abe at the end of the trial, and his threat never appears in the final court transcripts.

Yet, the following day the papers were filled with bold headlines such as "Orders Thug to Name Gambler's Killers."[4]

None of this trial made sense to me. Kovner had no reason to lie about Beitler not being at the candy store. Beitler had killed himself during the Times Square shootout. If we are to assume the bookie's story is true, Beitler had the gun and made the threats, not Kovner—who could have blamed the whole robbery on Beitler if he wanted to. Instead, a case where nothing had been stolen, turned into a 15- to 30-year sentence for Kovner.

It seemed to me that with Beitler dead and Kovner being silenced, Chief McGowan and the DA's office could easily wrap-up their robbery-murder theory of Uncle Abe's death by blaming it on Beitler. "The Killer" and Kovner were looking more and more like the perfect fall guys for the authorities.

The newspaper coverage of Kovner's trial abruptly stopped. There was no further information whether he had revealed details of Uncle Abe's murder to the Judge before his sentencing. I wondered if Kovner even knew anything about Uncle Abe.

Assuming Kovner did the minimum 15 years, he would have been 43-years-old if he was released in 1957. That would make him about 93 today. Could he still be alive? I Googled him.

The result was an article from *New York Magazine*, 2005, "Multibillionaire commodities king Bruce Kovner is the patron saint of the neoconservatives, the new Lincoln Center's crucial Medici, owner of a vast Fifth Avenue mansion—and the most powerful New Yorker you've never heard of."[5]

As I read through the article of hedge-fund multi-billionaire Bruce Kovner, it mentioned his family roots.

The Kovners were big, physical men. Moishe Kovner [Bruce's father] played pro football for a time. Moishe's older brother, Sam, known as "Big Sam," was a player in the Jewish underworld…Sam pulled a long stretch

in Sing Sing—"the only member of the family who went to music school,"
cousin Abraham Kovner says jokingly.[6]

These Kovners were bound to know what happened to Sam—but I
had no idea how to contact a multi-billionaire recluse in New York City.
I did a search for his cousin instead.

Quickly, I had found Abraham Kovner's address and phone number in Manhattan. As I contemplated calling him, I was reminded of
the threatening message to our family—*Don't try to find out what happened to Abe or we'll kill the whole family.* I rationalized that petty thugs
like Kovner and "The Killer" Beitler probably wouldn't have bothered
to make a phone call like that—they wouldn't have wasted the nickel.
I dialed Kovner's number and left a message asking him to contact me.

Three days later he called me back.

"This is Kovner," announced a deep, low voice. "What's your game?
Why you diggin' up stuff about Sam?"

At first he was skeptical about my motives. When I mentioned that I
was doing genealogical research about my Great Uncle, Abe Babchick,
he opened up.

"Ahh…,well, my Uncle Sam was a petty foot soldier, nothing more.
Honestly, he wasn't very bright. He couldn't have orchestrated anything
on his own. I'll tell you this much though, he was scared to death. He
never told anything about anything. He kept his mouth shut."

"What was he scared of?"

"That he'd be killed, whether in jail or not, by higher-ups…the police
and the DA's office."

"So he was silent and did his full jail term?"

"Yup. The only Kovner to go to music school!" The old man laughed at
his joke about Sing Sing prison—the same line he'd used in the magazine
article.

●————————●

A year later, in March of 1943, Kovner was back in court with a new
lawyer seeking an appeal. Maurice Edelbaum Esq., had pointed out the

many flaws of the first trial to the court. It was revealed that two detectives had visited the candy store owner at home and had coerced his identification of Beitler during the robbery. Although the new defense had made a strong case that Kovner's trial had been unfair, an appeal was denied.

My theory that keeping Kovner quiet was essential for allowing the police the cover story they needed, was plausible after I discovered an incredible connection to the renowned Malinski Murder Trial.

Detective James A. Bell, Jr., of the Brooklyn District Attorney's office, gave a shocking testimony in 1946, that three years earlier he had taken long-term convicts from their Sing Sing prison cells for weekends of partying in Manhattan. Bell's testimony came during a cross-examination at the second murder trial of Morris Malinski, charged with slaying a patrolman in 1941. The convicts that Detective Bell took out of prison included none other than Sam Kovner, along with David Yellin and Nathan Spielfogel, who were all star witnesses against Malinski at his first trial in 1943.

Once a month, Bell said he took Kovner out of prison to visit his sweetheart and to be wined and dined in Manhattan—all paid for by the DA's office. He also took Yellin to visit his girlfriend, and later when she gave birth to a baby, the DA's office paid the hospital expenses—all while Yellin was giving testimony for the State against Malinski. Detective Bell admitted to taking the third convict, Spielfogel, in a chauffeur-driven car, every month for two years to visit his wife. At no time were the convicts handcuffed on these trips, whether in the streets, hotels, or restaurants. They also received monthly stipends from a DA fund while in prison.

Bell's testimony that Sam Kovner was being taken care of by the DA was startling, but I wanted to know how Kovner was connected to the Malinski case to earn such rewards. I did some digging into the original Malinski trial of 1943. The further back I went to the root of the crime, the more baffling it all became.

It all started on the evening of February 15, 1941, when Coney Island police inspector Leon Fox went to Loew's Coney Island Theater on Surf Avenue to escort the theater manager with the evening's money deposit to the Brooklyn Trust Bank a few blocks away. According to the theater manager, suddenly a man came out of the shadows and shot the officer in the chest, demanding the theater manager turn over the bag of money, and then ran to a waiting car 30 feet away. Officer Fox, lying on the ground mortally injured, managed to shoot at the car. The gunman turned and fired again, hitting Fox a second time, then zoomed away. Officer Fox died the next morning.

Two days later, after a 200-officer processional to Fox's funeral, a new version of what happened surfaced by unknown witnesses: they claimed there were actually two or three men participating in the robbery, and one man waiting in the getaway car. In the following months a legion of potential suspects were brought in and marched before the court. Every month there was a new group of thugs who had their names and addresses printed in the papers as potentially responsible for the robbery-murder of Officer Fox. Ultimately, no one was charged and the crime was never solved.

A year-and-a-half later, on October 26, 1942, acting Brooklyn DA Thomas C. Hughes (O'Dwyer was on leave in the Armed Forces) and Assistant DA Edward Heffernan—both of whom had been the prosecutors at Sam Kovner's trial—announced they had solved the Fox case. They proclaimed in a press conference that "The Killer" Beitler was the murderer—even though Beitler had been dead for over a year. The DA's stated they had been "secretly" investigating the Fox case all along and Sam Kovner had supplied the information that "The Killer" Beitler was Fox's shooter, in cahoots with Morris Malinski and two others.

This was perplexing. The press had been announcing monthly, throughout 1941, a slew of different suspects the cops were picking up for the Fox murder. It wasn't being investigated in secret. So, how *did* Sam Kovner get involved?

In November of 1942, Morris Malinski, Sidney Rudish and Joseph Indovino were indicted for acting in concert with the dead Beitler for the Officer Fox murder. Police charged that Beitler and Malinski each possessed revolvers, but Beitler fired the fatal bullet. Rudish was accused of driving the getaway car and Indovino was said to have been the "finger man." They all pled not guilty to first-degree murder charges, but were held without bail to await trial.

During the initial 1943 trial, along with the damning testimony given by Kovner and the other two "paid" convicts, the only piece of evidence that placed Malinski at the crime scene was a felt fedora, found in the stolen getaway car. Inside the hat was an imprint of the haberdasher, who was able to identify the owner. It was traced to a man in the military, who stated he'd lent the hat to Malinski. The three men were found guilty and sentenced to die in the electric chair based on the fedora.

An appeal to the U.S. Supreme Court revealed that Malinski's confession had been coerced, the conviction was reversed, and a new trial was ordered for Malinski. Rudish and Indovino were set free.

The real craziness started at Malinski's new trial in June of 1946, when the jury heard the amazing confession by Detective Bell that during the two years of appeals, the convicts Sam Kovner, Nathan Spielfogel, and David Yellin, who were the star witnesses against Malinski, were taken out of Sing Sing and well taken care of by the DA. Acting Police Captain on the case, James McNally, said they also extended favors to Malinski, letting him stay in a hotel before his arraignment in 1943. When Captain McNally was asked why they let Malinski stay in a hotel, his ridiculous answer was, "It was done at Malinski's request. He preferred the hotel to jail."[7] It came out that Malinski's hotel "stay" was really a beating by the cops, where he was stripped naked and told to confess or else.

Over the 13-day retrial, it was revealed that Kovner and the other paid convicts were coached and coerced by both the DA and their detectives on what to say when they appeared on the stand. Convict Spielfogel was actually Malinski's brother-in-law, and on the stand recanted his original testimony against him saying, "Malinski couldn't shoot anything but dice."[8] He was innocent. Never did the crime. Spielfogel said he had been told to lie by Brooklyn DA's Thomas C. Hughes, Edward Heffernan, James A. McGough, and Captain McNally. The three years as a state's witness, Spiefolgel said, "were just a round of crap games, liquor and women,"[9]—with the DA's office supplying them with the good times and weekly funds.

DA Edward Heffernan admitted that he, "recommended a series of payments"[10] to the witnesses—after discussing it with DA Clerk James Moran—but denied knowing what the amount was or about the women they were allowed to see. Over $9,000 in payments were given to the convicts by the DA's office when they were preparing the Malinski case for retrial. Captain James McNally, who was in charge of the police investigation, added on cross-examination "all stool pigeons receive money,"[11] claiming it was common practice.

The piece of evidence that finally freed Malinski from his death sentence was the same fedora hat that had first convicted him. On the stand, Malinski was asked to put the hat on his head. It was so big it fell over his eyes, leaving only the tip of his nose and chin exposed—it was not his. Never borrowed. When Spielfogel learned that his brother-in-law Malinski was found innocent, he was so guilt ridden over the lies he had told, that he attempted suicide by cutting his wrists.

For me, the big question was why did the authorities need to bribe the convicts to begin with? Did the DA or the police have something to do with Officer Fox's murder? Was Fox a "clean" cop and the "dirty" cops wanted him silenced during John Harlan Amen's corruption investigation, which was in full swing in 1941? If that was the case, they already had their scapegoat with "The Killer" Beitler, who was now dead and couldn't say otherwise.

Morris Malinski was freed on June 29, 1946. The DA's and detectives that testified, or were exposed for bribery and corruption during the trial, were never investigated or saw any repercussions for almost sending three innocent men to the electric chair—from what I had researched. By the end of the appeal trial in 1946, Amen's investigation into official corruption was long over.

The common factors in both the Uncle Abe and Officer Fox murders were Sam Kovner and "The Killer" Beitler, along with the DA's and detectives that ran both the investigations. Beitler was an easy—and dead –fall guy for police cover-ups, with Kovner backing-up the concocted stories. I question if Beitler really fired the shot that hit the songwriter standing in the window or committed suicide that day in Times Square. I theorize that it may have actually been Detective Bowe who killed the onlooker while aiming at Beitler. Only Detective Bowe knows for sure, but I have a feeling both Beitler and the onlooker were met by the officer's bullets.

Following the threads of Sam's story, and cases such as the Maliniski trial, strengthened my belief that this was the perimeter of the Uncle Abe cover-up by the same officials.

13

Brooklyn's Finest

I knew I was on to something. I buried myself in research for the next few months, locating documents and trying to grasp the law enforcement landscape in 1940s New York. I even reached out to experts in the field. One of those was Alan Block.

The renowned professor of Criminology and Jewish Studies at Penn State had written the only reference to Uncle Abe that I'd ever been able to find in a published book. Block's *East Side, West Side: Organizing Crime in New York*, mentioned Abe's murder in only a single paragraph, but he had written important and rather disturbing information about the authorities of that time period.

I was eager to connect with Professor Block, hoping that he might share some of his unpublished research with me. Unfortunately, his wife said he had Alzheimer's disease. She was kind enough to invite me to rummage through their basement in Pennsylvania, filled wall-to-wall with Alan's research—until I mentioned that I lived in California. She was regretful that she couldn't help and suggested I contact a lawyer named Jeremiah McKenna who had done research with Alan. She gave me his phone number.

I was crushed that the one man who was a leading scholar on Jewish crime in the 1940s was now lost in his own inner world. Before I gave up all hope, I looked up Mckenna on the internet. He had been the Assistant DA for Manhattan from 1958 to 1965 in the Organized Crime Bureau. My spirit was regained as I dialed Mckenna's number in Connecticut.

A cheery woman answered the phone, and when I mentioned that Alan Block had referred me for research purposes she exclaimed, "Oh, dear! Jerry has advanced Alzheimer's disease, I'm afraid he doesn't remember much of anything."

"I'm so sorry to have bothered you," I replied, now in shock for the second time within the hour.

"Hold on though, I'll let you speak to him…"

"No! Wait!" I begged, but before I could continue the woman had passed the phone over to him.

"This is Jerry Mckenna, how can I help you?" The voice was confident, even lucid, but I was hesitant to launch into my story. This was all very awkward, so I simply said I was doing research on old gangsters from Brooklyn.

"Manhattan was my territory, organized crime was my specialty," he answered with a clipped prominence. "But Brooklyn? Brooklyn was corrupt. The courts were corrupt! The police were corrupt!"

Before I could say anything else, his voice rose to a fevered pitch, "They were all corrupt, I tell you! All of them! Corrupt!! CORRUPT!!" He continued ranting madly into the phone until his wife took the receiver away.

"I'm sorry dear," she said with a soft giggle. "I think that's all you are going to get from him."

As we said goodbye I could hear Mckenna in the background, shouting 'Corrupt! Corrupt!' over and over again.

What was extremely evident to me was just how rampant corruption ran within the ranks of the police department and the higher authorities in the 1930s and 1940s. A pattern had developed. The cast of detectives and DA characters involved in Sam Kovner's arrest and prosecution, the Malinski Trial, "The Killer" Beitler's death, and "Kid Twist" Reles' death, were the same authorities involved in Uncle Abe's murder investigation—and they all worked for Brooklyn District Attorney William O'Dwyer.

O'Dwyer had questioned Uncle Abe several times in 1940 concerning Murder, Inc. He was well aware of Abe's stature as a policy king, yet after his murder O'Dwyer publicly called Abe a "punk who didn't amount to much,"[1] trying to minimize how powerful Abe really was. He also made John Harlan Amen's life miserable during the last two years of his corruption investigation—restricting him from exploring the murder of his witnesses and blocking his efforts to see important records and documents.

William O'Dwyer, also known as "Bill-O," had a remarkable career that began as a beat cop and swiftly moved from lawyer, to Kings County Court Judge, Brooklyn District Attorney, and Mayor of New York City.

As the District Attorney in 1940, the biggest investigation to transpire during O'Dwyer's tenure was the Murder, Inc. arrests and convictions—which were to fulfill his election promise to clean up Brooklyn. He appeared to be taking down the mob, but allegations of his own ties with mob bosses Anastasia, Adonis, and Costello, negligent homicide investigations, and evidence tampering would be brought against O'Dwyer and his staff in 1945 and again in 1949. The accusations ballooned even further during the famed Kefauver Senate Committee Hearings on Organized Crime in 1951.

O'Dwyer's tenure as District Attorney seems to have been a stepping-stone for promotion of his police pals during his early days as a beat cop. He placed his close-knit group of comrades into higher and higher positions of power as his own political career skyrocketed.

These comrades, who appeared in every case I was researching, included John J. McGowan, Frank Bals, Edward Heffernan, and James J. Moran. On the surface these men seemed stoic members of the justice system but they were, in fact, much more dangerous than their public personae appeared.

When O'Dwyer became DA he appointed a huge staff, which included naming John J. McGowan Chief of the Brooklyn Homicide Squad—for the second time. McGowan was somewhat of a legendary character among his fellow detectives, and by 1940, his 28 years on the force got him the nickname "The Old Man." McGowan received commendation for pioneering the use of forensic science in police work and was considered "a cop's cop."[2] But his "two-fisted exploits"[3] included beating suspects senseless and ignoring legal protocol.

In 1932, McGowan and another member of the "old boys network," William T. Reynolds, were promoted to the Brooklyn Homicide Squad under very shady circumstances. The current captain had been demoted and transferred only 40-minutes after arresting a thug in a stickup who was supposed to be under police protection. The vacancy was given to Reynolds and McGowan was made Lieutenant.

By 1936, McGowan had achieved the rank of Chief of the Homicide Squad, but was demoted for severe negligence, doctoring records, and giving false testimony on the stand during the highly publicized Druckman murder trial of 1935. Samuel Druckman was found viciously murdered at a Mob-connected trucking company where he worked. Three employees were found guilty of his murder, until it was revealed that police officers had destroyed evidence and delivered bribes to the grand jury. Several high-ranking officers and members of the DA's office were found to be passing bribe money from the Mob to police. The scandal was so tremendous that Police Commissioner Lewis J. Valentine came under heavy scrutiny from the Governor's office, and ultimately McGowan was stripped of his rank and sent to the Old Slip station house to perform uniformed duty. Whether McGowan was "punished" because of the Druckman case or the thirteen other unsolved homicides in the borough, the Commissioner wouldn't say.

McGowan remained in this disgraced position until 1940, when O'Dwyer resurrected him from the trenches and placed him back into the post of Chief of Homicide. O'Dwyer needed McGowan to round up the murder-mob to fulfill his campaign promise and knew "The Old Man" would get it done—by any means.

In another bold appointment, O'Dwyer removed the awarded Deputy Chief Inspector of Brooklyn Detectives, Michael McDermott, from his position and had him sent to the Staten Island station—a "Siberia" for officers. Interestingly, it was McDermott who had helped launch John Harlan Amen's investigation in 1938 by arresting a leader in the fur racket and uncovering two corrupt Assistant DA's. Undoubtedly, O'Dwyer didn't want McDermott anywhere near his new cabinet, so he had McDermott replaced by none other than Captain William T. Reynolds as head of Brooklyn Detectives.

O'Dwyer also appointed Frank Bals as the Captain in charge of his large, private detective staff, only having to answer to him, not the Police Commissioner or Mayor, as was the usual protocol. Much scandal followed Bals throughout his career, most noticeably the death of "Kid Twist" Reles, whom Bals had been responsible for when he died in police custody. The chaos that ensued the morning Reles' body was found had Bals in a dither and called McGowan to help him with the crime scene. He relied on McGowan to take control. However, "The Old Man" followed no protocols and collected no evidence.

All the officers assigned to guard Reles the night he died faced a departmental hearing, which was dissolved by O'Dwyer saying it was "the best we could do,"[4] when they were merely demoted to uniform patrol. But the flip side of O'Dwyer's statement was that he, himself, had volunteered to speak on behalf of the officers, and kept his friends McGowan and Bals out of the inquiry completely. Mayor LaGuardia demanded to see the day-by-day records of Bal's police unit investigation into Murder, Inc. and Reles' death, but Bals chose to retire rather than turn them over. When the Reles case was officially reopened in 1951, questions about McGowan's negligent behavior were front and center, but could not be answered as he had died in 1948.

O'Dwyer named Edward Heffernan Chief of Investigations for the DA's office. He was in charge of the probes into "Kid Twist" Reles, Malinski, and every other botched case that went down during O'Dwyer's reign. During the first set of accusations against O'Dwyer and his staff by a 1945 Grand Jury, Heffernan was forced to step down from the DA's office due to impropriety and took a job in the City Legal Department thanks to a childhood friend. Heffernan, along with John McGowan, had been at the forefront of Uncle Abe's murder investigation for O'Dwyer.

The most nefarious of O'Dwyer's cronies was James J. Moran. With only a high school education he went to work as a court reporter. His life and career had a lucky turn in 1938, when he was promoted to court attendant and assigned to O'Dwyer, then a Brooklyn County Judge. O'Dwyer adored Moran and trusted him completely, finding him to be loyal, and letting him handle his personal financial affairs.

When O'Dwyer became DA he took Moran with him, appointing him Chief Clerk of the DA's office, where he was known to have such great influence that if he said "no" you couldn't get O'Dwyer to say "yes." It would later be learned that Moran was responsible for making sure John Harlan Amen never saw the reports on the waterfront rackets. He also disposed of Murder, Inc. records and was in charge of Captain Bals, who was managing the detectives guarding Reles at the Half Moon Hotel.

In 1942, O'Dwyer took a hiatus from his DA position to be part of the war effort as Executive Director of the War Refugee Board. He left Moran in charge of many important matters in the DA's office, and gave him the power to open and close investigations at his whim. It was considered outrageous that a clerk was in charge, especially one with no education in law enforcement—but it happened.

Along with Assistant DA's Thomas C. Hughes and Edward Heffernan, Moran had the muscle to decide who went before a Grand Jury, such as Kovner and the convicts in the Malinski trial. It turned out that not only were these DA's discarding incriminating documents, but they were all extorting money from racketeers.

When O'Dwyer returned from the war as a Brigadier General in 1945, he resigned as DA within months, having received the support of Tammany Hall—the "Democratic Party political machine that played a major role in controlling New York City politics,"[5]—and secured the nomination for Mayor of New York City. Moran quit as well and became his campaign aide. Thomas Dewey—the famed Special Prosecutor of Manhattan who had taken down bootlegger Waxy Gordon and syndicate leader Lucky Luciano—was now Governor of New York, and he appointed Republican George J. Beldock to temporarily take over O'Dwyer's post as Brooklyn's DA.

During the four months Beldock was DA, he brought up corruption allegations against O'Dwyer and his staff. The focus was negligence in the waterfront rackets and the death of longshoreman Peter Panto, who was murdered while trying to start a movement against the waterfront gangsters and extortion rackets in Brooklyn—which meant Cosa Nos-

tra Albert Anastasia. The allegations claimed O'Dwyer was in bed with
gangsters and Beldock went so far as to air those allegations on several radio shows "to tell the detailed story of how William O'Dwyer as
District Attorney whitewashed the waterfront rackets and how his chief
appointees made it easy for one big-money branch of Murder, Inc. to
carry on."[6]

Some thought Beldock's rampage was a political move by the oppo-
sition, as O'Dwyer was at the tail end of his successful mayoral race and
about to be elected. But the Grand Jury charged O'Dwyer's former assistants, Edward Heffernan, Joseph Hanley, and Chief Clerk James Moran, with over 44 counts of basic ineptitude. Unfortunately, the statute of
limitations had run out and the charges were dropped.

Alan Block clearly states in his book *East Side, West Side* that "Moran
was the link between the underworld bosses and the Brooklyn authorities."[7] These accusations came under heavy scrutiny during Beldock's
investigation, as well as the Kefauver Hearings, when Moran was nailed
on the stand, not only for the Waterfront cover-up and the Peter Panto
murder for Anastasia, but also for his Genovese and Adonis mob
connections. He was known to often have dinner or drinks with Costello
and Adonis and for his extortion of many bookies and policy operators,
which included Uncle Abe and Abe Frosch (who had taken over Uncle
Abe's territory).

During the Grand Jury inquiries, Moran's 10-year-old son was mysteriously shot while walking home from school. He survived. The public
story was that a neighborhood teenager was suspected of the shooting
from a rooftop, yet no one was arrested and the case was never pursued. I
spoke with one of Moran's cousins, and his family believed the shooting
was a warning from the Mob to stay quiet.

A second Grand Jury presentment of accusations came into play in
early 1946, when Miles McDonald became the new DA, replacing Beldock. DA Joseph Hanley (who was excused of indictment) took the
stand and stated that, "The matter of Murder, Inc. and Anastasia was
handled exclusively by a little group headed by O'Dwyer, and included
Chief Clerk James Moran, Police Captain Frank Bals, and DA Heffernan."[8] One of the many theories of "Kid Twist" Reles' death was that

Anastasia had paid the security detail to rub out Reles before he could testify against him.

By February of 1946, the second Grand Jury requested an extension into the investigation, but O'Dwyer was tired of the circus and ready to start his new post as Mayor. James Moran "went to Judge Franklin Taylor and pointed out that there were technical flaws connected to the presentments."[9] The judge, in turn, shot down the entire case against O'Dwyer and had it expunged from the records. With that, O'Dwyer took his place as the 100th Mayor of New York City.

It's amazing that O'Dwyer was elected, considering the accusations, but he had made a name for himself as the DA who put away criminals, and it stuck. Historian Thomas Reppetto noted, New Yorkers were "tired of economic depression and war. They wanted to go back to the happy days…with a mayor who smiled a lot and dished the blarney."[10]

As soon as O'Dwyer became Mayor, all his cronies moved into new positions as well. Retired Captain Frank Bals was appointed 7th Deputy Police Commissioner under Arthur Wallander. This caused much controversy because of his past record, and police across the borough complained that he was bringing down morale. Once Bals was appointed Deputy Police Commissioner, he had no one to answer to, once again, except O'Dwyer. His new squad of covert detectives immediately started shaking down illegal gamblers and bookies for monthly payments, but the racketeers ran to their "political protectorates" complaining about the "big-money shakedown."[11] O'Dwyer was forced to look into the matter, and two months later Bals was released from his duties as Police Commissioner—although O'Dwyer had him stay in the position on paper for over a year, so he could collect plump retirement benefits.

Once O'Dwyer was elected Mayor he also appointed James Moran as First Deputy Fire Commissioner. Almost immediately after moving into his new position, Moran started a fuel oil racket that collected $1.5 million over a three-year period. It consisted of fire inspectors demanding money from installers of oil burners and refrigerators before permits for installation would be issued.

Meanwhile, new DA, Miles McDonald, still had an eye on O'Dwyer, continuing his investigation into the new Mayor from behind the scenes.

In 1949, as O'Dwyer was about to start his second term as Mayor, McDonald made his move with a presentment against O'Dwyer that shook him badly. He was suffering from dizzy spells, depression, and on the verge of a nervous breakdown due to the "dangerous, vexing, and deteriorating situation"[12] that was coming to a head. Whether it was the new indictment, personal problems, or the criminal doings of his pals, O'Dwyer quickly drafted a letter of resignation and then checked himself into Bellevue Hospital.

It is written that when Moran found out about this, he rushed to the hospital to see O'Dwyer and a tremendous fight ensued—Moran tore up O'Dwyer's resignation letter and demanded that O'Dwyer not retire before positioning Moran into a more lucrative government job. Although their bro-mance was coming to a close, O'Dwyer gave Moran a life appointment as Commissioner of the Board of Water Supply, and then resigned in the summer of 1950. It's no wonder O'Dwyer was sick, with the increasing criminal activities of Moran and his own involvement with mobsters. But Alan Block points out that with O'Dwyer we are "left with a picture of an enigmatic politician…who never got caught with his hand in the till."[13]

Upon resignation, Bill-O was given a ticker-tape parade up lower Broadway's Canyon of Heroes in Manhattan. Despite the slanderous allegations, and to keep up respectful appearance, the "much loved" Mayor, was appointed U.S. Ambassador to Mexico and promptly left New York.

It sounds like the end of his story, but a year later, in 1951, the U.S. Senate Investigation into Organized Crime and Interstate Commerce, better known as the Kefauver Committee Hearings, took place.

The five-member senate committee became a sensational traveling roadshow that went to 14 cities to take testimony from big mob leaders such as Frank Costello, Meyer Lansky, Mickey Cohen, Anthony Anastasia (brother of Albert), and Joey Adonis, as well as bookies, gunmen, racketeers, and others.

The televised hearings were highly charged as the committee matched wits with professional criminals and their defense lawyers. The hearings demonstrated, for the first time, that there was an organized and connected national crime syndicate comprised of mainly Italian and Jewish crime groups across the country. They also revealed the names of some of the politicians who were in bed with them. This brought O'Dwyer back to New York.

First up at the New York hearings was Frank Costello. The slick, well-dressed 60-year-old was currently one of the most powerful mob bosses in America, known to have great political influence. When Costello was called before the committee, "he promptly developed laryngitis in the midst of several embarrassing questions."[14] According to the *Brooklyn Daily Eagle* he "gave a final croak and defied the hearing when two questions were fired at him in rapid order: '*Do you know Frank Bals?*' and '*Do you know James Moran?*'"[15] Costello stood up and marched out of the room. He spent 15 months in jail for contempt.

Many riveting testimonies transpired at the Kefauver Committee Hearings, but what was of most interest to me were the players from O'Dwyer's District Attorney's office who were called back to testify.

Moran had been arrested and was in court for his oil shakedown as Fire Commissioner, while simultaneously being grilled about the death of Reles and corruption in O'Dwyer's office at the Kefauver Hearings. Both Moran and Edward Heffernan were exposed for their mob ties and called out as "inept" while running the DA's office when O'Dwyer was in the Army.

The climax of the New York hearings came when O'Dwyer faced the committee and was questioned about the mystery of Reles' death. O'Dwyer became so unnerved that a recess had to be called. When O'Dwyer returned for further questioning, he surmised that Reles was trying to escape. Senator Tobey asked why his statement contradicted Captain Frank Bals' testimony that Reles was playing a practical joke on the cops. O'Dwyer reacted as if he'd been attacked and went on to defend Bals' character, but was stopped by Senator Tobey who said, "Bals made a spectacle of himself before this committee…don't try to build Bals up, you'll only look ludicrous," and an angry exchange ensued.[16]

O'Dwyer admitted he thought that it was a mistake placing Bals and Police Commissioner Arthur Wallander in their positions, because "not much got done,"[17] about the gambling rackets. Brooklyn DA Miles McDonald, who had been on O'Dwyer's 1940 staff, verified that over

$12,000,000 a year was paid to borough cops and the DA's office for protection or "ice."

O'Dwyer was also trashed at the hearings for his association with organized crime figures. Charles Lipsky, an elder Republican statesman of Brooklyn politics, said he was an emissary between O'Dwyer and Frank Costello in an effort to "clean up" Tammany Hall. For many years it had been necessary to get Costello's okay if a man wanted to run for Mayor. These accusations would follow O'Dwyer for the rest of his life, and he resigned as Ambassador to Mexico in 1952.

But the fun wasn't over. O'Dwyer was called the following week to testify before a special Grand Jury about Moran's racketeering and political tie-ups in the Fire Department that equaled $1.5 million dollars between 1947 to 1950.

The big mystery was who Moran had delivered the fat sum of money to that he collected (he only kept $90,000 for himself). He refused to tell, stating, "I came into this world a man, and I'm going out a man,"[18] and was sentenced to 12 to 28 years in Sing Sing prison. But, after two years in prison, Moran wrote a 75-page letter to the State Court of Appeals saying that he would spill the names of those for whom he collected the $1.5 million if he would be granted an appeal for reduction in sentence. But the letter revealed no names, only that Moran felt there was a political conspiracy against him. Still, he was released from prison after serving only 10 years. Some historians have believed the money in question was going to Frank Costello.

Except for Moran, no actions were taken against O'Dwyer or any of his other men.

I was exhausted after researching all this. All I could think, just as McKenna had ranted into the phone, was "corrupt, corrupt, CORRUPT!" It was pretty clear to me that Uncle Abe's death was another cover-up by these diabolical men. But the bigger question was why.

I suspected there might be more to Uncle Abe's death than just silencing him from testifying for John Harlan Amen. Corruption is always about money and power, and Abe knew something about the higher officials that gave him power.

14

A Place in the Sun

New York, June 2007

Carnegie Hall was premiering an orchestrated choral piece set to Dad's poetry, so he was headed to New York. Since he rarely ventured to the family stomping grounds, I took the opportunity to tag along and orchestrate something of my own: family reunions.

We headed to New Jersey to be near my sister Valerie, her husband Steve, and their 3-year-old son, Zachary. Aside from the Carnegie Hall excitement, we planned to visit Aunt Carol and her family, have dinner with some newly discovered Marcus cousins, and upon my request, go graveyard hunting. Every genealogist loves to roam through cemeteries, not just to pay respect to ancestors, but to possibly discover new information. I was particularly anxious to visit Uncle Abe's grave with Dad. We had spent so many years talking about Abe, that it felt important to pay homage to him together.

Aunt Carol was now retired and living with her husband in Connecticut. It had been 15 years since I'd seen her, but at the age of 77, her jovial demeanor and dry sense of humor were alive as ever. Carol's daughter Sheila and several grandchildren were at her home when we arrived. She served lunch around a large oak table and we enjoyed lox and bagels, creamed herring, and every salad concoction imaginable that could be made with mayonnaise.

When I finally had Aunt Carol alone, helping her clean-up the dishes, I pushed her for more memories of uncles Abe and Frankie.

"I'm gonna charge you a dollar a question," she replied matter-of-factly, then a sly smile spread across her lips.

"Tell me the truth about Uncle Frankie. He wasn't really a cowboy, was he?" I asked.

Carol threw her head back in a gleeful cackle. "Did you really believe that baloney?" She was laughing so hard her eyes became wet with tears. "We made that up!"

When she finally caught her breath, she put her arm around me and leaned in to whisper. "Listen, it was like this—Frankie was in the rackets with Abie!"

She went on to tell me how Abe rented her parents, Bertha and Mudsy, an apartment on East Clarkson Avenue in Brooklyn. The deal was that no one was allowed into the house between 3 and 5 p.m., when Abe, Frankie, and Mudsy—who "cleaned" the money—would count the day's take. When 10-year-old Carol would come home after school, Bertha would scuttle her and brother Leo off to Great Grandma Anna's house on Avenue B for the afternoon.

"Great Grandma Anna would bake this delicious chocolate cake, which was especially for Leo, and I would meet up with cousin Selma, Dave's daughter, and spend the afternoons climbing the peach trees in the yard." Sometimes Carol and Selma would set-up a stand and sell what they picked from the burgeoning trees. Great Grandma Anna would always give them a few pennies to start their sales.

"The best times were when Uncle Frankie would come and play with us," Carol smiled as the happy memory flooded her thoughts. "He used to tell me and Selma he was gonna marry us. All the kids loved Uncle Frankie."

Abe may have been a sharp dresser and financially took care of the family, but he was quiet and serious around the children, usually attending to business and asking them to leave the room. Uncle Frankie was just the opposite. Gregarious, carefree, and always laughing, he would bring them presents, tell animated stories about his supposed cross-country adventures, and take them to Coney Island. Often Frankie would show-up at Bertha's house late at night. While Bertha fussed over feeding Frankie a four-course meal, he would slip his car keys to young

Leo with a wink, allowing him a midnight joyride around the neighborhood in his fancy coupe.

Carol had finally broken her silence and confirmed what I had learned—Frankie didn't ride those horses, but "played" the horses, helping to run Abe's pari-mutuel racing policy.

In his last years, Abe spent much of his "home life" with sister Rae, but Frankie spent much of his time with his older brother Dave's family. Dave and his wife Ida had a restaurant in Harlem during the depression and an ice cream stand farther down the same street, where the famous "coconut whip" was originally created, before they moved to their Brooklyn location. When the afternoon money count was complete, Uncle Frankie would pick up his niece Selma from Great Grandma Anna's house and take her for a ride up to 116th Street to pick up her parents. Frankie always worried about Dave and Ida traveling home from the restaurant after a long day. It also gave him the opportunity to try to get Dave to join him and Abe in the lottery racket. But the answer was always no.

Dave grew up with a different ideology than his younger brothers. In the old country, when his father left for America, Dave became the head of the family and took on all the responsibilities of a father figure. He was reared on sweat and blood to make a living and never understood why Abe and Frankie were mixed up in the rackets. At first he thought it was just youthful folly. As the years went by and the younger brothers were arrested several times on lottery and gun possession charges, he thought it madness. Dave felt they had been swept up into the easy moneymaking activities and he refused to join them.

Dave and Ida hoped Frankie would find his way. He was so wonderful with the children that they thought he should have a family of his own. But Frankie subscribed to Abe's feelings that "no woman should end up a young widow." At a family gathering one year, Ida's sister introduced Frankie to a neighborhood gal. Frankie dated her for quite some time but eventually ended it, knowing his life was too entangled with the underworld to give her the life she deserved. "You coulda had a nice life,

Froike, if it wasn't for the rackets," Ida would say in her broken English, hiding the sadness she felt for him.

As good-natured as Frankie was, I learned he also had a temper. The short, square man with the shining blue eyes was known as the enforcer behind Abe's well-conceived plans.

"Around 1945 Frankie called my father, Mudsy, to meet him at the deli they used to all hang-out at, somewhere off Pitkin Avenue," said Carol, as she concluded her stories. "After that no one ever saw or heard from Frankie again. They must have killed him, too. That was the finish." Her hands slapped together loudly then fanned out in a motion like a referee at a finish line. "The end."

Aunt Carol leaned her round body against the kitchen counter and studied me over the rim of her glasses. "Next time you want information, ask someone younger!" Then she erupted into a squawk of laughter again, pulling me toward the living room to rejoin the family. "Bubelah, you can say you heard it all from your beautiful Aunt Carol!" With that, she threw her arms around me in a giant hug, then went to join my father on the sofa.

•———•

The reunion with several of the newly-found Marcus cousins took place at a restaurant on West 58th street, around the corner from Grandma Rae's longtime residence on Central Park South. I figured her spirit was still guiding me in organizing this.

As we entered the dark, wood-paneled restaurant, I recognized several of the cousins from photographs they had shared with me via email. As we approached the large table where nine cousins were awaiting our arrival, several people gasped at the sight of Mort.

"You look so much like Max!" they explained apologetically.

We had a wonderful time getting to know each other, sharing old family photo albums, and hearing the cousins' stories about Max's shenanigans and his wild gambling habits. It bothered me that they always ended their tales of Max with head-throwing laughter, as if his gambling addiction was funny. Had no Marcus relative ever tried to help him with his problem?

I was anxious to find my long-lost Aunt Ruth, Max's daughter from his first marriage. I inquired if anyone knew her whereabouts. The cousins pointed out her picture in an album being passed around the table. She had died of cancer in her 40s. None of the Marcus cousins had seen Ruth's children since they were very small, but one of them recalled that her oldest son, Mark, was living somewhere in Albany.

The cousins were warm and gracious, and continued to help me piece together the torn fabric of the Marcus clan. There were more relatives than my father and I could have imagined—cousins, aunts, uncles, and their children. We had gone from 0 to 60 in the family department in one second flat. Overall, I was satisfied with my discoveries and Mort now had a sense of family history to reflect upon.

Later, I located Ruth's son Mark. He had never met any family from the Marcus side and told me he had always felt alone, with no known relatives or information about them. He was over-the-moon that we were cousins and he had an Uncle Mort. This new cousin worked for the state of New York, and I inquired if he might help me find John Harlan Amen's Grand Jury investigation report, which held important information about Uncle Abe. Cousin Mark was thrilled to see what he could find in the Albany State Library. He loved the idea of a notorious gangster in the family—even though it was not his bloodline and Abe was not notorious. I loved the idea of combining family resources, and he was immediately on the trail to find Amen's report.

The final family excursion on this trip was the graveyard-hopping adventure. I had planned three stops for our afternoon, which I had researched in advance. We would visit the final resting places of William and Esther Marcus, Abe and Great Grandma Anna, and finally Max Marcus.

We began by heading out to find Esther and William Marcus, the great grandparents of our newly-found clan. We took the Long Island Expressway to Flushing, Queens, where industrial smoke stacks eventually gave way to velvet green lawns spiked with tall gray headstones.

We drove through the massive, immaculate grounds of Mount He-
bron Cemetery and wound our way to section 37, which was quite old.
The headstones were at least five feet tall and beautifully engraved with
ivy, menorahs, and Hebrew script. With maps and plot numbers in
hand, we spread out to search. Valerie immediately started jumping up
and down with excitement. "I found them!"

William and Esther's graves were tall headstones next to each other,
streaked with time. William's stone had a faded picture on it that retained a trace of his piercing eyes. There they lay, the brave ancestors who
left Russia and brought their family to this country for a new life. All of
us felt deeply moved to be there in a way we hadn't expected. This was
our heritage, our roots, laid quietly before us in the warm afternoon sun.
Dad was restraining tears as he studied the image of his grandfather on
the granite stone. We took photos, placed rocks on the headstones, and
walked the elaborate grounds as Mort talked about Russian history and
birds flitted about in the peacefulness of the day.

As the afternoon heat intensified, we headed back to the car. Everyone now had a spirited attitude and Valerie, feeling particularly triumphant due to her quick discovery of the sites, was eager to reach our next
location.

Back on the Long Island Expressway, we headed east to Jamaica,
Queens, to find Abe.

The Montefiore Cemetery was huge, with an old and a new section.
The older section, off Francis Lewis Boulevard, held a sad presence. The
grass had turned to sun-bleached weeds and the plots had not been kept
up. It felt like no one had been to these hundreds of graves in years. The
stones were a sea of zig-zags with etched Stars of David in every direction. Although we knew the grave was located in block 84, the map we
had was cryptic and we couldn't locate row 10. I knew Abe and his mother Anna were buried next to each other, so we spread out, each in a different direction, to find the name Babchick. Valerie was hot on the path,
scampering up and down the narrow, overgrown aisles of headstones.

We couldn't find the graves. Back and forth we searched for over thirty minutes. With the blistering afternoon sun beating down on us, I was

afraid everyone would give up before we could find them. "Abe, where are you?" I whispered. "I feel like we're close, please help me find you."

A few minutes later, Valerie's head jutted up and down in a far-off row as she hollered, "Over here, over here!"

We ran to where she was standing, ankle deep in ivy and dry brush. Before her was a huge seven-foot art-deco monument engraved with menorah flames shooting skyward and the name BABCHIK spelled out in a large, vertical pattern.

Together, we started clearing brush, ripping up weeds and brushing away the dirt and dust. As we cleared the area two footstones were revealed in front of the monument, each graced with a Hebrew phrase and their names:

Our Beloved Mother ANNA. Died Dec. 20, 1946. Age 67 years
Beloved Son, Dear Brother. ABRAHAM. Died Sept. 24, 1941.
Age 35 years.

Valerie continued to pull ivy from the base of the monument and a beautiful inscription chiseled into the stone was revealed:

The Stars Shall Fade, The Sun Grow Dim,
But You Shall Be Always Remembered.

We were all in awe at the size of the monument. "Jesus, my mother never told me it was this big. I had no idea," said Dad, placing his hand on the warm gray stone.

"Remember that story Grandma Rae once told?" Valerie asked. "She said that red roses were left on Abe's grave every week for many years after his death, and no one in the family knew who they were from." Dad recalled the story, and it seemed vaguely familiar to me.

I knelt down and touched the surface of Abe's footstone. I had waited for years to come here and pay my respects. This was as close as I would ever get to the man. I wanted to just sit there quietly and be with him, but the others had started to make their way back to the car. Dad stayed behind with me.

I felt connected to Abe, on a level deeper than just something ancestral. I felt driven, pushed, to understand what happened to him. My heart felt so full—of admiration for what he had achieved and provided the family, and of sadness for his life being taken in its prime. "I will find the truth," I whispered. Dad reached for my hand and we stood silently together, before walking back toward the others.

We were all quiet and contemplative as Steve drove us back toward New Jersey. I stared out the window at the expressway and thought about Abe. *You shall always be remembered.*

We stopped for lunch at a greasy burger joint and Dad told stories about old Jewish gangsters like Meyer Lansky and "Kid Twist" Reles. I loved that we were all together, reminiscent of when Valerie and I were kids spending a weekend with Dad. It was rare that we had that opportunity anymore. Everyone was happy this day.

Max Marcus was buried in Paramus, New Jersey. We rushed to Beth El Cemetery before they closed for the Sabbath. *Why was Max buried way out there?* Beth El was very fancy, with a circular marble lobby and several attendants to assist us in finding the plot location. We received a map, drove about a mile into the property, found the section, parked, and split up to locate Max's grave. This was important to Dad, going to the grave of the father he never knew.

We marched up and down the gray aisles in the appointed section several times, but we couldn't find the grave. Forty-five minutes passed and the Sabbath was nearing. The gates would soon be closing. Steve and I jumped into the car and headed back to the office to ask for further assistance. The attendant rechecked her computer, acknowledged that we were in the correct area, and gave us another map marked up with red ink. Steve and I raced back to the group. They were spread out in different directions, heads bobbing among the tall gravestones like buoys at sea.

We regrouped and again went up and down each row, meticulously reading every headstone. Gottlieb. Brownstein. Cohen. Silverman. The five-minute warning bell sounded. Mort looked defeated, his posture taking on a rounded hunch. His search for his father seemed destined to be futile. The final bell rang and we had to leave. Max had evaded Mort in death, just as he had in life.

The following week, after we had returned to California, Valerie and Steve revisited Beth El Cemetery and insisted someone take them to the actual grave location. "I want my son to know where his great grandfather is buried!" Valerie demanded. The end result was the discovery that the headstone had sunk into the ground. No one had been to visit Max's grave since the funeral in 1975. This was poetic justice—In life, Max had cared about no one. In death, no one had cared about him.

The cemetery personnel asked if we wanted to have the stone raised. Dad grappled for several weeks with a decision and finally decided to leave Max, and the past, as it was.

15

Dark Victory

Santa Cruz, Autumn 2007

The year had been significant in the family mystery arena, as well as in my personal life. I had been dating my partner, Amy, for some time and we had recently moved in together. It had also been an eventful year for Dad, connecting with the Marcus clan, his work performed at Carnegie Hall, and completing his lengthy literary memoir. But his triumphant year suddenly took a dark turn.

We had just celebrated his 71st birthday in early September, when curiously I didn't hear from him for over a week. Dad and I talked on the phone every other day, so the quiet was a bit strange. When I finally reached him he simply said he needed to come over and speak to me and Amy. It sounded serious.

There was a sense of doom in the air when Dad arrived, seating himself on our sofa with an unnervingly calm demeanor. "I have cancer," he said matter-of-factly. Dad's calm appearance was simply masking his state of shock—he needed to have immediate surgery to remove a tumor on his kidneys, and we all needed to pray it hadn't spread into a main artery.

In spite of this, Dad was very worried about me. He knew I was particularly sensitive to the subject of his mortality. Although he and I had a very special bond, it had been deeply affected when I was ten-years-old. My parent's divorce was a very difficult time for both of them. Being a child, I didn't understand any of that when I was taken to see my father lying in a coma from an overdose of sleeping pills in the hospital. Peering through the glass of the intensive care unit at my unconscious father with tubes coming out of him was beyond devastating, and I never really got over it.

When he recovered, he took me for an afternoon drive through the redwood forest of Bonny Doon. He struggled to explain that his episode had nothing to do with me, and he loved me very much. Although I was happy he was alive, what stayed with 10-year-old me was a terror of losing him. I spent much of my teen years and early twenties worrying about him and becoming his surrogate keeper so he wouldn't "go away" again. We weren't able to talk about the residual effect that his attempt left hanging over our relationship, until we finally went to counseling some twenty years later to work through it. For the most part we had.

As Dad revealed his current cancer diagnosis, he knew this would bring up major angst for me and he was concerned. I surprised us both when I dealt with the potential reality of my childhood nightmare through proactive research and finding options for his illness.

Mort was soon rushed into surgery. He'd never been sick a day in his adult life and he was sure he'd die on the operating table. As he nervously waited to be taken into surgery, Valerie—who had arrived from New Jersey—and I sat with him. I knew the only thing that would calm all of us would be for Dad to tell one of his famous stories. He thought for a moment and then decided to tell us how he met our mother when they were teenagers in New York. We had heard this story many times before, but it seemed to relax him almost immediately. As we listened, his story connected us to each other and the past, giving comfort as we moved into an unknown future.

In the following weeks, as Mort slowly recovered in the hospital, I would visit late in the afternoons and often spend the night in a chair next to his bed. We would read, watch PBS, or play a strategic game of Gin Rummy, which led to an all-out championship battle by the end of his stay. Dad was frightened to be left alone in the hospital at night. His current wife had many of her own health issues and couldn't stay over, so I happily arrived daily, often with the latest news about my research on Uncle Abe. Dad loved the investigative aspect of my hunt, and at this point he was as invested in the outcome as I was. The family exploration kept both of us distracted during this difficult time.

On one of my evening sleepovers at the hospital, Dad was excited to have me read him a vital new piece of information I had received. Marcus-Cousin-Mark had been instrumental in retrieving John Harlan Amen's Grand Jury investigation into gambling from the Albany Archives, which held important details about Uncle Abe's organization.

I arranged Dad's blankets to keep him warm in the cool, air-filtered hospital room, grabbed him a jello from the nurse's secret stash, and curled up in the chair next to his bed to read the Amen report. It had a very long name:

Supreme Court, State of New York—County of Kings.
A Presentment Concerning The Enforcement By The Police Department of the City of New York of the Laws Against Gambling.
By the Grand Jury for the Extraordinary Special and Trial Term.

The investigation contained the evidence collected between 1938 and 1942. It basically stated that the chief operators or "bosses" of the gambling racket in Brooklyn were never arrested, only their subordinates, even though police knew who these "bosses" were. Plainclothes police officers were assigned to make gambling arrests, and they often fabricated unfounded circumstances in order to create a record of apparent enforcement in the borough. When they did make arrests, more often than not, a charge could not be proven.

Both uniformed and plainclothes officers were found to be betting on horses regularly and had substantial incomes far beyond their police salaries—buying houses, cars, boats, furs coats for their wives, and taking luxurious vacations.

In the *Presentment Concerning Enforcement of Laws Against Gambling* from 1938–1939, there was a description of the structure of Uncle Abe's organization, based on the testimony of an unnamed, former member of his policy ring. It detailed that Abe had an unlisted phone number at his policy bank headquarters that received over 100 separate phone calls from police officers who stated they had members of Abe's organization in their custody and requested that he, himself, should come immediately to a designated area to discuss the matter. Abe would later return to the headquarters with a package filled with their personal betting slips.

The report went on to describe the wide scope of Abe's outfit, which stretched into Jersey and West Philadelphia. He regularly paid for police protection in order to conduct his operations, which were estimated to have been established for many years, bringing in thousands of dollars a day, and had employed upwards of 700 people to maintain its smooth operation. Dad and I were awestruck at just how big Abe's operation was.

There were insignia rings, business cards, and special wallets used by Abe's men, to identify them as being under the protective eye of the police. The report named many of the officers who were charged with grafting and misconduct, and included surveillance stills that caught them in the act.

Amen revealed a broad picture of the gambling operations in Brooklyn in which there were as many as 1000 "protected" betting locations making weekly payments to the police. Gamblers and bookmakers—operating in hundreds of poolrooms, candy stores, cigar stores, restaurants, and busy street corners—would be warned by dishonest policemen of the presence and identity of plainclothesmen who refused to be bribed. There were accommodation arrests, designed to protect the records of police assigned to gambling details, and of bondsmen and lawyers organized to handle the dispositions of arrest cases.

The broad gambling picture also covered the entire police set-up. Brooklyn was divided into five divisions, with plainclothesmen in each division assigned to check on dice games, bookmaking, pinball machines, baseball pools, and policy rackets. Above them was the borough squad which checked on gambling throughout the borough. Above the borough squad was the so-called "P.C. Squad" or the Police Commissioner's Squad, which checked on gambling operations throughout the city.

Despite Dad's enthusiasm to hear the report, he had quickly fallen asleep. As the late hours of the night ticked on, comforted by the sound of his breathing, I continued reading and thinking about Uncle Abe and John Harlan Amen.

These two men were on trajectories that crashed into one another like speeding locomotives, producing an explosion with a fiery aftermath. No two men could have been more different. Abe was a poor Russian immigrant who had nothing but an eighth grade education and a lot of chutzpah. He used his astute and calculating mind to carve out a piece of the street action to support his family. He was a snazzy dresser and a force on the gambling circuit. He loved the prizefights, was pals with Slapsy Maxie Rosenbloom, and dated beautiful women. Abe was loyal and generous—to his family, to his friends during the depression, and to Reles.

Amen, on the other hand, was a privileged all-American guy. He graduated from Princeton and obtained a law degree from Harvard. He piloted sorties in World War I and eventually opened his own law practice in New York. He married president Grover Cleveland's daughter, Marion, and they had a son whom they named Grover. His personality was far from flamboyant. He was soft-spoken and always professional, but often absent-minded about personal issues—always forgetting his hat and coat. He was superstitious, known for wearing a white carnation every day as a good luck charm. The origin of this habit is not clear, but a local florist delivered a fresh flower to his home every morning. He was a chain-smoker and self-described "independent democrat" which helped him keep clear of biased ideology during his investigations. He was driven and methodical when it came to his examinations of injustice. He fought against the tremendous corruption in Brooklyn, which no one had ever done before. Later, in 1946, Amen would go on to be part of the trial counsel on the U.S. staff at the Nuremberg trials of World War II criminals.

As unlikely as these men were, their paths intersected at the corners of truth and justice. Amen needed Abe to testify to make his case clear-cut against the Borough police and Police Commissioner's Squad.

Abe, who had a lawyer negotiating with Amen, may have requested the only terms he thought truly valuable: to relocate the entire Babchick family into a witness protection program. The truth was that Abe had everything to lose. He was backed into a corner. If he decided to be a whistleblower for Amen, he might have received a deal to avoid prosecution of his policy enterprise, but there was no way he was getting out of this situation alive, after ratting out the cops. If he didn't cooperate with Amen he would go to prison for a long time, and probably still be silenced.

Abe was not a dangerous man. Sure, the lottery and horse-betting policies were illegal, but he was not a killer. The cops had taken an oath to protect and serve, yet in many cases they were more underhanded and deceitful than the policy gangsters. They were the worst kind of hypocrites. Perhaps he knew there was no way out of this mess except to hope that eventually justice would prevail against the dirty cops.

If Amen had been allowed to lead the investigation into Abe's murder we might actually have concrete evidence of his assailants. But Amen's hands were tied. He was forced to leave the investigation to Homicide Chief John McGowan and O'Dwyer's staff. That left me, decades later, to thread together the circumstances as best I could. I continued to believe the truth was out there.

16

Suspicion

Santa Cruz, April 2008

After reading Amen's report that Abe's gang used insignia rings and other identifiers to inform police that they were protected, I wondered if any relatives had these in their possession. My partner Amy, always wanting to be helpful, asked if I had contacted all the Babchick descendants. For the most part I had, except for a few cousins who hadn't responded to my emails. "You must try every resource," she encouraged me.

There was one relative I hadn't reached out to yet—Susan, the daughter of Abe and Frankie's younger brother Ike. None of the family had been in touch with Susan for over twenty years. I had no relationship with Susan other than a lovely letter she'd sent me in 1979, when I was a teenager trying to build my first family tree. When I reread her letter I was touched by its sweetness and sincere desire to stay in touch with family. I looked her up online and gave her a call. Now retired, Susan had taken to digital photography and spent a lot of her time scrapbooking via the computer. This meant she had the ability to scan and send photos, unlike many of the other relatives.

I told her about my genealogy projects, as well as my search into the uncles. Believe it or not, she had never heard of Abe and Frankie. Her curiosity was piqued, which was good, since I was hoping to get her to dig through her father's old belongings for anything that might be useful information. I mentioned that her father had signed Abe's death certificate back in 1941, and I was hoping he might have saved some of Abe's personal effects. I really wanted to know if Ike had saved Abe's wallet or anything else found on his person after the murder. Susan thought her father's things might be packed way in her garage someplace and she would look for them.

"Even if it doesn't seem important, take a photo of it for me," I requested.

"Well, I do have photos of my father with men I can't identify," she replied.

Susan immediately started sending me photos and a treasure was revealed in the very first round of emails. It was a photograph of the entire Babchick family surrounding Ike and his wife Rena on their wedding day—June 23, 1945. Aunt Carol and Cousin Selma were each 15-years-old, standing next to their respective parents, Dave and Bertha. Mort was 9-years-old, leaning on Great Grandma Anna. Rae was dressed to the nines, in silk and a feathered hat, and next to her was a short, happy looking fellow—Uncle Frankie.

There was also a second photo of Frankie and Rae smiling with joy as Rena and Ike kissed. Frankie was in a tailored suit and oversized yamelkeh, grinning from ear to ear, looking as jovial as every relative had ever described him.

This photo was significant because it was June of the year he supposedly disappeared. Frankie was free from his jail stint and still alive in mid-1945. This helped me to establish a timeline of his whereabouts.

The only two family members not present were Uncle Leo, who was away in the service, and Abe, who had been gone for almost four years.

Susan was very sad that her father had never told her about Abe and Frankie. Ike was a curiosity to me, as he had always been so tight-lipped and quiet. He must have known something about his brothers and the family racket—something he hid deep inside and never spoke of again. Cousin Terry, Dave's daughter, had posed the question many of the cousins wondered about: "Why was Ike such a loser in life? He had everything going for him!"

Ike's wife Rena was most probably not the cause of his failed professional life, as the family had insinuated. I think he was a broken man. Seeing his older brother laid-out on the steel bed at the coroner's office with two bullet holes in his head would have been enough, but then his brother Frankie disappeared. I think Ike knew a lot, and it destroyed him.

As the weeks passed, Susan wrote that she couldn't find her father's belongings. She recalled old 16mm films he had taken, but her mother had thrown everything out years ago. I cringed at the thought of all that lost history.

I was becoming more and more intrigued with Frankie. The family cowboy never went to Wyoming to break horses. He never died in a Denver hotel room of a heart attack, as one cousin had told Mort when he was young. All I knew for certain about Frankie was that he had taken over Abe's policy bank after his death, supposedly to track the killers, and was sent to prison on lottery charges. Mark-the-Cop and I couldn't locate any prison records to verify if he had served the full jail term. At some point, after Ike's wedding in June of 1945, he disappeared and was never seen or heard from again by anyone in the family. There was no death certificate that I could find under any family name combination.

Frankie was obviously the heir apparent to the policy throne. I wondered if Abe Frosch or a rival gang wanted him out of the way so they could take over Abe's policy territory. Uncle Leo and Aunt Carol believed that whoever killed Abe was after Frankie as well. I pondered if perhaps Frankie had been in hiding from the police and higher-ups

Frankie and Abe's story continued to expand. I had most definitely shifted from curious researcher to driven sleuth. Politics, law enforcement, and organized crime in the 1940s was so complex and corrupt. So much took place in the span of a single day in the press—it was like trying to put together a giant puzzle. Some pieces almost fit, but something was missing, something yet to be discovered, which was probably right in front of me.

There were originally three theories for Abe's murder: at first the DA's office claimed it was a robbery-gone-wrong, followed by the police stating he was rubbed out by a rival mob.

First, if Uncle Abe was robbed for his gambling victory on the night of the murder, the robbers would have taken action when he was still in Manhattan, fresh from his win in Mulberry Bend. They would not have waited several hours to stalk him in Brooklyn at Dubrow's Cafeteria Restaurant, where he was last seen with a couple of his buddies. The DA's robber theory seemed bogus—as did the claim that Sam Kovner and "The Killer" Beitler had anything to do with Abe's murder.

Secondly, Abe might have been rubbed out by a rival policy king, or maybe even Murder, Inc. commander "Lepke" Buchalter, who was trying to snuff out underworld figures in the Brownsville area who might testify against him or back up "Kid Twist's" confessions. Abe paid regular tribute to Reles, but once Reles was arrested who did Abe have to pay to stay in business? He may have been directly connected to the syndicate at that point—Costello or Anastasia.

Thirdly, John Harlan Amen declared Abe was silenced by "authorities" on his payroll. It was the only theory that made sense—especially after examining Sam Kovner's case and reading through Amen's investigation report. It seemed clear that the authorities killed Abe to keep him quiet. But it was the "quiet" I found unsettling.

The District Attorney's office had been on the take from policy czars like Uncle Abe for years and went to great lengths to cover up their transgressions. The police's eyewitness the night of Abe's murder, "Zoo" (probably Meyer Rabinowitz), had recalled that "two well-dressed men" took Abe away that night. Was Meyer coerced to give statements that steered suspicion away from the DA's office? Grandma Rae was sure Meyer was involved, and he had promptly left town after the murder.

Was the murder solely about the authorities on Abe's payroll or something more?

The *Brooklyn Daily Eagle* had run a story in July of 1943 titled, "Six Crimes Baffle Brooklyn Homicide Squad. Are They What You'd Call Perfect, Insoluble?" Abe's story was one of the six cases listed, making the cut as a "perfect crime." Were Abe and Frankie destined to go down in history as unsolved cases? I could only take encouragement from the article's closing statement: "No case is closed until the murderer is brought to justice."[1]

17

The Dark Figure in the Doorway

Santa Cruz, October 2008

Most of the year was a blur of images and sounds, of doctors and treatments. Mort's health was stable for the moment, despite side effects from the cancer drugs. He was such a strong force during this time, traveling to Europe with his wife, giving a book signing and reading with many of the literary giants mentioned in his newly published memoir, and vigorously continuing all his projects. But, he confided to me that he hadn't been able to compose poetry in the last year.

I got married in mid-October. Proposition 8 had passed and Mort eagerly went to city hall and became a Deputy for the Day, marrying Amy and me on a cliff as the sun set into the vast blue of the Pacific Ocean.

Amy and I were also house hunting, as the economic downturn had made it a buyer's market. Dad announced he wanted me to have my inheritance before he died. Despite the fact his cancer was at bay, such talk of his demise reminded me of my own painful denial of his mortality, so I shifted my thoughts to his offer. *There was money?* We were not a family of wealth, by any means, but certainly part of the comfortable middle class. Mort explained that he wanted to see me enjoy the money and make proper use of it while he was still alive. The financial gift enabled me and Amy to put a down payment on a home. He gave the same amount to my sister, and I inquired several times where the money had come from.

During one of our weekly lunch outings, Dad finally told me he had inherited Grandma Rae's trust when she passed in 2002. He had made a few investments here and there with it, that didn't amount to much, and what was left was divided amongst his wife, Valerie, and me. I found it surprising that Grandma actually had any money left when she died. She had lived very frugally her last years and I figured whatever money she had went into that fancy retirement community in Monterey. I was shocked to learn that Rae had left over six-figures to Dad. Didn't he find this strange?

"Well, I guess it is a bit curious," Dad nodded.

"Where do you think it came from? Could it be Uncle Abe's money?" I asked.

Dad raised an eyebrow at me and we both burst into laughter. But, maybe it wasn't such a crazy thought after all.

"Did I ever tell you the story about the money buried at Grandma's home in Westchester County?" Dad asked.

"No!" I replied, eager for a new gem from the master of stories.

"Back in 1948…," As I listened I realized this might be one of the last tales he would ever tell me. Life seemed normal on the outside, but every day I was counting my blessings that he was here and alive before my eyes.

"…Grandma had Uncle Leo bury money on the grounds of her country estate in Harrison, New York, to hide it from Larry Siegel (husband #4) during their very public divorce." Mort's expression became mischievous. "I was 12 years old at the time. I loved that house. It had an acre in the back with fish pools, a thick grassy lawn, and rock gardens. I would explore the woods around the house with my dog Nosey. It was one of the happiest memories of my childhood—and one of the few years I was allowed at home." He paused, smiling at the happy memory. Then his expression became serious. "Siegel wound-up being a madman. He drugged Grandma and had her sign away her rights to several bank accounts and the property. At some point she told Uncle Leo to bury cash on the grounds of the estate so Siegel wouldn't find it."

"That's wild!"

"There's more." He was grinning, the one eyebrow going up again. "By the time the divorce went to court it was making scandalous headlines in the newspapers. I remember it read something like 'Beauty Bites Husband.'" Dad let out a gust of laughter.

"Wait, go back to the money," I insisted. "Could it have been part of Abe's missing stash? Did anyone ever unearth it?"

"I assume she had Leo dig it up at some point. I have no idea how much money there was. By the time the divorce was completed, Grandma had nothing left but the Century apartment on Central Park West from her marriage to Max."

I knew the divorce from Siegel had been rumored to be headlines, but I'd never heard about Leo burying money. These tales just kept getting better and better.

By late October, Amy and I had moved into our spacious new home in Santa Cruz. I placed a framed photo of Uncle Abe in the front sitting room, in honor of the man whose money, I was sure, had somehow trickled down to me some 67 years later.

Santa Cruz, February 2009

I will never forget how bright the rays of sun were through the giant trees surrounding the Sesnon House as I waited for Dad to arrive. It was unusually quiet except for the squawking of a raven, high on a tree limb looking down at me as I stood in the parking lot in front of the historic mansion where I worked at Cabrillo College. Dad had called in the middle of my workday to say he needed to talk to me. His voice had that strained reserve, which usually meant something was terribly wrong.

Dad pulled up in his silver Honda. He was dressed in nice slacks, a maroon shirt buttoned to the collar and a stylish dark sport coat. *Why do I remember that?* He smiled as he approached me, his blue eyes shimmering as he put his arm out to embrace me and kissed my cheek. He took my hand and we walked in silence down the side path of the Sesnon House, which led to an expansive green lawn and flowering bushes.

"Brace yourself," he said in a low whisper. I wasn't sure if he was talking to me or to himself.

As we walked through the colorful garden he told me his cancer had returned, spread throughout his liver and lungs. I was confused, as was he. It was less than three months ago that we had received great news that his tumors had significantly shrunk due to the new drug Sutent. Though it made him very tired and he was losing weight, the drug had delivered positive results. Now it seemed to have reversed, the tumors doubling their size in the last couple months.

"I'm going to keep living my life for as long as I can," he said bravely, but there was a tremor of anger in his expression. He wanted to live. We sat on a wooden bench quietly together, a magnolia tree covering us with its long branches. I helped him write a list of questions for the doctor. Then we hugged, holding the embrace for longer than usual. I watched him prepare to drive away and waved. He blew a kiss to me through the open car window as he left.

We talked on the phone the following day. He was frantic that it was February 12 and my sister Valerie wouldn't get her Valentine's day card in time and he would need to express mail it to New Jersey. I reminded him it was only February 10 and he had time. Dad never forgot Valentine's Day with his children, no matter how old we got. The card was always in the mailbox, year after year, signed with the "xxxxoooo" he was known for—four hugs and four kisses—his lucky number. I asked how he was doing emotionally and he responded he was very depressed. I couldn't imagine the gripping fear of death lingering at the door. I didn't know what to say except I loved him. He told me he had started writing poetry again, "It may not be any good, but I'm doing it." We said good night, but neither of us wanted to actually hang-up, and a long silence ensued on the wire. "Here's four kisses," he finally said. "Here's four back," I replied.

Every gesture and word seemed so heartfelt and precious during this time. The roller coaster ride of cancer had only one upswing in its journey toward the end of life: we had the time to say everything we needed to say. The downswing was devastating—watching my strong, intelligent, humorous, loving father deteriorate before my eyes.

One by one Dad ended his commitments from an active and involved life. They were all countable in lasts—the last radio show, the last TV episode of *Cinema Scene*, the last lecture at the Nickelodeon Theater, the last speech at Cabrillo College's All College Day Convocation, and finally, the last public poetry reading. They were monumental events, with hundreds of people coming out to see Mort, showing their respect, and hearing his last words. The love was palpable from his friends, colleagues, ex-students, and the entire community.

By the spring I was helping Dad edit his last book of poetry, *The Dark Figure in the Doorway*, which was scheduled for publication at a future date when he would no longer be here. I was with Dad every other day—taking him to the doctor, running errands, editing and designing the cover art for the new book. The eerie title, which seemed so macabre to me at that time, was inspired by Diego Velázquez's famous painting *Las Meninas*, a mysterious behind-the-scenes look at the Spanish court. In the painting there is a dark figure in the doorway, unclear to the viewer if he is coming or going. For me the dark figure was symbolic of a force waiting to take my father away.

By June, Dad had decided to stop all medications. They seemed to be killing him more quickly than the cancer, and dying with dignity on his own terms was very important to him. He was becoming thinner and frailer and only had energy for a few hours a day.

A letter came in the mail that it was time to renew Mort's driver's license with a written test. He hadn't driven himself for months, but insisted I take him to the DMV. We stood in that godforsaken line for well over an hour. He refused to sit down and stood with trembling legs to take the test he had studied tirelessly for. At first I couldn't figure out why he was so determined, but during the time we stood in that line I realized it was a marker of independence he was not ready to relinquish. When the DMV ordeal ended, Dad was exhausted but overjoyed at receiving the slip of paper stating his autonomy had not been stripped away. I assumed he was ready to go home, his face was bright red and fragile legs weak. But his expression was one of a big kid. "Let's go to Dairy Queen and have a sundae to celebrate!"

Valerie came to the West Coast for the summer months with her son Zachary to spend time with Dad and to help with the enormous task of cleaning out his garage. A lifetime of paperwork, letters, and manuscripts needed to be sorted and organized—all of which were to be archived at the University of California Santa Cruz's McHenry Library Special Collections in the Morton Marcus Poetry Archive.

I went to join them in the dusty garage one day and paused in the doorway, watching them analyze every piece of paper and discuss its significance. Looking at the scene from afar, I wondered what these last months of life must be like for him, organizing pieces of his own story that would be left behind. It felt abstract and surreal as he prepared for an upcoming, unknown journey.

How do we prepare for leaving this life? Dad was courageous, his attempts vigorous, to keep things going as normally as possible during this time. It was a testament to his spirit. I admired his tenacity to finish his book of poetry. At least he had this time to prepare. I thought about Abe and Frankie. They didn't have that luxury, taken away so young, caught up in such a thick web of corruption. And what did they leave behind besides a grieving family? Only two unsolved murder mysteries. They were not at peace, and I was reminded that I needed to finish their stories, but there was no time to do that now. I had to face the final curtain call of my father's life.

18

The Glamour Girl's Secret

Santa Cruz, August 2009

As family on the East Coast caught wind of Dad's failing health, relatives were calling. One of those calls was from Aunt Carol. After a short catch-up, Dad became tired and handed the phone to me, so he could nap in the overstuffed chair he was propped up in.

"Well, if isn't Jana—How ya' doin'?" Carol asked in her usual upbeat fashion. I moved to another room and we spoke of Dad's health, her family, and more mundane topics like the weather. While I had her on the phone I asked if I could jog her memory a bit.

"Yeah, yeah, go ahead…I know you've been doing research…sure… ask me," she pretended to grumble, then quickly started to giggle.

I mentioned I had recently been in touch with Uncle Ike's daughter Susan who'd sent me her father's wedding photo with Frankie and Rae standing together in the background. I was hoping Carol might remember something regarding Frankie's disappearance.

"Listen, I was just a little girl…," she replied in a silky Mae West tone, then started to laugh. "It was like this—my father told me the last time he saw Frankie, they met up at some deli they used to hang out at, somewhere off Pitkin Avenue. It was around '45 or a little later."

"Did Mudsy ever mention anything they may have talked about at that last meeting at the deli?" I asked.

"I remember my father mentioning Frankie being worried…something to do with papers at their old business place…but I don't know. Then a few days later Frankie disappeared. I'm telling ya', whoever whacked Abe, whacked Frankie too."

"And Abe was living with Rae on Eastern Parkway then?"

"Yeah, yeah…Rae with all her comings and goings," Carol chuckled. "I told you how she came in that fancy chauffeured car in diamonds to clean Grandma Anna's floors, right? You know, your grandmother was a real pip," she asserted.

I asked if she remembered anything about Rae's husbands. She remembered being told that in the late 1920's Rae married Bernard "Jack" Neufield (husband #2), whom she'd met through Abe and Frankie. That was new information—I'd tried to research Neufield and could never find anything about him. Carol insinuated that he was involved in underworld schemes and was ultimately killed. It seemed Rae had met at least two of her husbands through Abe.

"I remember in the '30s or '40s she went with this guy named 'Red' for a long time. Some gangster guy who was madly in love with her. Then came the unfortunate day for Max Marcus when he met Rae." Aunt Carol sighed and rehashed their extravagant lifestyle. She concluded how her mother, Bertha, was exasperated with Rae in many ways and did not approve of how she flaunted her wealth.

"My mother told me that Rae didn't want to have children because she thought she'd lose her figure. My mother convinced her—*'What respectable Jewish woman has no children?'*" Carol reenacted. "So, she had Mort, but then she spent all her time worrying about Max's gambling —*'What's it your business? He takes good care of you and still has money to throw away. Let him gamble!'*—my mother would say to her."

Grandma Rae had told me she left Max because he was a womanizing gambler, but Aunt Carol told it differently.

"Ah, please, Rae drove Max crazy. He left her!" she declared. "My mother told me that when World War II broke out Max thought he would be called into service for the men over 38, which would get him away from Rae's constant nagging for a while. But Max wasn't called, so he left her instead. Rae got a big settlement," Carol's voice dropped to a whisper, "but she probably stole from him on the side as well."

"Carol!" I exclaimed at her suggestion.

Aunt Carol was silent for a moment and then let out a sigh. "I think she sent poor Morty away to school because she went with so many different men after she broke-up with Max. She was very vain and didn't have the attention to give a child. It was terrible what she did to Morty. How do you abandon a small child like that?" Carol mumbled some Yiddish. "She was not a good mother, but in her mind she was giving him an education by sending him away."

"I've often wondered about all those photographs of her with different men in restaurants and night clubs," I added.

"Listen, she was not a respectable woman. I can tell you now—because she has passed, God rest her soul—she was a high-class call girl." Carol paused dramatically, then started shouting. "There were too many men! She never paid for anything! Her fridge was always empty...nothing in it...she was a call girl!"

"Wait a minute, are you really saying this?" I asked in shock.

"Sure...everyone knew," she crooned.

I asked her to hold the line and ran back into the family room. Dad was still awake, and I handed the phone back to him. "Carol is saying Grandma was a call girl...you better hear this."

His face turned ash gray as he listened. "So, you're saying you know this to be true?" Mort asked, gasping for breath.

"Sure, sure—before and after her marriage to Max. Look, we weren't going to mention it to you back in the day...but now that she's gone..."

We were dumbstruck by Carol's declaration of certainty. Carol adored Mort—she would never have intentionally hurt him with idle gossip.

"Look, she did what she had to do...she was a single mother...it was hard times," Carol continued, as if somehow the reason was justified. "Look, she was always good to her mother...and us, when we needed her. She paid for Leo when he had appendicitis and Dave's eye surgery," Carol added.

Dad and I sat for a long while after the call recounting past incidents that had brought this idea to our attention before, but we had always dismissed the thought. Rae herself had mentioned how she'd sit in bars with her English girlfriend Christine and wait for men to buy them dinner and what not, when they were traveling through Europe in the early 1950s. A distant cousin had once confessed that Rae had taught her how to attract men, and even on my mother's side of the family there had been rumors about Rae. "Your grandmother was a prostitute," one of my mother's cousins had blurted out on the phone to me once. I was so angry at the insinuation that I hung up. Finding that ancient sex manual after Grandma's passing didn't help either. I knew she was a conniver, even a gold-digger…but this? It was stunning.

"Remember the story about Siegel," Dad said slowly, catching his breath. "It's in my autobiography." In the section of Dad's book about his childhood memories of living in Harrison, New York, he mentions that Larry Siegel had claimed in divorce court that Grandma was a call girl and he possessed a document with signatures of over 270 men who had supposedly slept with her during their marriage.

"The claim was later thrown out of court when the signatures were found to be false," Dad continued. "Signed by bums on the Bowery in exchange for a bottle of muscatel."

"Do you think any of this is true?" I questioned.

"Who knows anymore," he sighed, resting his head on the back of the big leather chair and closing his eyes. "Siegel had abused Grandma terribly. That's why she had Leo bury money, remember? Jesus…who knows. When I was younger I asked her doormen how many visitors she had in a day. I was suspicious, but never found anything out."

Dad drifted into sleep while I sat thinking about the many aspects of Rae. I would keep this to myself for now. I wasn't at all sure how I felt about it.

19

La Mort

Santa Cruz, Autumn 2009

In late September we marked Dad's 73rd birthday. Close friends and family gathered in his backyard under the massive redwood tree to share food, drink, and a huge white cake topped with flowers and candles. Frail, but effervescent, Mort laughed and smoked cigars with his buddies. It was the final celebration. Hospice was arriving to set up camp in two days.

The remainder of the week was spent moving Dad from his upstairs sanctuary, where he wrote and often slept, to the spare bedroom on the first floor. This was difficult. His private space, filled with books, paintings, tchotchkes, and constantly streaming symphonies, was his magical haven. Luscious scents from his pipe or cigars streamed down the stairs to the main house. This was where he said the voices of his ancestors spoke to him and his poetry flowed. The sanctuary door was about to be permanently closed.

Amy and I set up his computer in the small spare room, installed a flat screen TV, and arranged a little garden outside the window with flowers and metal letters that spelled out *I love you*, so when he looked out the window he saw something beautiful, opposed to the neighbors' fence.

I cried often when I was alone or when I met with the hospice social worker. She would tell me to think about how I wanted to say goodbye. I cried because I didn't know how to do that. There were moments when I was conscious that death was a natural process, but after two years of fighting cancer, and wrestling with dashed hopes, it all just seemed unreal. Especially since I could still pick up the phone and talk to him at any time.

By mid-October a night nurse was brought in to take care of Dad. His wife was taking anxiety meds to get through the day and sleeping pills to get through the night. I had a heavy workload at the time, acting as the interim marketing director for the local college and preparing for the grand opening of their $80 million arts complex. After a full workday I would race across the county to Dad's house to be with him.

Amy and I celebrated our first wedding anniversary with Dad. I photographed his last portrait for the back of his upcoming book. We made food that he didn't eat, and laughed together playing cards and letting him win—though his head was too foggy to remember how to make sets in Gin Rummy. He grabbed our hands at the table and told us how much he loved us both, imparting words of wisdom for our futures, which left us all in tears. Dad gave me his lucky St. Seraphim necklace. The nice Jewish boy had worn it every day for years, rarely taking it off except to polish it. He kissed the medallion and handed it to me. "Give Jana as much luck as you have given me." Then he handed me a stack of mystery books to read. I felt out of my body, knowing a hard rain of tears was approaching fast.

On October 26, during one of my visits, he seemed particularly distracted. He sat near the window, looking out at the big redwood tree, gazing off and gasping for breath. His gaunt expression turned to a smile as I entered the living room.

"Jana, my love," he whispered in a raspy tone, waving me into the family room. I pulled the ottoman next to his chair and sat close to him. He was tired, the skin taut over his skeletal face.

"I didn't sleep well last night. I had these dreams…," he said. I held his spindly hands in mine and stared into his exceptionally clear blue eyes. "Everyone was here last night. Grandma, Abe, Leo, Frankie, aunts and uncles. I woke up shouting…they were all crowded into my bedroom and talking very loudly at each other. I thought it was real. Why were they all there?"

I just smiled at him.

"Jana, you are a great person and you've been a great daughter." He looked at me seriously. "You've asked me if I was afraid of dying, and I'd always said no. But today I am afraid, because I don't know where I am going." His eyes became glassy and we held the moment in silence.

My father, for all the mysticism in his poetry, did not believe in life after death, neither religiously or spiritually. I always found that puzzling. To him, the end was the end. But this day he had a different approach. Seeing the deceased family members gathered in his room had affected him, and now he was entertaining the thought that he might be "going somewhere." Maybe it was just the workings of the mind, the urgency to not let go, to believe there was something else.

I tried to lighten the moment. "You're going on a great adventure, Dad. Soon you will know all the secrets of the universe. And, when you realize you can come back, let's have a secret knock so you don't scare the hell out of me!"

He smiled and rolled his eyes, "That's ridiculous." But his expression turned serious again and gripped my hands tightly. "I never deserved to have you as a daughter. You and your sister have been the light of my life. Promise me you will live your life fully and not mourn me."

I couldn't promise him either of those things. Tears started to roll down my cheeks, but my eyes never left his. "I don't want to say goodbye, Dad. I don't know how. I'm not ready."

"Let it out…go ahead and cry," he said. And I did. "Just know how much I love you and enjoy your life while you have it. I'm ready to go."

I didn't realize that would be the last time I would see my father alive. He died 36 hours later.

●━━━━━●

In the Jewish religion it is noted, somewhere in the phases of mourning, that losing a parent is the hardest loss someone can go through.

Because of this, children are allowed a longer time to grieve. Psychologically and spiritually, our connection to our parents is the essential relationship that defines who we are as people.

The loss of my father was enormous for me. Though he had asked me to not mourn him, the request was not one I could fulfill. There was a private ceremony and many public memorials—radio show remembrances, awards in his name, and an annual poetry reading in his honor that still takes place every November—but my private mourning was an empty and lonely place. These became my Dark Ages.

The first six months after his passing it was hard to grip the reality of it all. I kept thinking he would walk through the door, having been away on vacation, or I would suddenly think it was time to call him and check in…but he wasn't here anymore.

I tried to visit Dad's gravesite. He had picked the plot himself, on a peaceful hill above Grandma Rae's plot, where he thought people would enjoy visiting him. I went several times, and then stopped. I felt horribly guilt-ridden for not going and talking to him more, but I hated it there. It took me some time to realize that my resistance was due to the fact that I couldn't think of him as disintegrating bones and flesh six feet in the ground. I remained hopeful that he was a guardian spirit that walked with me every day.

In the seventeen years I'd been back in Santa Cruz, since leaving New York, we had worked on many book and art projects together—spent many years researching, talking and hypothesizing about the family history, the murder of Uncle Abe, Max, and the secrets of Grandma Rae. With him gone, my desire to solve the family mysteries was gone as well. I had nothing creative to give to it, and I couldn't even think about Dad without a river of despair flooding over me.

As months turned into years, I made attempts to sit at my computer to research and write, but I couldn't. I stared at my collection of old family photos and history files, realizing I had spent years with dead people, trying to string their lives together to make sense of my own. The research had been a long and sad road—rich with information, but also thick with loss and unknowing. I had grown numb thinking about dead relatives—thinking about their lives, what they must have been like, and trying to piece documents together that would awaken their stories and bring them to life.

I couldn't bring myself to put Dad's death date on the family tree. Grief stricken, the immediate family having disintegrated, and befuddled by the new information on Grandma Rae, I needed to walk away from the faces of the past.

Abe "Jew Murphy" Babchick, circ. 1925. (Author Collection)

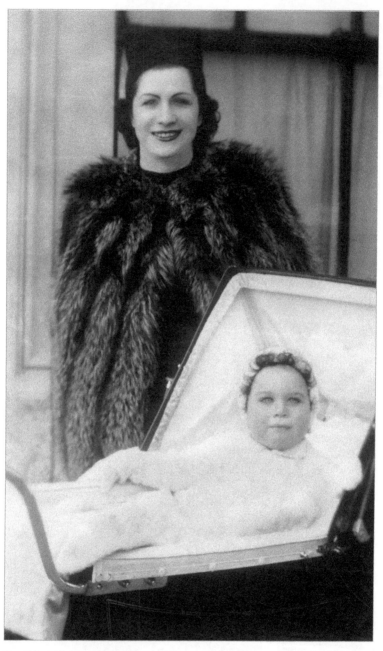

Rae Babchick Marcus and Morton Marcus, circ. 1938. (Author Collection)

Brothers Frankie Balzack, circ. 1935, and Abe "Jew Murphy" Babchick, circ. 1940. (Author Collection)

Abe and Rae vacationing in the Catskills, circ. 1934. (Author Collection)

Pincus Max Marcus and Rae Babchick Marcus at Atlantic City, circ. 1939.
(Author Collection)

Max and Rae, circ. 1935. (Author Collection)

Rae Babchick Marcus, circ. 1935. (Author Collection)

Morris "Mudsy" Hecker (left) with son Leo (right), wife Bertha Balzac, and daughter Carol (front). Circ. 1943.

Mort and Leo, circ. 1946. (Author Collection)

Abe "Kid Twist" Reles, ringleader of Murder, Inc., December, 1940. (Brooklyn Public Library, Brooklyn Collection)

Brooklyn DA William O'Dwyer greets "Kid Twist" Reles (center) and Murder, Inc. member Albert "Tick Tock" Tannenbaum as they return to New York after testifying before a Los Angeles Grand Jury. December 21, 1940. (Brooklyn Public Library, Brooklyn Collection)

Top: Midnight Rose's candy store, the Murder, Inc. headquarters at 779 Saratoga Avenue, Brownsville, in the shadow of the El train. circ. 1938. (New York Municipal Archives)

Bottom: Mark chats up the locals in front of what once was Midnight Rose's candy store. August, 2015. (Photo by Jana Marcus)

DAILY NEWS

Copt. 1941 by News Syndicate Inc. NEW YORK'S PICTURE NEWSPAPER Reada Mark Reg. U. S. Pat. Off.

Vol. 23, No. 79 | New York, Thursday, September 25, 1941* | 68 Main + 16 Brooklyn + 8 Queens Pages | 2 Cents

MARTIAL LAW RULES PARIS, VICHY REPORT

Story on Page 3

Bullets For Breakfast

The Mobster Died at Dawn

A detective looks over the corpse that was Abe Bebchick, crap-shooting mobster, in front of 675 Empire Boulevard, near Albany Ave., Brooklyn. Bebchick was slain at dawn yesterday by two bullets behind his left ear. Special Prosecutor Amen says Bebchick may have been murdered to forestall exposure of a tie-up between police and policy racketeers. District Attorney O'Dwyer labeled Bebchick a cheap punk who was trying to muscle in on a dice games combine. Police said Bebchick had begun to operate as Brownsville's "policy king" and suggested he may have been exterminated by rivals.

Story on page 4.

(NEWS foto)

Cover of the Daily News, September 25, 1941. (*New York Daily News* Archive)

Interior of Dubrow's Cafeteria Restaurant on Eastern Parkway, from the back looking toward the front. May, 1941. (New York Municipal Archives)

A detective looks at Abe Babchick's body, found on Empire Boulevard on the morning of September 24, 1941. (*New York Daily News* Archive)

Special Prosecutor John Harlan Amen on his way to Brooklyn Felony Court to present the case against Lt. Cuthbert Behan for stealing police records. Amen is accompanied by prosecution team members Moses Lewis (l) and Deacon Murphy (r). October. 29, 1938. (Brooklyn Public Library, Brooklyn Collection)

Edward Heffernan, Chief of Staff, District Attorney 's office under William O'Dwyer. 1939. (Brooklyn Public Library, Brooklyn Collection)

James J. Moran, O'Dwyer's Chief Clerk, arrives at Federal Court for his perjury trial. May 3, 1951. (Brooklyn Public Library, Brooklyn Collection)

John Harlan Amen, Special Prosecutor for the Attorney General, investigating law enforcement bodies in Brooklyn, and J. Edgar Hoover, FBI Director, as they confer at FBI headquarters. November 4, 1938. (World Wide Photo, Brooklyn Library)

William O'Dwyer appearing at the Kefauver Committee Hearings on March 21, 1951. (Brooklyn Public Library, Brooklyn Collection)

Ike and Rena Balzac's wedding, June 23, 1945. Back row (l to r): Carol, Bertha, Dave, Dave's daughter Selma, Rae, unknown, Frankie, Dave's wife Ida. Front row: Mort, Great Grandma Anna, Ike, Rena, Rena's parents. (Author Collection)

Above: Rae dancing with underworld figure "Red Bill."

Right: Drawing of unknown witness in the Lucky Luciano trial of 1936. (Author Collection)

Rae with fourth husband Larry Siegel, circ. 1946. (Author Collection)

Rae, Leo, and Mort, 1991. (Author Collection)

Carol and Jana, 1981. (Author Collection)

Jana and Valerie, circ. 1993. (Photo by Paul Schraub)

Jana and Mort in 2008, a year before his death. (Photo by Dina Scoppettone for *Metro* Newspapers)

Session with Maria via Skype. Flash of blue light over her head just as she said Abe's spirit was present. January, 2015. (Video still, Author Collection)

Abe's headquarters on Lincoln Place, displaying the empty lot, black doors, and narrow windows as described by Maria. June, 2016. (Author Collection)

Maria and Cousin Michael explore outside the Lincoln Place basement. March, 2015. (Video still by Jana Marcus)

The old gate at St. Matthew's Church on Eastern Parkway across from Dubrow's Cafeteria Restaurant, where Abe met with Amen the night he was killed. August, 2015. (Video still by Emery Hudson)

Top: Mark and Maria in the Lincoln Place basement. March, 2015. (Video still by Jana Marcus)

Right: Cousin Jared and Jana on Van Sinderen Ave, Brooklyn. August, 2015. (Video still by Emery Hudson)

Investigation Team on Van Sinderen Ave, Brooklyn. August, 2015. (l to r): Emery, Mark, Jana, Maria, Eric, and Jared. (Author Collection)

Mark explores inside the dumbwaiter at Lincoln Place. June, 2016. (Video still by Jana Marcus)

Maria channeling on the dirt road off Van Sinderen Avenue, Brooklyn, where Abe was murdered. August, 2015. (Photo by Jana Marcus)

Top: Mark, Jared, and Zach digging on the empty lot at Lincoln Place. June, 2016. (Video still by Jana Marcus)

Left: Jana takes roses to Abe's grave on her final visit. Montefiore Cemetery, Queens, NY. June, 2016. (Photo by Mark Basoa)

PART
III

20

Back to the Future

Santa Cruz, October 2014

On the eve of the 5th anniversary of my father's death, I got a phone call.

A scratchy-voiced woman introduced herself as Jeannie. "I got your name and phone number from your stepmother." She mumbled something about not having called me sooner.

"How can I help you?" I asked impatiently.

"I'm the daughter of Meyer Rabinowitz, your Uncle Abe's driver."

She had my attention. *Was this a joke?*

The woman's aunt had been Birdie Sunkin, Grandma Rae's life-long best friend. Birdie had told Jeannie many times to call Rae's family in California. "But you know how it is, when your aunt tells you something and you don't know the people, so I never called. Then I found out your father died and I didn't want to impose, so all the years went by," she said in a raspy, yet cheerful tone.

To make matters even more strange, it seemed Jeannie and her husband had lived in the county of Santa Cruz for over 40 years and raised their children here. I was pinching myself. *Why had I never heard of this woman before? Why now?*

Jeannie explained that she'd been thinking a lot about her father Meyer, and over the years had become more curious about his early life in Brooklyn. She hoped I might have information about him. I forwarded a few newspaper articles via email about Abe's death and her father's arrest, and we arranged to meet for lunch the coming week.

●───●

Jeannie and I met at a crowded rosticceria. She appeared to be in her late 60s, with long, wispy strands of gray-blonde hair framing her tanned face. She was personable and extremely excited to be connecting with me. She gushed about how everyone loved Uncle Abe. "He kept the entire Rabinowitz family employed during the Depression. If it wasn't for him, we'd have had nothing."

She didn't have any new information to add to my research, but we did come across something puzzling: Where had Meyer actually been the night of the murder?

Jeannie was confused about "Zoo," the police-protected witness who claimed, under shrouded identity, to have been Abe's driver and with him the night he was killed. Jeannie explained that her older sister was born on September 22, 1941, and she had always been told that her father stayed several nights at the hospital with her mother. Back then, women stayed in the hospital for several days after delivery. Because of this, Jeannie said her father hadn't maintained his usual morning routine of grabbing a newspaper and bagel before heading to Abe's headquarters on Lincoln Place. If Meyer had read the paper the morning of September 24, he'd have learned about Abe death and wouldn't have gone to the headquarters with the collected money bags, where he was ultimately arrested with Mudsy and the other men. We went over the scenario several times, but Jeannie couldn't reconcile what the papers had recorded versus what she had been told about her father's whereabouts.

Jeannie was also struggling with the dates when Meyer had left the East Coast for Los Angeles. She was under the impression that her family had moved to L.A. in 1947. Jeannie's cousin Mickey had told me, as had Grandma Rae, that Meyer had moved to LA within a month or two of the murder and changed his name to Rabin. Jeannie said that her father had changed his name to Mike Robinson, and often went by the name Eddie, to appear less Jewish.

Most intriguing to Jeannie was the insignia ring that Abe's gang wore to signal police that they were under paid protection. She had been obsessed for many years about a pinky ring her father wore and quickly drew a sketch of a square-shaped gold ring with her father's initials engraved next to a small diamond in one corner. She attempted to show it to me in some old photos, but they were too washed-out to see any detail. When one of Jeannie's sons grew into adulthood she gave him the ring, but it was stolen at a youth hostel in Europe during a summer vacation. Jeannie had never seen such a unique ring again—until the early 1980s when she and her husband were neighbors to Marge Heinold who owned the famous bar First and Last Chance Saloon in Oakland's Jack London Square. Once, on a visit to the bar, Jeannie had been served a drink by an elderly bartender who had a ring exactly like her father's, except for different initials. She was amazed to see the ring pattern and asked the bartender about it, but he gave no details other than he was from New York and dating Marge. That was all Jeannie remembered, but now it was plaguing her if it might have been the gang insignia.

I had given Jeannie much to ponder as we parted ways a few hours later. Except for his arrest records, I wasn't able to shed much light on her father's exploits of the 1940s. She would have to unlock the secrets of her family history on her own.

A much-needed rain was descending as I drove home. My mind wandered as I sat at a stoplight, transfixed by the rhythm of the windshield wipers. In a flash, I had the revelation that it had been on the 5th anniversary of Grandma Rae's death in 2007, that my journey into discovering the Marcuses had begun, and so much of my research had taken off. That had most definitely been some sort of a sign. Now, as I faced the 5th anniversary of Dad's passing, I felt that something was shifting again. *What was it with this family and 5th anniversaries?*

It was only recently that I had mustered the strength to read Dad's poetry again or watch his videos. The grieving process had been difficult and incomplete for me. The pain of such a great loss never really goes away, it just mutates over time.

I couldn't fathom the anguish the Babchick family must have felt from the loss of two brothers taken down in their prime. The killers were suspected, but nothing could be done when the culprits were most probably the authorities. It was no wonder my generation didn't know anything about Abe and Frankie—the events were too violent and terrifying.

It may have been the romanticized notion of being related to a mobster, the mystery of unsolved murders in the family, or the fact I was in great need of a creative project to take me away from the grief of losing both my father and my longtime job, but I was once again feeling passionate about my research since the unexpected call from Jeannie.

I had never shaken the dreams, from years ago, of Abe at the foot of my bed trying to wake me. Wanting to talk through me. I had been obsessed with the circumstances of Abe and Frankie's deaths for the last 26 years. That was half of my lifetime spent hunting for the poetry in their lives.

I was reminded of Dad's words, which had always resonated so strongly with me:

> I don't know how I write what I do most of the time—it's like there are voices inside me that want to speak…and those voices are the voices of my ancestors who could never talk. Suddenly their voices come out and they speak their dark secrets, or their joyous secrets, or what they wanted to say about their lives. It is my job to shape it, so it becomes an alive experience or communication for the reader, and it enriches their lives.[1]

I was confident of what had happened in the wake of Abe's murder, but questions remained: What happened leading up to the murder? Was Abe's death solely about the cops on the take? What happened to the missing Uncle Frankie for whom I could find no death certificate?

Returning to the research was also a way for me to stay connected to Dad. I needed to get back to uncovering Abe and Frankie's story—to finish it once and for all, whether I could solve the murders or not.

21

Winter is Coming

Santa Cruz, November 2014

I jumped back into my research, trying all the new avenues available on the internet. I contacted family friends and a myriad of other sources for additional clues, including filing Freedom of Information Act papers with the courts and FBI, scanning websites full of old Brooklyn memories, online newspaper resources that weren't available five years earlier, history books, and more. I even considered working with a crime scene psychic.

That thought started for me back in 2010, when Amy and I had gone to the Flint Center in San Jose to see Lisa Williams, the renowned TV medium who had a series on the Lifetime Network called *My Life Among the Dead*. I loved her show. She seemed very authentic in her sessions, helping people talk to departed loved ones and solving cold cases. It left me curious to investigate if this sort of work might help me.

The night we saw Williams, she came on the stage and started channeling spirits. She told of a man who had been shot in a nearby town who needed to tell his daughter what really happened to him. Amy had worked in the town where this murder had occurred and knew the family, including the daughter, who was now weeping on the stage. Williams gave important and insightful clues to the case that night, which ultimately led to solving the murder a few months later.

After that I was aching with curiosity to see a medium about Uncle Abe. Could Abe himself come through with information? It may sound like a silly idea to some, but the thought was beyond intriguing to me, if I could just find a medium who was authentic. I've always considered myself a skeptical believer—I believe, but it has to be proven to me. There are so many phonies out there making money off people who are at their most vulnerable. But, I also believe there are some truly gifted psychics as well. Lisa Williams had jolted my imagination and I dreamed of visiting the scene of Abe's murder with her.

But, William's private sessions were way beyond my budget and she was booked a year in advance, so I put it out of my mind—until the day I received a surprising and timely email. It was from Maria Saganis, an acquaintance from long ago. I was shocked that she remembered me after so many years, but her note said I had been on her mind and she hoped to reconnect.

Nineteen years earlier I had been in New Orleans working on my first photo documentary book, *In The Shadow of the Vampire*, and had the opportunity to join author and forensic psychologist Kathryn Ramsland on a late night ghostbusting case with several psychics at Le Petit Théâtre in the French Quarter. This was not a commercial tour, but a private group of paranormal investigators. On that hair-raising excursion I met Maria. The attractive, dark-haired woman was a psychic healer and medium, helping spirits tell their stories and transition to the other side. I witnessed her channeling during my visit and had been amazed by her gifts. We had made a friendly connection, but lost touch. Maria's email was like a beacon from the other side, and as I read it I knew exactly who to call for a connection with the dead.

I quickly sent her a reply which led to a phone conversation. Maria still sounded like the sassy, straight-shooter I remembered. She had fond memories of the adventure in New Orleans and felt something had pushed her to reach out to me. That's when I mentioned I could use her help on a family murder. She was immediately interested and insisted I give her no details. We worked out a price for her services and made plans for her visit to Santa Cruz. She was already getting rumblings about my case just from talking on the phone. She sensed I had lot of misinformation and kept seeing the trunk of an old car. She jotted down some notes and looked forward to seeing me soon.

Maria arrived at my home on a blustery December day. She was as I remembered her from all those years ago, although her dark hair was now gray, cut in a short style that swept across her forehead and behind her ears. Maria was of Greek origin, originally from St. Louis, and the third generation of her family to display the gift of talking to the dead. She had worked on missing persons cases with the St. Louis and Los Angeles police departments in the past, and currently had many clients.

Dressed in yoga pants and a long purple top, she wore miles of jingling silver bracelets that sounded like small bells as she gestured and moved. Maria always had an engaging and dynamic personality, and we immediately clicked despite the passage of time.

Twenty minutes into our reunion she started to get a sharp pain in her chest and was developing a headache. I was afraid she was getting sick, but she assured me it was due to paranormal activity happening upstairs in the house. Maria described herself as an empath—sensitive to the physical pains and sensations of the spirits she interacted with.

My cat, Max, crept down the stairs from the second floor and peered at us with suspicion through the wooden railings of the banister. Maria whispered to Max and then mentioned there was a light anomaly next to him that rose and went up the stairs and to the right. As we continued to catch up she became more and more distracted until she was practically unable to finish her sentences. Her headache had increased, becoming more and more intense with pressure and pain on the left side, from the back of her neck to the front of her lobe. I offered her some aspirin, but she responded, "No, it means they are ready to talk. I think we should start."

I had not told Maria any details about Uncle Abe's story. She only knew I had a relative who was murdered. Nothing else. I asked where she would be most comfortable. She was inclined to go upstairs, so I followed her. She was feeling a lot of energy and stopped at the landing of the second floor and sat on the carpet, which gave her an obscured view of the other rooms, the doors only slightly open. She explained there were a lot of "people" present who wanted to talk, and a lot of the energy was coming from the room to the right—the spare bedroom. Maria didn't know, and could not see, that the room she referred to was where I had my St. Michael angel collection and a large altar with photos of Dad, Abe, and other deceased relatives. I asked if she would like to go in there, but she shook her head, explaining she had not been invited by the spirits—they didn't know her—and she was being respectful, happy to sit on the floor outside the rooms. She was also happy to sit on the floor because she was starting to feel faint and her head was continuing to throb on the left side—the exact spot where Uncle Abe had been shot. I said nothing.

I turned on my video recorder and sat on the floor across from Maria, who had closed her eyes and was concentrating in silence. "I'm getting information from your family. Obviously, you've done research…," Maria stopped, asking something invisible near her to back-up and get off her, then continued. "I don't know anything about your story, but the image I received when we spoke on the phone was of a police car. There is a large number on the car, which reads 69. I picked-up that there is a lot more involved with this murder than what the public perceived, or that you have currently found. There is also much more to be learned about the police and people of power who were respected by the public, but were actually very dirty. This is being told to me by a person who has a very clenched jaw, and I'm having a lot of pain there."

Maria started to rock back and forth in silence before she continued.

"This person with the tight jaw is telling me that everyone was stealing from everybody. He keeps using really ridiculous old terms, like 'everyone was on the take,' including these people of power. I don't know if they were judges or what…what's bothering me is the trunk of this cop car. It's troublesome. The spirits are screaming about it right now…they are saying there is more to this than what you have documented, but you'll be able to find the truth because you'll be given names and information about the people who have lied. The man with the clenched jaw is telling me this…he has a little name…I keep getting told something like 'Ned' is his nickname."

Maria alternated between speaking directly to me and speaking to the entity that was giving her messages. "Dude, you are killing my teeth, back up!" she exclaimed, then returned to speaking to me. "This Ned guy is chewing on a cigarette with his teeth…he's so clear right now… young guy, hook nose, hair parted on the side…looks like the penguin in the TV show *Gotham*…deep set eyes…he chews his cigarette after he lights it. His hair is straight…he's darker, maybe Italian…his nose stands out…it's very hooked. He's a thinner man…the cigarette is driving me crazy. He's sort of disheveled with a loose tie and shirt. It's almost like he is a seer…he watches. He doesn't speak much. I don't know if he was a witness or worked with somebody…I don't know where he belongs in all this, but he's watching the police car and is adamant about the trunk, and adamant that you don't have the whole story…'*there is more to this*'… he keeps saying, '*you ain't got nothin*'…there are names of men involved that have been protected because of their stature back in that time.

"Can you open the trunk for me?" Maria asked the spirit. "Can you show me what's in there?" Maria continued rocking her body to and fro. "He won't let me move on from the car, so bear with me for a minute. He's showing me two scenarios. One is a red brick building with windows that are cut narrow and close together like a factory…the building is not tall, maybe three or four stories high…it has a main door in the center and many windows above and there is an empty lot next to it."

Maria went on to describe a locked black door and black windows on the lower level of the building. The second vision was of the police car, sitting under a bridge, and the road next to it dropped off as if into water, but there is a fence there now. Maria started to feel nauseous and had an acidic taste in her mouth, as if Ned had been punched in the stomach.

"What does he want me to know?" I asked.

"I'm not sure yet. He's adamant about showing me the trunk of the car…I get the sense there is a body in the trunk. When I asked him to show me inside the trunk, he went straight to the building with the empty lot…and something is there. I don't know what it is yet, but something is buried on this ground. It feels tangible like a ring or a watch is buried there…they keep showing me a black door and it's locked. I don't know if it's a locked door on the premises or another part of the building…but they are very adamant about showing this to me…it leads to a basement and I have horrible, horrible pain in my spine, like I can't breathe. Someone was taken down there and '*business*' was handled. I'm being drawn to the basement. That's what Ned jumped in to say."

Maria was quiet for several moments, and then looked up at me. "It's interesting, because the spirits feel they can all talk about it now, so information may come freely. Sit at your altar and ask the spirits for guidance. That room to the right is very much a doorway." She pointed to the spare bedroom again.

"Speaking of doorways…I'm seeing another doorway, a round door that's open a little bit and a glow is coming out of it." Maria was quiet for a long moment and then asked me directly, "Do you have your father's desk? A woman wants to know where the desk is. Did you sell the desk? She wants to know what the problem is that you don't have the desk."

"Oh my God, It's Grandma Rae!" I blurted. *That was exactly what Grandma would say to me!* I was stunned, but tried to contain my shock.

"She's showing me the desk…she's being a real noodge…she's livid about this." Maria spoke to the spirit in a sarcastic tone, "Seriously? Why are you being like that right now?"

I asked Maria to tell Grandma not to worry, that the desk was O.K. and it didn't matter.

Maria chuckled, "She's not having it…her perception is, '*why did they take it away and break it*'…'*why is it gone?*' She's fussbudgety about it… it feels like something may be attached to it. She's adamant about this little piece of furniture. It's not even a desk, it looks like a card table with folding legs."

I couldn't believable this. I explained to Maria that Grandma was always mad that I left a gate-legged table with my friend Anne in New York. There was no way Maria could ever have known about that.

"Can you contact your friend and ask her about it?" Maria suggested. "Your Grandma is cute, but very demanding about this. I'm also seeing a piece of paper, it's yellow with age, but I don't know what it means. Maybe it's connected."

"Why is that the only thing my Grandmother has to say to me from beyond the grave?" I laughed nervously.

"Listen, just handle this so we can move on." She rolled her eyes and we both laughed.

Maria continued to be shown the table, with a vision of a man sitting at it with a little girl on his lap, who she felt was me. "The table is a connection to creativity, there is a muse present and there is a creative energy that is being given." Maria was being shown the scene from the perspective of someone who was watching this. "They are telling me that you have information about this case in your possession…you have the clues you need in papers you have…'research and review.'"

Maria went back into a trance-like state and then looked up at me. "I'm receiving a man who is contemplating…what's in that room?" she pointed toward my home office. "He's sitting in the big chair in that room with his feet up. He's watching us very intensely. He's trying to understand what's happening right now…trying to understand how he can speak through me."

I asked what he looked like and Maria pointed at a painting of Mort in the hallway. "He's a younger version of this painting. He's very inquisitive and watching us. He's trying to figure out how to communicate…'what do I do?'…'do I talk?'…he's watching carefully…'so this is how it is done?'…when the spirit of your grandmother came through he materialized and walked into your office and sat down. It's a father figure. I sense your Dad has passed and may come to you and give you information as you're writing. Your Dad has people up there he is in contact with. That's a nice conduit to bring through."

Maria had no way of knowing that my father had passed away or that the painting in the hallway was of him. It could have been of anyone—just another piece of art.

"Can we go in there?" Maria asked, pointing toward my office. I jumped up from the floor to enter the room first and take down a photo over my desk of Abe's crime scene. I tucked it away in a corner, to the left of my desk, so she wouldn't see it. When Maria entered my office she sat on the ottoman by the big chair, steadying herself as she received messages. "The man in here is definitely your dad. He sits in here while you work and communicates with you…he's very comfortable here. Now that we've moved into this room there's a lot of frenetic energy…a sense of excitement. Your father is pacing around your desk."

Maria saw a portrait photograph of Abe on the wall and walked over to it. "This is what Ned looks like, but it's not Ned. This is your murdered relative, yes? Ned's nose is more hooked and his hair is straighter, but both have dark circles under their eyes…they look very similar. Everyone is frantic to talk right now…your Dad opened a doorway for all of them to come through. Your Dad is walking around your desk and is adamant about showing me something to the left of your desk. Are your files here?"

Maria looked around my desk area. "There's something here, in this area, that your Dad wants me to see," and she went straight to the pile of papers where I had tucked away the photo of Abe's crime scene. "What's here?…you're adamant about me being here…" she asked the spirit of my father.

I retrieved the crime scene photo from its hiding place, but Maria had closed her eyes. "There's something in that police trunk, I'm telling you." She opened her eyes and I handed her the crime scene photo. She stared intensely at the image, then shook her head excitedly, "This is not right! I'm telling you something isn't right, this whole photo is wrong…there's a fucking cop car involved in this!" Maria held her head in pain. "Who are you? Why does my head hurt so much on the left side?" she asked the silent air.

"I'm very faint right now," she declared and sat down in my desk chair. "Ned saw all of this….and he's telling me again about the police vehicle…this crime scene photo is all wrong. He's getting very emotional about it right now…two people are jumping in and out to give messages…there's Ned, and I also have pain in my frontal lobe that belongs to your relative…an uncle. I'm going out on a limb right now, but it feels like his death was a hit from a group of people…it's not what happened in this picture. Ned is adamant that a cop or several cops killed your uncle. They were summoned to do the hit."

I told her that Uncle Abe was shot in the head exactly where she was having pain. Again, Maria excitedly pointed at the crime scene photo and started speaking very quickly, "This story is wrong…it's not right… it's not right …I keep hearing *'I was taken away to here'*…*'taken here.'* There is an overwhelming sense of frustration and anger that he was taken away…I'm getting a large amount of chatter…a lot of people are here now saying *'let me tell you what happened'*…they are really emotional about this…*'I was taken away'*…your uncle's photo triggered their talking." Maria explained that when they all start talking at once it feels like her head is exploding, like a flash of white noise—images and words streaming in front of her.

"The whole scenario of his body sitting in a car is not right…Abe didn't die immediately…there were several seconds of aliveness in his body after he was shot." Maria had her hand over her heart as she continued. "It feels like he had a breath or two in him…he didn't die right away…he had the wherewithal of what was happening."

Slowly she started to calm down and appeared more present. "Everyone is backing away now. I'm seeing the room in a normal fashion again. Your Dad is here with you, and will continue to be here. This is where he's going to hang out for a while. He probably has his own space in the afterlife, but his comfort level is here…writing is what your Dad knows about, and this space reminds him of his own space when he was alive. He's here and he's inquisitive. It was important that I asked permission to first come in this room."

I shared with Maria that my office was set-up in a similar fashion to Dad's home office, and I had several of his personal belongings in the room. Recently my partner Amy had started to come into the office when she arrived home after a day at the flower shop she owned, and would plop down in the big chair, smoke a cigar, and ask how my day was, in the same way that Dad used to.

"She's channeling his energy. It's time for you to get this story told," Maria declared.

I acknowledged that the details she had given were true. I told her that my uncle's name was Abe and that some of the newspapers stated he was robbed or taken-out by a rival gang. "The only gang that took him out were the ones in office. I'm telling you, it was the cops," Maria insisted.

"I have always thought the police killed him, but I don't have the proof."

"You will be given names," Maria stated with confidence. "This Ned is a guide, and he is adamant that there's something in the trunk of the cop car we have to see, so the crime scene photo you have doesn't make sense. Your uncle was killed somewhere else and they moved his body. We will have to continue to see what's in that trunk."

Although Maria said the spirits had started to back away, I made one more request of her, "I'd like to know about someone named Frankie."

She closed her eyes and was silent.

"He is an unsolved case as well, yes? I'm getting sharp pains in my skull...I'm seeing a triangle...it seems he disappeared in the same fashion as your Uncle...he worked for your Uncle. I'm feeling pressure and pain in my whole body...I keep hearing *'they forgot about me'...'they forgot about me'*...this is a family affair...is he Abe's brother? I don't know the story, but it's not just about Abe and Frankie...the higher-ups started to take everyone out so they could stop something...This doesn't make sense to me, Maria—I'm having trouble understanding." Maria referred to herself in the third person when she was channeling, to differentiate between her personal feelings and what she was hearing from the spirits.

She concentrated with her eyes closed, as if listening intently to a conversation. "It feels like the higher-ups started to cut all these people down because of whatever they were doing...I don't know what that is, but I can tell you a cop has money in this car...Frankie is telling me this. Pockets are turned inside out...Hands with the money aren't Frankie's hands...something's in the trunk...Frankie's confused...he doesn't know what's happening to him...feels like they got him after Abe...he died after Abe...Abe was in the wrong place at the wrong time...but I can't tell where Frankie is...it feels like he faded to black very fast. Could mean he was covered by something...he's very discombobulated."

Maria asked Frankie to back up and calm down a little bit. "Frankie's not as cut and dry as the others...he feels different...Abe was shrewd... Frankie's a softer soul...he's sweet...very scared...he doesn't understand what happened. There's almost an innocence to him. He was either jumped or knocked unconscious."

"Where was he when Abe died?" I asked.

"'*Earlier*'...he saw him earlier...during the day...Frankie is still looking over his shoulder...he doesn't feel comfortable here right now...I see him backing off. I don't know if he's scared or if he's backing away for your protection. I feel his nervous anxiety coming through...he's saying '*I can't talk about this right now.*' I can only see black around him. I don't know what kind of damage he had done to him...a knock on the head... my ears are ringing. He's still here with us, but he's backing away slowly and nervously."

"Where did he die? Where was he?" I asked anxiously.

"My throat feels water-logged...he died in water...it's fade to black and I can't breathe. The hit to his head was so traumatic he fell into water...my hands smell chlorinated...he's being very careful...it seems he knew about or overheard threats being made to the family...he has an overwhelming sense of determination to get to the bottom of this case without getting anyone else involved."

As Frankie faded away, our session came to an end. I was flabbergasted and Maria was exhausted. She had been right about so many things I knew to be true. It was remarkable to watch her process and witness how she took on the physical symptoms of the spirits that came through.

I thanked her immensely for the information. Maria was very interested in the case and as soon as she settled in her new home on the East Coast we planned to continue with a few sessions in the new year, and then a potential visit to the actual Brooklyn locations in the spring.

After Maria departed, I watched the video I had recorded of the session. There was no way she could have known about that desk and how angst-ridden Grandma had been about it in the last years of her life. Maria was also accurate about the Abe situation—and knew that Frankie had been Abe's brother, was killed after Abe, and that the cops had done it. She also picked-up that there was more to the story than the newspapers revealed.

The Uncle Frankie connection was particularly fascinating to me, as I knew little about him. She had been told by Frankie's spirit that threats had been made to the family, and he took it upon himself to find Abe's killer, which I knew to be accurate. It hurt my heart that Frankie thought we had forgotten about him, as if Abe's case was more important. I had never forgotten about Frankie. There had just never been any clues to figure out what happened to him. With Maria having been so accurate about other details, I was hopeful she might be able to reveal what happened to Frankie as we moved forward.

This was a whole new vein of investigation. I currently had the time and wherewithal to look at the old information with a fresh perspective, and I was ready to tackle it.

There were no words to describe the elation I felt that Dad might actually be with me—guiding me to finish the research and finally piece together the truth behind the family secrets.

I had a sense this was going to be a very wild ride.

22

Shadow of a Doubt

At the top of my to-do list was a call to my friend Anne about that damned gate-leg table which seemed to be haunting Grandma Rae from beyond the grave. Anne thought the table was probably in storage at her mother-in-law's house, and her mission was to find it in order to put Rae's spirit at peace.

I used Google's Street-View to look at the Brooklyn locations that were mentioned in my early research. I don't know why I'd never thought to do this before. There was Dubrow's Cafeteria Restaurant, which once stood at 1110 Eastern Parkway, where Abe was last seen alive; 675 Empire Boulevard, where Abe's body was found in his car; and 626 Lincoln Place, Abe's headquarters.

To my amazement, the Lincoln Place location fit Maria's description exactly. It was a four-story red-brick building with narrow rectangular windows, a black door in the middle, and an empty lot adjacent to it! The empty lot was actually the backyard area of the neighboring building which faced the parallel street, Eastern Parkway. *This was eerie!* The Google view showed that Lincoln Place had a black gate leading to a lower level and black basement windows. Maria's vision had been spot-on.

Next, I sifted through the garage for my old notes on Abe's case. The gorilla racks were stacked with cartons of decades-old notebooks, datebooks, and journals. I plopped the boxes onto a makeshift worktable and started reading through them, finding the folder of my original research from 1988 and some family photos. Spreading the materials out, a box teetering on the edge of the table finally fell over, scattering papers and datebooks across the floor. As I knelt to pick them up, an old spiralbound datebook was overturned, loose papers protruding from all angles. One of the papers was an old napkin scribbled with notes from a discussion I'd had with Uncle Leo at my sister's wedding.

It had been the summer of 2002. Valerie and her husband Steve were married in the Berkshires on the weekend of June 22. Family and friends had gathered at the rustic Race Brook Lodge—some coming for the day of the wedding and immediate family staying the entire weekend. The ceremony took place in the shade of large maple trees by a creek, followed by festivities in a 2000 square foot barn with exposed beams and wide plank floors.

I went to sit with Uncle Leo and Aunt Carol, gathered around a table with their spouses watching the dancing in the center of the barn. Leo was sporting dark glasses and looked very mafioso-ish. I only saw him on occasions such as this or at the family gatherings that once took place at Grandma Rae's apartment in New York City. I asked, yet again, about the uncles. Leo had told me that Abe kept a list of the people he was paying off to insure that his policy and gambling racket stayed alive. He had kept it at his headquarters, in the basement, where they counted the money and the day's lottery numbers.

I had scribbled his responses on the napkin. It was coming back to me now—Leo had mentioned a few names of authorities who were on Abe's list and had been pursuing him in his final days. I had jotted at the bottom of the napkin: "DA's office–corrupt," "Dewey," and "Police Captain."

Leo had passed away in 2005, and I had forgotten all about that conversation—I never imagined my research would get so far as to allow me to be able to figure out who the police involved might be. But now, in light of the information coming from Maria, it seemed substantial.

As I prepared for the next session with Maria it dawned on me that I needed a way to record our Skype video sessions. It seemed to be a normal practice for Maria to do sessions via video calls, and recording them would allow me to revisit the information after the sessions were over.

Eric, my trusted pal, tech guru, and soon-to-become research assistant, set me up with a recording device so that I could capture the calls as a movie file. This was a hi-tech lifesaver.

Maria had been settling into her new digs for the last month, and as the video call came to life, she was sitting in the tower room of her Victorian home in Connecticut where she had set up her sacred space. She was cheery and spunky, waving into the camera, her silver jewelry jingling. We were both enthusiastic to delve deeper into the messages she had received.

I asked how she wanted to handle the session—in what order she wanted to work. But she was ahead of me. "I was awake between 4 and 6 a.m. this morning with visions, some very strange…about tunnels and things. We were walking and someone unlocked a black gate, where we would have to walk down stairs to get to some sort of platform…then I jumped to other visions. Interestingly however, a woman in black came through. She was older and in mourning and had a message for you…'*the family is grateful and overjoyed that their story will finally be told, to heal long-time wrongs and find the truth. We're proud of you and will assist in your exploration. Continue to pursue.*'" Maria looked at me, nodding her head. "Your family is with you on this journey." All this ghost talk made me feel a bit uneasy at first, but I had to remember that this was my family coming through and I shouldn't be scared.

Maria said that the spirits had shown her a path connecting different locations, as if a route were revealing itself in regard to what took place the night Abe was killed. "They showed me an aerial view and keep telling me something is underground." Maria was not that familiar with New York and couldn't decipher the aerial view they were showing her.

I was anxious to get her impressions of the Google Street-View of the key locations in the case. When she looked at the still photo of Lincoln Place her demeanor abruptly changed. She sensed something bad happened there and it made her feel sick to her stomach.

"Spirits are coming through now…they are all talking at once. When I look at Lincoln Place I'm absolutely drawn to the basement. They are showing me a locked black door again, that leads to a basement and I want to go there. I don't know if it's locked because…," she suddenly yelped and bent sharply to her left, as if she had been poked in the side.

"I don't know if I'm feeling the pain of…someone was very hurt in that basement. They're showing me people counting money…files…it's like a 'war room'…a place where they would strategize. Something is down in the basement…serious things happened in there. I keep seeing the locked black door and that's where they want me to go."

Maria doubled over in pain. She moaned, rocking back and forth as if she were going to be sick.

"Maria, are you…"

"I have to get this guy off me…I don't know who it is…"

She attempted to regain her composure, then doubled over again. "He won't let up…I have to follow this," she explained between deep breaths. "Is there something in the basement that caused you pain? Is there something down there?" She asked the spirit, bobbing back and forth, grunting in agony.

"It's Frankie. He is saying there are two offices…a headquarters used as a façade upstairs…I'm sensing the 4th floor…but the basement is the 'nerve center.'

The papers had reported apartment #4D had been Abe's headquarters and Leo had mentioned the basement.

"Frankie took some horrible hit to the back…feels like something went through his back and exploded on the inside…the ribs are not right…it is a hit of great force…not a bullet…it feels like a board or a pipe that went across his back. Horrific pain. He couldn't get the black door open fast enough…he couldn't get in there…he's saying…'I don't have what they are looking for.'

"He's showing me a full aerial view of the empty lot next to the building. It feels like there is something under it. A sublevel to this building… in there is another door that leads into this basement, or used to anyway. I don't know if it's someone's apartment or a laundry room…but it's making me very uncomfortable. I see rats, it's musty and hard to breathe down there. Frankie is in a panic to get to the stuff buried in there, but he can't get to it. That's where you are going to find some important stuff.

I don't know if you're going to find bones, or a ring, or paperwork, but there is a hidden trove of information there.

"I'm sensing that there are two overlapping stories happening. I want to drive down the block…things have been built up over the years, but somewhere to the right of this location is a fence and water…I know at Lincoln Place there isn't this…Frankie was downstairs in a panic and knew he was going to die. But over here," she pointed away, into the distance, "there is a road that goes down near water. The cop car with the body inside of it is there, with Abe…" She stopped, then started asking the spirit questions.

"I'm conflicted because I'm picking up what happened to the brother, and I don't understand why we are back at this building after Abe was killed. He is showing me his panic…and he's saying, *'I don't know what you want me to do'.…'I don't do this anymore'…'I'm not here anymore'…'it isn't here anymore'*…and there's pain, and he says *'I don't have anything…I don't have it…what do you want me to do?'*"

Maria was quiet for several moments. "I'm having trouble breathing…something is punctured in my throat…I have a gritty, rusty taste in my mouth." She closed her eyes and swayed back and forth, asking the spirit, "Why would you go back to Lincoln place?"

She moaned, shaking her head, as if the response was very bad. "He's showing me an image of a white man, bald, wearing a gray suit and tie… someone of power. I'm seeing the man looking down at him…he's tall in stature. He looks like President Gerald Ford, but paler and his eyes are a deep blue. He has a speech impediment or lisp. He's a real prick."

Maria continued groaning and rocking. "The man looks about 55-years-old, white-gray hair shaved close. There are numbers or something on a gold pin on his jacket. He's watching the pain being inflicted on Frankie…awwwww…" Maria moaned. After a few minutes she took a deep breath. "He's gone now…God, that made me sick."

"This was happening in the basement at Lincoln Place?"

"Yes, at Lincoln Place. It was very vivid. The pale man was looking down and smirking…he was looking for money or documents. He was pissed he couldn't find them. Feels like he was a cop, but no longer is and still works in law, in a high-ranking position. What was happening to Frankie in the basement was horrible. He was frantic to tell us what happened, as if he wouldn't be here much longer to do so…"

Maria suddenly held her hand up to her face and burst into tears, which quickly turned to uncontrollable sobs. She covered her eyes and wept.

"What's happening?" I asked softly.

Maria could barely speak, but between sobs she squeaked out, "I don't know…I'm sorry…this is what happened when the woman in black came through…there's an overwhelming sense of pain…and relief." She wiped her eyes, rocking back and forth. "The pain is tremendous. As if it had been held on to for so long and is finally starting to come out."

Maria inhaled deeply and took long breaths. "I don't know if this emotion is from the brother Frankie who was hurt, or the woman in black again…but all of a sudden I got flooded with emotion." She wiped her eyes. "they're gone…for now."

She paused to have a glass of water.

"My shirt is soaking wet…my God, I didn't expect to get hit so hard. I thought we'd be able to ease into it, but noooo…holy shit, dude! It's like the whole family came through at once, desperate to show what happened…"

"Can we look through some more photos?" I asked. I still needed her thoughts on some of these photographs of the locations from Abe's final night.

She nodded. We looked at the image of 675 Empire Boulevard, but she got no vibe about it. "We are stuck in the basement of Lincoln Place, so to speak. Something happened there."

I revealed that Frankie was sent to jail for running Abe's business after his death, but had not been arrested at Lincoln Place. When he got out, a few years later, he mysteriously disappeared and the family never heard from him again.

Maria shook her head. "That story doesn't jibe correctly. What you're telling me doesn't sound right. Maybe it was a lie that he was back in the family business. Or, if he was caught…it doesn't feel right. There are false statements in whatever documentation is written, as if it's a cover-up. I keep hearing the word '*justice*' and then '*it's not.*' These people, these cops, did a lot of damage to your family…but did a lot of damage to other people as well in the name of justice. There was no justice because these are unsolved cases…the spirits are saying, '*how can there be justice?*'"

"I'm picking up that the cops were lording their power over them. Frankie was being beaten down…this was unbelievable pain…it was harsh, abusive, and inhuman. He showed me the man who was hurting him and then came this huge release of emotion. The most important part of today's session was Frankie showing me that man." Maria wiped her brow, then started to laugh. "He kicked my ass, though!"

Maria was exhausted and we ended our session, but agreed to reconvene at a later point. I was amped up. This had been another astounding reading. While Maria didn't know that Abe was a mobster or anything about the whole policy-graft police tie-up, she still saw right into the heart of the situation. We were getting close to the truth.

I spent the next couple days combing through articles that listed police, district attorneys, and other officials in the *Brooklyn Daily Eagle* between 1935 and 1945. Whenever I found someone of official stature, I dug deeper into the article or searched the web for a photo, looking for someone based on Maria's description.

I came upon a listing of police commissioners of New York City. Lewis J. Valentine had been the commissioner from 1934 to mid-1945, during the years Abe was operating and killed. But, if Frankie presumably died in the mid-1940s, who was the commissioner then? As I scrolled down the list I learned that Mayor Fiorello La Guardia appointed Arthur W. Wallander as Police Commissioner in 1945. Wallander had trained Brooklyn DA William O'Dwyer at the police academy back in the day, and they had remained close friends. When O'Dwyer was elected Mayor of New York, he kept Wallander on as Police Commissioner with his new administration. The papers stated this was the first time in history that a commissioner stayed in office with a new mayor. When O'Dwyer retired from his mayoral term due to corruption allegations, Wallander retired as well. He had been part of O'Dwyer's infamous posse.

I punched his name into a Google picture search. My screen came alive with a black and white studio portrait of Wallander in his late 30s. He was pale, of Swedish origin, with piercing light eyes, bald on top with nubby, close shaved hair, and he looked like Gerald Ford!

I took a screen shot of the image and immediately emailed it to Maria. No one else came even remotely close to the physical description of the man beating Frankie. And, Wallander had been a cop who went on to hold a high-ranking position, just as Maria had indicated. He was also connected to several shady characters that had come to the forefront of my investigation, such as Captain Frank Bals. I sent his photo to Maria as well.

A few days later, Maria and I connected. When she saw the images she got very excited. "Arthur here is exactly, to a 'T,' who I saw in our last session."

"So, you are confirming Wallander is who you saw?" I asked.

"Yes. Arty, here, is a son-of-a bitch," Maria said firmly, rubbing her jaw. "He's slippery. The photo of Frank Bals makes me physically ill. He has told so many lies, that I don't know how he kept anything straight. Bals seems to have taken over and done whatever he wanted to do."

Maria was correct. My earlier research revealed Bals was assigned by O'Dwyer to be the 7th Police Commissioner under Wallander and had free reign to run his investigations as he pleased. What was most fascinating about Maria's take on these photographs was that she had no idea who they were or their positions of power in the 1940s.

Maria became quiet and started rocking back and forth.

"Our guide Ned is back, which is why my jaw hurts. He's showing me stacks of cash being put into an inner coat pocket. I still don't know who Ned is, I guess he's going to help us," she smiled and continued to massage her jaw. "Ned is showing me the car trunk again in regard to Wallander...he's showing me the black police car again and the two numbers, a 6 and a 9, on the car."

Maria suddenly hollered, "*he's a liar...I'll prove it, he's a liar.*"

"Who's a liar?" I asked.

"Frankie is saying to look at the money...see how Wallander's family lived after he died. He's telling me he hid money. The money you couldn't find in your family...your boys had money on them and in the building with the black door...there was cash, stacks of money with string around it...it's torn...old money...not pristine...I keep hearing, *'check the records.'*"

Maria closed her eyes and started to tap her forehead quickly. "Abe's coming through...I don't want to feel all his pain!" she exclaimed, vigorously rubbing her head and swaying back and forth. "Abe is here and I'm hearing *'they robbed me'...they robbed ME!'* He's saying it over and over again. Two other spirits are here...they have weird nicknames with quote marks around them...they sound something like 'Lup-key' and 'Tweaky Twist.'"

She bent over in concentration. "I got a bunch of people here...hell, we got the whole goddamn gang in here!...there's an overwhelming sense of excitement...'Lup-key' and 'Tweaks,' or whatever the hell their names are...they too had money taken or they were constantly having to pay. They are saying, *'there were no good guys and there were no bad guys, everyone was in the same shit as everyone else...you just tried to get one up on the other, and if you were smart enough to do it, you did it. One had a badge, one didn't. That's the way it was. Everyone exchanged money, everyone had territories, the cops were no different'*...this is what they are saying to me. The minute we started talking about the money all of them started to come through."

She bent over to concentrate. "'Lup-key' and 'Tweaks' came through, but they aren't directly related to this incident with Frankie, as it seems they were in prison and/or dead when this happened...but they came through and said the same thing. Everything had to do with money...*'You bought what you had to buy in order to live your life.'* They are not saying they were right or they were good...but they want to tell their story because they never got to. They're saying that the police muddied the waters for everyone…'*so who's going to listen to our side?*'" After a short silence Maria thanked them for their message.

"Does Abe have anything to say?" I asked.

"He's here. When he jumped in they all wanted to jump in…okay, he's showing me something…it's a steno pad, weather beaten and old. Do you have anything like that?"

"I have some of my Grandma's old paperwork, but nothing from the family."

"There's names and numbers…like a numbering system, or code of some sort…Abe just said he has it '*all up here,*'" Maria pointed to her head. "There are cop names on it. Looks like one column is numbers… amounts of some sort…I can't read his handwriting…it's very old-fash-ioned, precise writing." Maria traced the air with her finger, trying to spell out what she was seeing.

"I'm seeing a name…an E, sounds like Effer." She wrote it down and showed it to me. "This is not my handwriting, but how he's telling me to write it…the numbers are in a corresponding column. This name is the next name of a bad cop we need to look at. I see a big 'E,'…then a little letter 'H'…'E'…'F'…'F'…'E' again. An important key to this case is this guy. Abe is telling me you have his name in your research…Abe is show-ing me you and your father reading this name…he is adamant about it. I don't know what this person's capacity in law enforcement was…but he was being paid by your boys and was present when things went south. He was with Wallander when Frankie got hurt."

I had an idea whose name it might be, but I stayed quiet. It *was* in all my research—Edward Heffernan, Assistant DA to William O'Dwyer.

I reiterated to be clear. "So you are saying that Frankie was hurt in the basement of Lincoln Place and Wallander and this Eheffe guy were there."

"Yes, this is confirmed." Maria nodded. "I can see Wallander grab-bing the money…I see stacks of money and they are going right into his chest pocket. The boys are saying, '*that's the son of bitch.*'"

"Can Abe tell us about his death?" I asked.

She lowered her head in concentration, tapping the back of it. "Abe is saying that the guy he usually had drive for him was not there. He's saying he *'was taken'*...he wasn't shot in his car...someone is lying in the back seat of the cop car...I don't know who it is, but Abe's showing him to me."

She buried her face in her hands, rocking back and forth. "Abe is like this...," Maria repositioned herself on her knees, with her arms extended behind her. "My arm feels like it is dislocating...his arms are back behind him...someone is yelling at him...someone with a white fedora, but I can't see his face, it's covered in shadows...it's a light colored hat... Abe is down on the ground, they are interrogating him, yelling at him, doing something awful to him...they were looking for something. Everything on his person was removed...I keep getting hit on top of the head...my eye sockets hurt...people are screaming...it's chaos...it wasn't well planned at all...someone in this group got over zealous and fired the gun."

Maria was in a trance-like state. "The ground is wet and gravelly...I'm seeing the fat numbers 6 and 9 again...I'm against the cop car and there's the numbers, 6 and 9...the license plate is not in the center...it's off to the side. Abe had nothing...everything was taken off of him...nothing in his pockets...there's a very odd, almost weird sense of quiet...there's a calmness...and then a deafening noise...he's showing me his death." After a long silence Maria looked up at me. "That's all I was given right now."

She demonstrated again how she saw Abe leaning against the car. "Over to my side is the man in the white fedora...the light is shining down from behind him...the ground is wet like it rained. Abe's suit was disheveled...his hands were tied behind him. He couldn't move. I would like to see the autopsy report, to verify if there were any markings on his wrists.

"The pain that shot through the front part of my face was horrible... The whole thing is really awful...his death should have never happened. That's what your boys were saying about the cops...*'you aren't any better than any of us, you aren't better than any crook on the street.'*...that was the big message today...*'the cops were no better than us...who were they to play God?'*"

"Just so I'm clear, there's a difference between Frankie's beating with Wallander and Abe's murder, correct?"

"Yes. This is verified." Maria replied.

"I'm curious about this piece of paper with names and numbers," I mentioned.

"They showed me an old beat-up briefcase...an old satchel that was worn, with papers inside it that have numbers and corresponding names, like this 'Eheffe' name."

As the session was wrapping up, Maria reflected. "It made me very sad to see Abe on the ground...I felt his transition through death. Abe did have a rough go of it, but he had no pain upon his departure leaving this world. Your boys are starting to work with me now. The doors are opening and I think we are getting key components that are going to make all the pieces come together properly."

Maria suggested we do our next session during evening hours, as spirits tend to be more intense at night. She requested that I make a specific list of questions. "I want to focus on getting only Abe and Frankie to talk...I'll set the room for a séance or door opening for them." She requested photos of Abe and Frankie to put on her altar for the next session.

●————●

I was floored by Maria's precision and wowed that "Lupke" Buchalter and "Kid Twist" Reles had made an appearance. All the new information had me spinning. I had a copy of Abe's death certificate, but I'd never thought to look for an autopsy report. I would have to figure out where to get that. I spent hours the next day going through every piece of paper I had from Grandma Rae, but there was nothing that resembled an old steno pad, or a paper with columns of names and numbers on it.

The 'Eheffe' name Maria saw on the steno pad was amazing. If it was code or short hand, as she suggested, I was sure it stood for O'Dwyer's corrupt Assistant DA, Edward Heffernan. He was often quoted in the newspapers about Abe's death and was part of the murder investigation. It sounded like this "list" may have been what Leo was referring to as hidden or missing at the headquarters.

This whole thing was making me think that whoever got rid of Abe in 1941 had to make sure Frankie was silenced when he got out of jail around 1945 because of this list of names—or else—they had to have Frankie lead them to the stash of money in the basement that was left after Abe's death. Still, it was not clear if Frankie's beating in the basement was when he died, or if he had been killed later.

I recruited Eric to help me verify the threads we were getting from Maria. He is a superb researcher—almost intuitive, and he had been a big help on my first book in New Orleans, many years ago. He started researching tunnels around Lincoln Place, and looking for the present owner of the building so we could gain access to the property for a spring visit.

I built a crime board in my office. I posted lists of police officers and police authorities of that era and cross-referenced their cases and precincts. I was confident the "69" on the car was the precinct number. Historic photos showed that police cars of that era had the numbers in chunky letters on the lower part of the front doors, and the 69th precinct covered the Brooklyn area of Canarsie, which included where Great Grandma Anna lived on Avenue B, as well as "Kid Twist" Reles on Avenue A, and Frankie's last address at 375 Vermont Street.

My sister Valerie wanted in on the research mix as well. She was back in grad school, studying library archiving and wanted to help from the New York end of things. My partner Amy was very supportive about my picking up the research again—she made the connection that everyone who assisted me on my first book, in New Orleans 20 years ago, was coming together again to work on this research—Maria, Valerie, Eric—it was serendipitous. As Maria said, "Doors were opening." I called Mark-the-Cop and scheduled a trip to New York for late March to visit the Lincoln Place headquarters and the crime scene. It would soon be time to launch an on-the-ground investigation.

I had two more sessions with Maria in January of 2015, most of which revolved around Frankie, tunnels, and descriptions of cops. Frankie's spirit had a big message for me: "follow your heart and change your perspective," which Maria interpreted as the need to think about the crime differently. For me that meant looking beyond what the newspapers had reported.

During these sessions Frankie came through and described his beating at Lincoln Place, as well as further descriptions of the basement with black windows and a black door leading to a lower level. He detailed the physical pain he endured, including his ribs being broken, and that there were two uniformed cops present as well as Police Commissioner Wallander and Edward Heffernan. Maria saw that Frankie had met with Wallander several times in an office, where the exchange of money took place.

I posed the question of where Frankie's body was. The answer came in fragmented sentences. He described being released from jail, which was "central" and located "up the river," and that he was followed everywhere he went once out of prison. He insisted the same people who killed Abe had killed him, just as Aunt Carol had told me.

Maria became filled with emotion when Frankie described where his body was. "It's dark…sludgy, cold…a tunnel, near water. I can see the brick of the tunnel arch. I heard, *'I traveled a long way'*…I don't know if that means he went with a current…it feels like he was under something for a long time, and then there's a tunnel. Not a sewer or drainage pipe… it's a brick tunnel. Frankie showed me what was evidently a police station that had some sort of a disposal, something to get rid of things the cops didn't want to have found…he was adamant in saying to be careful because if we discover the truth they will come after us too."

When I asked who killed Frankie the reply Maria received was "Shamus," the Yiddish word for cop. Neither of us had heard that old-fashioned term before.

I didn't know where Frankie had gone to prison, but "up the river" and "central" could mean Riker's Island Prison. Eric and I theorized that "central" might mean central booking. We discovered that the historic police headquarters for all of New York City, from 1909 till the early 1970s, was at 240 Centre Street. The block-long building in lower Manhattan had a tunnel that accessed Callahan's speakeasy at 140 Grand Street, so the police would not be seen accessing the illegal bar during prohibition. We also discovered there are still several police precincts that have underground tunnels connected to them throughout Manhattan and the other boroughs.

Another correct fact that Maria delivered came when I asked what kind of work Frankie did for Abe. She responded that Abe said the word *'enforce.'* "Something to the effect of, *'he kept things safe.'*...an enforcer...I'm hearing *...'Frankie made sure things were handled.'*"

Maria experienced a unique set of physical sensations when Abe and Frankie became present. Abe would tap Maria on the head or she would experience a headache in her frontal lobe and down the left side of her neck, where he had been shot. Frankie would playfully poke her in the side, or Maria would experience horrible pain in her ribs and back, on the right side of the body.

She called them "the boys." She described Abe as "calm, cool, and collected," with a calculating mind. Frankie, she felt, dealt with things in an emotional way. Rarely did the messages come in full sentences. They were usually short phrases or single words. Maria explained that it took a huge amount of energy for the spirits to talk, and they usually showed her images.

"I wish they could come through and just tell us exactly what happened," I sighed.

"They don't understand the concept of time anymore, so that part is hard...my type of channeling is, *'this is what happened to me'*...it's bits and pieces of the story, and names. Frankie's accent is thick and hard for me to understand."

I wondered if all spirits were somehow stuck, or how this whole thing worked. Maria explained that often spirits are stuck if they experienced an injustice or were wronged. "We, as mediums, tell their story and then try to do a soul healing so they can move on." But she also explained that not everyone is stuck. Once someone moves on you can still bring them back. "They can come down and visit, like the way your father is guiding you."

I needed to make sure Abe and Frankie didn't remain "stuck," waiting for the day they would see justice for their deaths. I felt more strongly than ever that it was up to me to find peace for them.

23

We Know Who You Are
and We Saw What You Did

Each new session with Maria produced increasingly stunning information, which either confirmed or coordinated parts of the scenario I knew to be true. She also revealed information into unknown areas, giving significant clues that Eric and I were able to verify through hard research.

I had no doubt that Maria was authentic and connecting with something I didn't understand. She never had the full context of Abe's story told to her and she could not have looked this information up online—it was not a case that was in the history books. Only if one knew to look at the week of September 24, 1941 in a New York newspaper would they have known that the murder of Abe "Jew Murphy" Babchick had happened—and most of those newspapers, except The *Brooklyn Daily Eagle* and the *New York Times,* were only available on microfilm.

The sessions were also fascinating regarding how Maria talked to unwanted spirits. She would often curse or talk back to them. She was tough. She didn't take crap, either from the living or the dead. Strangely enough, I was able to hear sounds and words come through the computer audio once in a while during our sessions. Maria attributed this to spirit interference, utilizing the electronics to communicate. I would send these video files to Eric to analyze through software. He was able to slow the strange sounds down to actually make out a word here or there, or the spine-chilling resonance of low rumbles.

During one of our February sessions, I showed her photos of Detective Frank Sarcona, who identified Abe's body at the crime scene, and Assistant DA Edward Heffernan. When she saw Sarcona's photo, she said a spirit came through whose name was Hull, first initial F. "Something happened to this Hull guy with Sarcona," said Maria. "The cops were part of covering something up. Hull keeps saying, *'they were all in on it'*...they finagled a crime scene. I don't know who Hull is, but he's saying Detective Sarcona is always involved and he's dirty." I had no idea who Hull was either, and put the information to the side.

When Maria looked at Heffernan's photo, she tasted blood in her mouth and suddenly became very agitated. A large entity had entered her space and was walking with heavy footsteps, shaking the windowpanes. This scared her, and she kept repeating, "*'Shamus'...'Shamus is present'...,*" in a trance-like state. She was then shown the image of a table, and this large shamus approaching it, exuding tremendous authority and evoking fear. "I hear someone crying, like a guttural howl...is this who hurt you?" she asked Abe's spirit. "God, I had a cop in my room!... he made me feel panicked, I was afraid...I was told *'he's at the table'*... and that's when I felt a police officer literally take over my room." She described the massive energy as a large male cop with a big square head wearing a long coat, who walked in with another cop, not wearing a uniform, but a suit, overcoat, and fedora.

Maria was very rattled and started burning incense to clear the space. "I need to set new boundaries here...holy crap...if I didn't know better I'd tell you it was Heffernan...when we started talking about him my windows shook and bam! Maybe two cops came through at the same time...but they sure made their presence known!" The spirit energy of the cops had been threatening. Maria's head was throbbing with pain as she yelled at the random spirits again, "Seriously, everybody back up!...I wanted one person in here tonight...one person!" She continued burning incense to cleanse the room and then focused on bringing Abe in.

"Abe is here." Just as Maria said the words I saw a sudden flash of blue light streak above her head on the video transmission. The streak, like a far off shooting star, happened in a nanosecond.

"I feel someone tapping on my head," Maria continued, unaware of the light streak. "Hi Abe, is that you? I just heard him say *'they're gone,'* so let's work with Abe now that the air is clear of those cops."

Maria received bits of messages as Abe started talking about the day of the murder, saying that something was *'cleaned out.'* Maria was shown the ledger book again, with a black hardcover and red corners, with screws that held it together. There was a ruler that moved across the ledger with names and numbers written in it, showing money received and spent. "I can't read what the writing says...I see it, but it is illegible...I don't know if it's code or what." After a long silence Maria slapped down her hand in frustration, "He's saying shamus again!"

Maria suggested I ask Abe questions, and I started with Meyer Rabinowitz. What was his part in all this? Maria answered *"He went back to the nest'...'he circled back'*...I'm being told that Meyer told someone in passing, *'yeah, he's there,'*...he gave Abe up quickly...he walked past people and said *'he's there'*...he went to the nest and then circled back. Abe's telling me that he, himself, was followed all day...people around him, on him...and not his people...he was constantly followed...but this had been happening for a long time...same thing with Frankie...every move they made someone was following them."

"So, who was in the restaurant with him if Meyer had left?" I asked.

"Abe's telling me about the White Fedora Man again...the guy that was at the scene of Abe's death...he's showing me that White Fedora Man is there, across the diner...Abe knows he's there." Maria retreated into silence for several moments.

"Oh my goodness!" she suddenly exclaimed. "Ok, someone said *'cop driving, cop driving'*...are you in the car? He's being a smart-ass...he said *'usually.'* He's saying he is...*'confined.'* Oh, man...he's describing being confined in the cop car when he was taken...is a cop driving your car, or are you in a police car? I'm hearing Meyer say he had a meeting with White Fedora Man...he had to clean something up...*'I'm cleaning'* he's saying ...it's almost like he has to report back to someone and confirm something..."

"Did he give Abe up?" I asked. Suddenly the audio started echoing and Maria was writhing in pain, nodding her head yes. "He said *'title'...'rank'*...he got some sort of payout...they are talking in little bits and pieces...he's saying *'I didn't want it to happen that way'* or *'I didn't want it to happen to me.'"*

●———●

Later that same day, I connected with Eric and told him details of the session, after which we both continued doing individual research. I didn't receive his frantic, middle-of-the-night email, titled in bold letters, "OH MY GOD!" until the next morning. Eric had discovered something he wanted me to see for myself. He had been scouring 1940s articles in the *Brooklyn Daily Eagle* about Heffernan, when suddenly a neighboring article caught his attention entitled "Changes Story on Druckman," which he directed me to look at.

"DID YOU SEE IT!? OH MY GOD!!!" He wrote in his email.

In the adjacent column there was a story that started with the name Frank Hull. I leaned closer to my computer, as if that would make it clearer, and then I had my own "Oh My God" moment: F. HULL! I was as shocked as Eric had been. It was the name Maria had channeled in the last session. It turned out that Frank Hull had been a murder suspect in the custody of Detective Frank Sarcona during the infamous Druckman murder trial of 1936. The scandalous case, which almost sent three innocent men to the electric chair, was another one of those stories of cops covering up evidence. It was the case that had gotten Homicide Chief John McGowan demoted from his position for destroying documents. Though not directly related to Abe's story, it was amazing that Frank Hull came through to say Sarcona was corrupt.

I sent Eric the video clip with that nanosecond of blue light streaking over Maria's head as she mentioned Abe. I wanted him to make a still image so we could evaluate it in Photoshop. He excitedly returned the freeze-frame to me within the hour. It was there…a long glowing trail over her head. As I lightened it in imaging software, I could see strange patterns inside the bluish haze. Maria had been high up in the tower room of her Victorian—it could not have been oncoming headlights from the street below or anything that obvious.

The most astounding of the February sessions started with a photograph of Abe Frosch, the fellow that ran a bail bond racket for "Kid Twist" Reles and supposedly took over Uncle Abe's policy turf when he died.

"When I looked at Frosch's image he came right through and is a total chatty-Cathy," said Maria. "He's talking a mile a minute with Abe, who is here also. I keep hearing the name of *'Murphy'* with these two guys, but I don't see a third being, I'm just getting the name of *'Murphy'* as they talk." I had a sense that what she was hearing was the reference to Abe's nickname, "Jew Murphy," which was why there wasn't a third spirit.

"Abe and Frosch are having a conversation about money. Frosch has a lot of information about the money aspect of it all. These guys were making millions upon millions of dollars. The line gets very blurry between them and the cops who are on the take. I'm hearing them say *'amen'* I don't know what kind of term that this...it sounds like a prayer...they are saying *'something, something, amen.'* Whatever it is, it has to do with the reason Abe passed away."

A shiver ran down my spine as I told Maria that "Amen" was a name.

"They are taking me back to the diner on the night of the murder. It seems Abe is supposed to meet someone...Frosch is talking about Amen...and someone named *Behine*...it's spelled differently than it sounds...I don't know who he is but his name is making me feel sick... he's a cop. Whatever meeting was supposed to happen, this Behine guy stopped it."

Maria told the spirits to slow down, they were talking too fast. "I'm hearing white noise and then I get names. They are saying *'Amen, Behine, Connor, Sweeney, Kelly'*...it's a stream of information that is being discussed between Abe and Frosch...Frosch just said something about *'Atlantic'*...and *'no body'*...not nobody, but *'no body.'*

"They are talking about some kind of meeting on that same night. Whatever information your Abe had, his death was the beginning of the end for many others...like the names I just gave you. With his death, police officers were nailed for bribes and doing other bad things. They are mentioning something about a *'Dwyer'* as well. They're giving me numbers...Abe said 41...then Frosch said 36 and 38. Don't know what it means, except it is related to the cops."

She started to rock back and forth.

"I'm trying to get Abe to explain what is happening here...it's like a triangle effect...Abe was supposed to meet with someone, then another meeting he was supposed to go to was cut short, and that was the beginning of the end for him. It seems he was going to talk to someone about the cops, explaining how they were on the take. This Amen has some direct correlation with World War II," Maria continued. "He's a cleaner... he's cleaning things up. If he couldn't clean something up, he would take care of it his own way...Abe and Frosch don't like him...the spirits are coming through fast and furious right now."

Everything that Maria was saying was correct. Assistant Attorney General John Harlan Amen went on to be part of the American team at the Nuremburg trials of World War II criminals. Abe and Frosch had every reason to dislike him. As much as Amen seemed to be the man cleaning up Brooklyn corruption, it was because of him that Abe ultimately met his demise.

Maria instructed me to ask them questions.

"Does Frosch know who killed Abe?" I asked.

"Frosch says to look at the names...'Kelly, Sweeney, Connor, Behine'... the killer was a 'cop'...'no body'...he keeps saying 'no body.'"

Maria was told to "discover quickly," and then a new spirit chimed in. She hollered back at it, "Fuck you!...someone just told me to leave everyone alone. I see what I need to do!" She quickly lit a smudge stick to clear the room of the negative energy. "This is about getting answers," Maria said to the intruding spirit. "This is about truth...has nothing to do with you so don't tell me to leave it alone." She turned toward me shaking her head, "Every time we talk about the cops I get nailed by something negative.

"Going back to the boys, they are giving me the number 20. They are showing me the ledger book again. There are names and numbers: 1, 2, 3, to 20. Some of the names are the names I gave you before."

Maria started her rocking motion and went into deep concentration. She reached for her head and let out a gasp of pain, continuing to rock to and fro. "I got you Abe, how ya' doing, buddy?" She said. "He wants to tell you about a guy named *'Zoo.'"* Maria was experiencing a huge amount of pain, moaning and taking deep breaths to get out what Abe was trying to say. "I'm hearing *'accounted for'*...he's talking really fast. I don't know why there's so much pain right now. He said *'Fin'*...it's part of a name...it's *'Fen'*...yes, *'Fen.'"*

Could this mean Theodore Fenner, who was the registered owner of Abe's car, was "Zoo?"

"I know this is draining," she whispered to Abe.

I asked who "Cappy" was—another protected witness who talked with Amen.

"Got the name of Sheldon," replied Maria. "There's a lot of crazy energy right now...a lot of people talking all at once. Abe wants to tell you what happened at the restaurant that night. I'm being told there was a social meeting. Someone dropped by that he didn't really want to talk to. Fen and Meyer left. I'm getting two pictures: one is of the diner, and the other is a gate...it has several padlocks on it...he's saying *'gate.'* It's very rustic and ornate looking, it's very old...where is the gate?...he's showing me the restaurant and then the gate...there is a triangle of events happening...I see a man with a white carnation at this gate...the man has a white flower in his lapel and is waiting there. I see the restaurant and the gate, as if they are layered on top of each other...it's very film noir-ish." She looked up at me, "It's 30 degrees in my room right now...Jesus!"

Maria started to rock back and forth, holding her head. "Abe's supposed to meet the man with a flower in his lapel...he says it's Amen... he's showing him figures, showing him a page from the ledger book... Abe is saying *'mine'*...*'these are my figures'*...these are Abe's numbers, he's showing them to Amen before the cops come and take him away."

Maria was silent for a lengthy amount of time. My heart was racing.

"He's giving Amen a piece of paper from the ledger book ...it's a copy of a page...the paper is folded in threes, it looks like ledger paper with a double red line down one side...there are odd holes on the side, lines going across and lines going down...the paper is yellow or light green... that's what's in his pocket and it's folded...he pulls it out...something was said I can't hear it….it was brief…I have the taste of smoke in my mouth…I can actually taste cigarettes in my mouth…'*Amen*' …'*not here, there's cops.*' I'm hearing about 15 conversations happening at once. I have smoke in my mouth again. Then the man with the white flower leaves and Abe goes back into the restaurant…I hear the word '*snake*'… Abe is having trust issues…someone is across the street that catches his eye as he's going back to the restaurant…he clearly hears the word '*snake.*'

"I know this is hard, I'm sorry," she whispered to Abe. "Abe's not happy with the outcome of the conversation…he feels Amen had an angle… some sort of disagreement…Abe is getting pulled in many different directions…he's in turmoil…he's being torn apart, everyone wants a piece of him…"

Maria was silent and then continued. "Abe's back in the restaurant and he sees the White Fedora Man in the restaurant…I'm hearing '*fight*'… there's going to be a fight…like getting ready to have an argument…he sits down. The White Fedora Man is standing over at a counter or bar… and he has his foot up and leaning on the counter, looking over…there's a brief interaction…an exchange like '*I know you're there*'…he's saying a word I don't recognize…it sounds like '*putz*' or something like that…I'm getting an overwhelming sense of emotion…Abe is panicking right now, a nervous feeling…he feels out of sorts because something happened in the meeting with Amen…there's an '*oh shit*' moment happening for him and he's trying to play it off like nothing's wrong. I can hear him say to himself, '*be calm everything is fine*'…he's having a moment where he's just trying to get through this…he's being calm about it, but panicked on the inside…like a cold sweat."

"Is this the same moment when the two cops come up to him at the table and one is the 'shamus' that made you nervous? Is White Fedora Man the shamus?" I asked.

Maria nodded her head and moaned in pain. "Yes…you asked about the two men who came up to the table…they weren't dressed like cops… they were wearing dark clothes…one with a long coat is thick like a bulldog, and relatively tall. The other man next to him looks a bit younger and has dark hair and a smirk on his face. He's wearing a suit, not a cop outfit. He's a police officer or higher up. It seems like he's saying, *'come with us,'* or *'we will wait for you to finish.'* They are waiting for Abe. White Fedora Man is over here…," Maria pointed to the right. "…he's wearing lighter colored clothes…that makes him a third man."

"Are these the men that took Abe?

"I'm being told they *'followed'* and *'watched'* him."

Maria was quiet and then a sudden sadness washed over her. "I don't understand why Abe is alone…it's really fucked up…Abe, you are alone aren't you?" I suddenly heard a chirping sound emanate from the computer audio. Maria stared up at the ceiling in silence for a several moments. When she spoke again her voice was soft. "For a brief moment I encountered Abe's sense of loneliness and abandonment. He realized he was fucked…*'I'm alone'*…*'there's no one here'*…*'my people aren't here'*…. it was a fleeting moment I was privy to, like a scent of jasmine…it was there and then it was gone." Maria dipped her head down. "It's so sad… it hurts my heart…there's an awful feeling of abandonment. There is no sense of security."

Maria fell deep into thought. It seemed the session was ending. The usual pain and headache Maria experienced when Abe was present was dissipating…the spirits had backed away.

I showed Maria a photograph of John Harlan Amen wearing a white carnation. She was stunned, and verified that he was who she had seen. I always thought that Amen was one of the good guys, but Maria replied, "I don't feel comfortable with him. Maybe that's because the boys weren't comfortable with him. Or, that something was going to happen with him. I get the sense he was cleaning up the town…I don't know what his deal was. He may have had some alternative ways of taking care of things. He feels like an interrogator…he just wants to pull up a chair and talk to you and then take that information and run with it…and do whatever it takes to clean up a mess his own way. I think he intimidates me because I get worried when the cops come through—that's when I get physically hit hard. If Amen's a cop or something, I don't know. Don't tell me yet."

We had never spoken about Amen before and she had no idea who he was or his part in Abe's story. How could she have known that Amen wore a white carnation every day or the fact that he was a chain-smoker? As we had our post-session conversation, I stared at my crime board in contemplation. The bold headline of the *New York Word Telegram* read "Gambler Slain to Seal Lips Amen Hints: Paid 20 Cops." A thought hit me: How did Amen come-up with the number 20 the day after the murder? How would he have known that Abe paid 20 cops unless Abe had actually told him? If Abe did meet with Amen and gave him the names of the corrupt officials before he was killed, this was huge new angle! The papers had said Amen's men were looking for Abe but couldn't find him. A lawyer tried to negotiate Abe coming in to see Amen, but the demands were "too extreme," the papers said. But, from the onset of my research I have understood that the papers told a skewed story, often fed to them by the police.

The events of Abe's last night seemed to be shaping into a meeting with Amen near some old gate, then the White Fedora Man and two detectives stalking him at the diner, followed by another meeting cut short by Behine, and finally the abduction.

Maria was trying to figure out how Amen fit into all this. She didn't want me to tell her, but as our post-session hypothesizing went on, I felt she should know the context, and explained that Amen needed Abe to testify against the cops.

"Oh, Shit!" Maria cried out, closing her eyes and rolling her head back in amazement.

After our session, I scoured through Amen's *Presentment Concerning Enforcement of Laws Against Gambling*. This document is hard to find unless you go to the New York State Library in Albany. The final wow factor from the session was shocking—every name Maria gave me, channeled from Uncle Abe and Frosch, was in the Presentment. The names she mentioned were cops that were either indicted or retired early in lieu of testifying before Amen's grand jury for taking bribes: John E. Kelly, Robert E. Connor, Charles Jeffrey, John Sweeney, and Lawrence Beine. *This was undeniably supernatural.*

There was also a Lt. Cuthbert J. Behan—the same Behan that Frosch had testified against in 1938 for Amen regarding Behan's involvement in the bail bond racket case. He had stolen 7200 pages of police records from the Brooklyn police station. Maria had mentioned the numbers 41 and 38 in the session—1941 was the year Abe died and 1938 was the year Frosch testified for Amen against Behan.

I wasn't sure if she meant Beine or Behan. But both men were listed in Amen's Presentment. Behan had already been tried and acquitted for his corruption case and removed from the force by 1940. I wasn't sure he fit into Abe's death scenario in 1941. Maybe he still had a beef with Abe and Frosch and was extra muscle that night for his old cop buddies.

In the final February session Maria channeled further information that continued to clarify Abe's movements on his last night.

Again, she saw the White Fedora Man at the restaurant tracking Abe's movement, and also at the murder scene with four other men. She said the murder took place somewhere under a bridge on a dark dirt road, near a factory-like building and oil drums. The big mystery for me was, if Abe was killed somewhere else, how did his body get back into his car and then left on Empire Boulevard?

As it got closer to the March trip to New York, I had a solid scenario of Abe's final night, as well as what may have happened to Frankie at the Lincoln Place headquarters. Meyer, Abe's driver, might have been some sort of pointman for the police, just as Rae had said decades earlier. Fenn, a.k.a. Theodore Fenner, the black garage mechanic that Abe had befriended and bought his car from, might have been "Zoo," the protected witness from that night. Maria had supplied the names of cops who may have executed the order for Abe's death. They were listed in Amen's investigation and the same names were recorded on Abe's infamous ledger, which Maria kept seeing in a leather satchel.

On the research side, Eric was trying to contact the landlord at Lincoln Place for our March visit. He was having no luck. He was able to find their name, Horus Realty, but the company made itself rather invisible when it came to contact information.

He was also investigating the terrain around Eastern Parkway, trying to figure out where there might be an old gate similar to the one in Maria's vision, where Abe supposedly spoke to Amen. Eric discovered there was an old Catholic church across the Parkway from where Dubrow's restaurant once stood. It was right next to a bank where, according to reports, Abe had parked his car. Eric felt there must be an old gate there somewhere, but on Google Street-View we could only see a modern wrought-iron fence that wrapped around the church. We couldn't imagine why Abe would have a clandestine meeting with Amen so out in the open where they could easily be seen. We would have to investigate the church when we were on location, so I added it to our itinerary.

I was hoping to find the original notes or papers that Amen gathered for his investigation—including 100 letters from tipsters about the murder. Where were the files from the interview with "Cappy the Scientist" who was singing about Abe's organization? They had to be somewhere, right? Wrong. I had a national library/archive search conducted by the Albany State library which came up blank. So, when I can't find information in the usual places what do I do? Make phone calls to their relatives. I tracked down Amen's son, only to find that he'd passed away, but I located his grandson, of the same name, who was a poet and writer. That struck me as lovely irony, as Dad was a poet and writer. I made contact with him and he tried to be helpful, but had none of his father or grandfather's papers. I was stuck again.

Meanwhile, there was also the question of the satchel. Maria channeled that Dad came through saying, "*go the family route*' to find the satchel." Maria was insistent that the satchel was a key to many unanswered questions. "There is a tangible satchel somewhere and someone has it." That prompted me to contact relatives and ask if they remembered an old leather satchel in their parents' belongings. Cousin Selma remembered her father Dave had an old satchel that contained a mysterious vase she currently had on display in her living room—but no papers. No one else remembered any such item.

Something made me return to my father's 1988 book about the family, *Pages From a Scrapbook of Immigrants*. The poem written about Abe was especially moving, juxtaposing him with his biblical namesake and his sacrifice. It was a long poem, most of it factual, but half way through I was struck by the following passage about the murder:

> Eventually the police unearth the satchel,
> but not the money or the triggerman.[1]

Stunned, I must have reread it five times. Where did Dad get that information? Was there actually a satchel or was he using poetic license?

I sent the poem's passage to Maria for her thoughts. Her response was that my father had channeled it, being deeply in tune with the spirits of the family. I laughed because she was so right. Mort had always said he heard the voices of his ancestors when he wrote. But did the satchel actually exist?

During my calls to relatives about the elusive satchel, I spoke with Cousin Michael, Aunt Carol's son. We had recently reconnected after 20-plus years, and he was now a well-to-do antiques dealer in Connecticut. Abe and Frankie were his great uncles as well, and he had always been interested, though on the periphery, about what had happened to them. He was eager to join us on the investigation at the Brooklyn locations and I was thrilled to have a family member come along, since Valerie couldn't make it. But, Michael made a request: "Ask the psychic what my secret word with Aunt Rae was." Michael and Grandma spent a lot of time together, and it seemed they had a code word "in case she tried to contact me after she died." For God's sake, this was embarrassing—but Michael was serious. I didn't know what the code word was, and he didn't tell me.

The week before the New York trip, Maria and I had a logistics meeting via Skype. Bashfully, I relayed Michael's request to her. She smiled, "I get it. I think it's just his way of proving to himself that all this is real. We'll see if we can connect with Grandma today."

We agreed upon the major locations we would visit based on newspaper reports, eyewitness accounts, and Maria's visions: Abe's old headquarters on Lincoln Place, the location of Dubrow's Cafeteria Restaurant on Eastern Parkway, and 675 Empire Boulevard, where Abe's body was found in his car.

"Abe and Frankie keep showing me a series of events from that last night, like a quick slide show—flashing images of a brick tunnel, an old gate somewhere near the restaurant, which I realize may not be there anymore, and lastly they keep showing me Lincoln Place with the empty lot next door." Maria rehashed.

Suddenly she paused. "Wait, they just walked in and started talking." All at once our conversation had become a session. Maria explained she was unexpectedly getting flooded with information because it was getting close to the date of our physically walking the area in Brooklyn. Then, our transmission on Skype was disrupted and went dead. I redialed.

"Holy crap!…seven people are walking around here right now!" Maria shouted as the video reconnected. "I don't know who they are…it's like a Peanut's gallery in here! I need the specific people for this journey!" Maria's comic frustration became serious. "I'm getting two words 'Pennsylvania' and 'Atlantic'…but I didn't know what they mean." She asked me if it could mean Penn Station. I shrugged. I had no idea. *A state and an ocean?*

"Oh!…someone is saying it again…'Pennsylvania'…'Atlantic'…they are showing me a bridge, and then the satchel and ledger again….your grandmother is here…she's showing me an old basement or storage locker…like an old vault…she's saying 'bank vault'…the satchel is locked in something…it looks like an old storage place."

"Is this at 626 Lincoln Place or somewhere else?" I asked eagerly.

"Rae keeps saying 'bank'...'bank'...someone else said 'under a tarp,' another said the satchel was 'jammed' somewhere, then Rae said it was 'stuck' under something. They're all offering their opinions. What they need to do is have a coffee date with Abe and Frankie and everyone needs to get their shit together!" shouted Maria in frustration.

Then it dawned on me that back in the 1940s the command post for a numbers racket was called a policy bank. Maybe Rae was referring to the basement of Lincoln Place as the "bank." Maybe that's where the satchel had been hidden all these years.

Out of the blue, Maria started sniffing and closed her eyes. "The scent of coffee is becoming very strong in here and I can hear a conversation between a man and a woman." She listened intently to something I couldn't hear and kept sniffing, saying it was like the aroma of a strong Greek coffee or espresso. That made me think of Dad and how he used to always drink Greek coffee that he prepared on the stove in a small metal pot.

"This is funny!" Maria blurted. "It's your grandmother and your dad...they are sitting in a café drinking coffee and talking about meta-physical stuff...like how to talk through someone like me...hell, I don't even need to be here...I'm just listening to them talk ...and the smell of coffee is so intense!"

Suddenly I heard a continuous clinking sound coming through the computer and then two words that sounded like...'it's hot.' Maria and I looked at each other with surprise. "Did you hear that?" we said simul-taneously. I nodded in shock. The clinking sound went on for another minute or so and then faded away.

"Well, there ya' go," Maria said sarcastically, slapping her hands on her thighs. "We never know what we are going to get. I purposely set the space to be informative for our trip, but it was interesting your Dad was here, so prevalent with your Grandmother and family...you are getting a lot of support...that's what came through today, it's awesome! I don't know what's going to happen when we're on location, but I can't fucking wait to find out!"

After we hung up I sent Cousin Michael a text message, letting him know that unless his secret word was coffee or café, I had no answer for him.

Less than I minute later I received his text reply: "Call me now!"

When he picked up the phone he shouted, "How did you know? That was our word! 'Coffee shop!'" Michael was in shock, he couldn't believe it. He explained that he and Rae always met at a coffee shop and chose the word together decades ago. What this demonstrated to me was that sometimes Maria's messages needed to be deciphered, like a game of charades. But games aside, I had been blown away by Maria's accuracy on so many levels during the last three months, that I couldn't imagine what else might be revealed.

24

New York Noir

My first day in New York I jumped on the A train to meet up with my sister at the New York City Municipal Archives in lower Manhattan.

Valerie was already at a table that had been prepared for us. Boxes of the original Murder, Inc. files were piled high. We air-kissed, not wanting to break the silence of the archive reading room, and then whispered our plan of attack. We were looking for threads—anything that might mention Uncle Abe or help piece together his story. Any small clue could be crucial evidence.

We sat in the still of the room, holding bullets from Murder Inc. cases, reading typed police reports with 70-year-old coffee stains splattered across them, and scouring through mug shots—which in the 1920s and 1930s were full-body photographs of entire groups of men. The files contained all the investigation reports into Abe "Kid Twist" Reles' death—testimonies, court records, and the names of many of the same crooked cops that kept appearing in my research. We looked through Mayor La Guardia and O'Dwyer's papers, district attorney investigation reports, and found many interesting tidbits and facts—but nothing on Uncle Abe.

Sitting at a table behind us, buried in paperwork, was a woman who was curious about what we were working on. She introduced herself as author Stacy Horn, who was conducting research for her current book on the history of Blackwell Island, which was later published as *Dam-

nation Island. Previously she had written a book about New York cold cases, and we commiserated on the lack of access to police files. She suggested I contact a Detective in the NYC Cold Case Squad who had helped with her book, and we exchanged information.

Valerie and I realized, after several hours of reading police reports, there was nothing to be found here on Uncle Abe. It left us curious.

We were given Abe's autopsy report, which I had requested before our arrival. The Medical Examiner's report was filled with details and was the first official information on Abe that I had accessed in years. Maria had requested to see this report during our sessions, curious if there were any mention of ligature marks on Abe's wrists.

Valerie and I anxiously looked over the long report filled with descriptions of the car, the clothes he wore, and the police who recovered his body. Much of the report was in medical terms we didn't understand. One fact that grabbed our immediate interest was that Uncle Abe was recorded as a mere 5' 2" and 130 lbs. I found this shocking, as no one in the family was that short. Also of interest was that there was no record of marks or wounds on the outside of his body. Only the two gunshots to the back of the head and the condition of his internal organs. That seemed unusual.

In the file was a xerox of the toe tag from the morgue, which was smeared with dried blood. Seeing that was dreadful—more gruesome than the matter-of-fact description of the bullet wounds. The whole report made me queasy, and I couldn't shake the image of the tag hanging from Abe's big toe as his body was pushed into a steel vault. I would go through this information more carefully when I returned to California and had an Alka-Seltzer to accompany me.

March 20, 2015

A snowstorm was expected to swing into full force by late afternoon and the sky was already an ominous gray as I exited a taxi on 59th and 8th

Avenue. Wind gusts burst umbrellas into inverted shapes as I elbowed my way to the entrance of the Time Warner Center at Columbus Circle.

I was having lunch with my friend Anne in a bistro that looked down on 59th street. She rehashed how she had found Grandma Rae's gate-leg table at her mother-in-law's home—but the woman was sure it was actually her table, not Grandma Rae's, and Anne was having trouble getting it back into her possession. After lunch, I persuaded Anne to take a walk, and we headed down 59th Street in the delicate snowfall, which was starting to stick.

Strolling down 59th Street had deep meaning for me. It had been my home away from home for so many years. As we walked past Grandma's Rae long-time residence at 116 Central Park South, it seemed fitting to pay homage to the location where the Uncle Abe mystery had started some 27 years earlier. I stopped and looked through the heavy glass doors at the renovated lobby, ignoring the inquisitive expression of the doorman. I was an outsider now, looking in. The presence of the whole family lingered like apparitions—Dad, Leo, Carol, Grandma Rae—I missed them all terribly. I could just imagine the sound of their laughter, emanating down the hall from Grandma's apartment during a family dinner, the smell of cabbage soup drifting in the air. Sometimes I felt very alone these days, now that much of the family had passed away. There I was, standing on Central Park South in the snow, looking into the past, hoping its secrets would soon be revealed.

I contacted Detective Wendell Stradford at the suggestion of Stacy Horn. He was very friendly and forthcoming with suggestions about researching old cases. He explained that he didn't usually bother with a case from the 1940s because everyone involved had certainly died. Still, he was willing to look through some case files to see what he could find. I gave him all the information I had about Abe, including the autopsy report and death certificate numbers. His search would yield more information than a generic Freedom of Information Act (FOIA) request by someone in the general public. He could bypass the FOIA restrictions and give me the entire report—but he warned it might take several weeks.

That evening, I made my way through flurries of snow to meet Mark and Maria for a late supper. They were meeting for the first time and I wanted them to establish a level of comfort before our adventure in Brooklyn the next day. Mark had been retired from the force for many years now, but he maintained informational privilege to many things through his current position as an intelligence analyst. He had been listening to my stories about Uncle Abe for decades and was just as amped as I was to take this journey to Brooklyn. I always felt safe with Mark. No one knew the Brooklyn terrain better than he.

As always, Mark was a gentleman, with an inquiring mind, quick wit, and engaging New York accent. I had no idea if he believed in this psychic stuff or not, but he appeared to be very engrossed in Maria's process and I deeply appreciated his openness. After a couple drinks our basic plan was set for the next day.

Maria and I sludged through the ice and snow back to where we were staying. "Mark is key to tomorrow," she said. "The spirits will explain some things we need to know through him."

March 21, 2015

The morning sun slowly melted the previous day's snowfall as Maria and I waited outside the car rental outlet on 68th and Amsterdam to meet our fellow adventurers. She was quiet, preparing for a day of channeling. I was contemplating how our gang of four was now middle-aged. I had known each of them for decades. Now we were all in our 50s—older and hopefully wiser—my past relationships with each of them, though very different, had brought us together for this voyage into the past.

Cousin Michael arrived, sporting yellow tinted shades that framed his wide face. He greeted me with a hug and shook Maria's hand. He was uncertain what to expect upon meeting the psychic. He had been impressed that she hit on the secret word he had with Rae, but remained politely reserved, holding at bay his usual sharp wit.

Mark pulled up in the rented bright red 4-door Ford Fiesta and the three of us piled in. Mark and Michael immediately engaged in animated conversation in the front seats. Maria was jazzed to be going on location—this was the kind of psychic investigating she thrived on—and she planned to open herself up as a conduit for anything that would come her way spiritually. But, she was concerned she might pass out if she experienced Abe or Frankie's final death moments. "If that happens," Maria explained, "my son's name is the code word that usually brings me back from a trance-state on the other side." We all raised an eyebrow at her remark.

As we made our way down the Henry Hudson Parkway toward lower Manhattan and the Brooklyn Bridge, I noticed Maria was starting to shiver as she gazed out the window. When her shivers turned to a violent shaking I placed my hand gently on her knee inquiring if she was okay. Michael suddenly shouted, "Look, it's the new Freedom Tower."

None of us had thought of the fact that we would be driving past the site of the World Trade Center. From the West Side Highway there was a clear view of the memorial pools and the modern architecture of the Oculus transportation center, which resembled an eagle's wingspread. As we paralleled the tragic location, Maria burst into uncontrollable sobs. She was not prepared for the intense amount of psychic energy that hit her as we drove past. I hadn't thought about how our route would affect her. Selfishly, I didn't want her totally drained before we got to Brooklyn, so I tried to comfort her, but she had to absorb it. "Do we need your code word?" I whispered. She shook her head and continued sobbing. Mark looked at me in the rearview mirror, his expression contorted with question marks.

Maria started talking very fast. "Thousands of voices are screaming for help…1300 bodies that hadn't been found…1300 bodies…why are the bodies in a landfill?…they threw them all away." She was seeing horrifying visions of a landfill where the remains of the unidentified were being covered. Mark asked her to describe the landfill, as he exchanged another serious glance with me in the rearview mirror. Maria continued to sob, as she described what she was seeing.

"Everything she's saying is absolutely true," Mark responded. He explained that several years after 9/11, more body parts and fragments were discovered, and several forensic anthropologists and NYPD detectives, including him, were assigned to go through the debris and recover fragments of the people killed in the attacks. He verified that tons of material were taken to the Fresh Kills Landfill on Staten Island and sorted. Thousands of remains were found, but only a few hundred bodies were actually identified. Eventually the remaining debris was buried on the site of the landfill, which did contain human fragments. Mark was paying close attention to Maria now, who was wiping her eyes and attempting to steady her breathing. She had just verified something not many people knew about.

We crossed the Brooklyn Bridge, and exited somewhere near Grand Army Plaza. Maria started rapidly repeating the name "Jones...Jones-y." As we weaved our way to our first location, off St. Charles Place on the edge of the Crown Heights neighborhood, the regal old brownstones exuded a sadness in their current state of disrepair.

626 Lincoln Place at Bedford Avenue, in apartment 4D, was where Uncle Abe's headquarters had been. Maria had envisioned black doors and windows, and several rooms on a subterranean level—all locked—with wet floors. This was also where she saw Frankie being beaten with some sort of metal pipe by a couple of men being instructed by Police Commissioner Arthur Wallander and Assistant DA Edward Heffernan.

We parked across from the building and walked over to the empty lot, which was covered with snow and random cars parked at scattered angles. I had Google-walked this area with Street-View many times, but it was surreal to actually be on site.

Toward the back of the empty lot was a recessed apartment building that faced the parallel street, Eastern Parkway. 626 Lincoln Place, to the right of the lot, was a red brick four-story building with heavy white mortar. The door leading to the basement area from the street was black, as were the basement windows, which had been sealed with black painted bricks, just as Maria had described.

Maria stood before the empty lot shivering, intensely studying the recessed building toward the back. "Someone saw something happen here," she finally said, pointing toward a top floor window. She continued to survey the surroundings as Mark noticed an elderly man standing on the steps of 626 and went to speak with him. I put Michael in charge of the audio recording device and turned on my camera's video function to start documenting.

"Something is down in the basement," Maria whispered to me. "Shit...my ribs are starting to hurt...," She pointed to the blacked-out windows of the basement area, her body starting to shake violently. She turned toward me, pale as the snow, "I need to lean on something, I feel like I'm gonna pass out. Abe and Frankie both have so much residual energy here...Fuck!" Maria clutched the wrought-iron railing leading to the basement's locked black gate.

There was no superintendent on the premise, but the old man agreed to unlock the gate for us. He was rather amused that we wanted to see the basement, scoffing at us in a thick Haitian accent that there was only a laundry room, and all the other basement doors were locked from the inside.

As we descended the snow-covered steps, the black gate opened to a narrow alleyway. Garbage cans caked with white ice were lined-up to the left. To the right was the door leading to the basement area. The alleyway was about 40-feet long ascending four steps to a higher alleyway flanked by a retaining wall which separated it from the vacant lot to the left and the towering windows of 626 above.

After unlocking the black gate, the old man scuttled away. He had no intention of opening the basement door.

Maria was shaking and cursing, placing her hands on the outside wall of the basement. "I'm seeing the room...and the man Jones-y crawl in through the black window...it's wet. He's younger, wearing a leather bomber jacket, jodhpurs, and boots...he's watching Frankie being hurt on the floor and there's blood everywhere...there's stuff overturned on the floor."

Maria was speaking very quickly. "Frankie is on the ground…It's re-sidual energy, like it's playing over again…he's cold from the inside…cold from the inside…the water is all black…I'm seeing two things hap-pen at the same time—Frankie's beating and also people rummaging through here looking for things."

"What are they looking for?" I asked.

"Money…'money'…'lists'…'Jones-y'…'Jones'…it's a money list. Frank-ie's saying 'I don't have it'…'I don't have it.'" Maria kept repeating the words, shaking. She looked up at the building at the edge of the empty lot, which we could see from the basement alleyway. "There's a woman in that building who saw this…eye contact was made as they drag some-thing out…they're dragging something out of here…" Maria turned and stood in front of the locked door to the basement and continued. "The room is torn up, it's not what it used to be. There's blood everywhere, and a bucket. There's stuff buried in the lot next door," and she pointed feverishly in the direction of the vacant lot. "I don't know who Jones-y is but he's with this group of people beating Frankie, which included Wallander. This is the first time I'm getting someone watching this… it's Jones-y. I think they dumped Frankie somewhere. He was near death here. This was his end. My ribs are caved in, my lungs have collapsed, I can't breathe…Frankie's in and out of consciousness…and then it goes black…like black water."

We continued down the alleyway and peered into the closest window, which was a laundry room.

"Look, there's another room in there!" Maria pointed excitedly. Mi-chael and I gazed through the wire window mesh and saw a closed door beyond the laundry room. "They are showing me an open room through one of the doors in there. The room is to the right and it's almost like a library…they had money there…I'm seeing it as a fully functioning room…people working…this must have been when Abe was operating it…they are working and doing stuff. Upstairs was an office…that was the legit part…but down here was where everything happened, where they counted the money…where the ledgers were. That's why there were two offices. This is where a lot of things were stolen. Things were kept down here that they brought Frankie back to find. There's still stuff here...there's stuff here!" Maria nodded her head anxiously.

We emerged back onto the street. "It's so weird to see this place through 2015 eyes...they show it to me as in the 1940s," Maria said.

Just than a Caucasian man in his early twenties exited the building. "Go ask him if he'll let us into the laundry room...quick!" I directed Michael.

Michael kibitzed with the young man for a few minutes then waived us over. He introduced us to Jason, who happened to live in the basement apartment and agreed to let us into the basement.

As he unlocked the door we peered inside. There was the laundry room to the left, and two locked doors—one ahead of us and one to the right.

Jason explained that the locked door straight ahead led to a corridor that connected to the backside of his apartment and a storage area. The door to the right was the boiler room. Only the laundry area was accessible to the tenants.

Mark and Michael assessed the sheet rock and what areas of the basement were renovated compared to what was originally there 70 years ago.

"Maybe if we tell Jason why we are here he'll let us see his apartment?" I suggested.

"My girlfriend is still sleeping and I don't want to wake her, or I'd invite you in," Jason replied, poking his head through the doorway. Trying to make the scenario simple, I started to explain that our uncles used to live in the building, when Michael interrupted, "I already told him they were gangsters!"

"I guess that would explain the bumps in the night," said Jason sarcastically. "Exactly!" Mark laughed. Maria quickly turned around. "Do you hear bumps in the night?"

"Well, my roommate Tina has seen orbs, and so has my girlfriend, but I've never seen anything and I'm pretty hip to the metaphysical," replied Jason. "I've heard knocking in the walls, which I attribute to pipes."

"Do you ever hear bells?" Maria asked.

"The doorbell does ring out of the blue sometimes. We have two bells between the front and interior doors."

"There's water down here," Mark interrupted. "Do you get water in your apartment?"

"Yeah, and we have a pretty serious mold problem," Jason answered. "Our lease is up in October and we're out of here. It's a pretty bad situation with the landlord. I had water damage so bad that the sheet rock was bubbling in my apartment, but that's a whole other story."

"See!" Maria exclaimed, "There was a water problem down here...I see them looking through things and there's puddles...and it's cold."

"They refinished the basement with two levels. I live on the bottom half and my roommate Tina lives on the top half," Jason explained. "She's lived here a long time. She's a good person to talk to." He motioned toward the second door—the boiler room. "It's usually open. You can go in there."

"We're just trying to pick-up the vibes where we can," I mentioned, jiggling the door handle, but it was stuck. "Well I'm interested to hear." Jason replied.

"The energy is frenetic and crazy down here," said Maria. "Abe is present...someone else is also here saying, '*don't do this*'...There's some sort of argument going on right now between two people...one is saying '*you don't want to do this*' and he's pissed...and then there's Abe and he's backed away a little bit...Abe's showing me the ledger again...and money being placed into a vest pocket. Abe is saying '*we have a meeting*'...'*Jones, Jones-y...Jones, Jonesy*'...I'm getting an ache across my head." Maria grabbed her head in pain and walked outside to the alleyway.

Mark managed to open the jammed boiler room door and dashed in, Michael at his heels, and they started rummaging through stuff, looking for a satchel or anything old. A single fluorescent tube on the grimy ceiling lit the small 12x12 storage area cluttered with objects—boxes, paintings, chairs, hoses, ladders, air conditioners—strewn everywhere. Dirty gas meters and decrepit lead pipes lined the walls and ceiling, their rusted coats illuminated by the green fluorescent light.

Maria returned, approaching with great caution, and then stopped. "I can't go in here yet…I can't even walk in here." She was pale, swaying as if she might pass out. She bent over and tried to rally. "Something is pushing me to stay out of the room."

"These are the sealed-up basement windows." Michael pointed at the dark charred brick walls of the original basement and the newer black painted brick that filled in the once narrow horizontal windows.

Mark found a small four-foot crawl space that expanded to the left. He bent down to explore it using his cell phone as a flashlight. "This leads somewhere. It's very old and there's something on the other side." The crawl space was so wet and corroded he turned around immediately.

"I remember the walls and the windows…I know this corner…it was wet," said Maria.

"It's always been wet, this is the natural ground," replied Mark, gesturing to a hole in the concrete base.

"I'm so dizzy I can't even…I feel like I'm going to pass out…my ears are ringing…I got this sharp hit on my back…like a diagonal hit up, with a pipe…and my chest and everything hurts…I feel sick to my stomach… like I'm going to puke…," Maria turned and hurried outside.

I heard the sound of dry-heaving coming from the alleyway and went to check on her. "I can't be in that room right now…I can't do the dry heave and blood thing that Frankie is experiencing," she insisted.

A few moments later Jason opened the other locked door from the inside, which revealed a small hallway straight ahead that opened into another large, disheveled storage room. To the left was the white, dirt-smeared back door to his apartment.

Maria rejoined us to search the second large storage space. The room's old musty odor smelled like a dank swamp in summer time. Against part of the original brick wall Mark discovered an old dumbwaiter with the letter "A" spray painted on it. Michael read the building permits from the 1970s posted on another wall as Maria and I started turning over boxes of junk and moving an ancient motorcycle. To the right was a crawl space that led back to the first storage room. At one time this had definitely been a singular, large room.

"Maybe they threw something back here," suggested Michael, discovering a long ledge that ran the length of one wall and spread back into darkness. "I throw crap in my garage, just like this." We continued shifting around boxes of tile, old electronics, and brushing away cobwebs.

"Everything here is disintegrated. I don't want to get back there without a mask," said Maria. Everything looked toxic. We needed hazmat suits to dig through the disintegrating garbage for the potential satchel. We decided we were better off to just leave, and thanked Jason for his help and exchanged contact information.

As we drove through Crown Heights to our next destination, I caught glimpses of shrouded women and black-hatted men of the orthodox Lubavitch order strolling down the street. The sun disappeared behind a hazy gray sky as we approached Eastern Parkway at Utica Avenue. We parked half a block from the site of the old Dubrow's Cafeteria Restaurant at 1110 Eastern Parkway, where Uncle Abe was last seen alive.

The site was now a discount clothing store that sported a large blue awning that read "Rainbow's" in enormous white letters. Large circular racks of clothing lined the sidewalk leading to its front door.

Maria stood with her back to the building, mentally blocking out the noise of the buses and traffic, as she gazed across the Parkway to the site of the bank where Abe's car had been parked, nestled next to St. Matthew's Church. She started speaking her visions immediately.

"Abe is sitting at a table inside. He sees White Carnation Man standing in front of the church…It's Amen…I don't understand how he sees him, unless the front of the restaurant had large windows…I see Amen right now, he's standing there, over a bit from the statue in front," Maria pointed at the church.

"Abe runs across Eastern Parkway to meet him and almost gets hit by a car…there was no fencing back then blocking the lanes, you could run straight across the Parkway. He's with Amen for several moments. I will have to go over there to hear the conversation they had. Then I see him run back toward the restaurant."

Having seen photos of the restaurant at the Archives a few days ago, I'd learned that there were indeed large windows on the front side of the restaurant that would allow Abe to see straight across the four-lane parkway. And, there was no median in 1941—Abe could have just dashed across the parkway as Maria was seeing.

"Abe sits down again. White Fedora Man is there with two other men…well-dressed, dark suits, long coats. They come up and say something to Abe…I can't hear them…and then they leave."

Maria pressed her fingers deeply into her lips and concentrated, looking off into the distance. "Abe comes back outside and says, *'No, no, I've got this, go home.'*"

"He's telling his driver to go home," I interjected, as that was exactly what was said in the eyewitness testimony. Maria repeated the statement several more times, in a trance.

"He leaves and goes over to Utica Avenue, to the right. I don't know why he doesn't just run across the Parkway like he did before, but this time he walks to the corner and crosses to his car in front of the bank. He's alone. Then two dark figures come up behind him." Maria traced Abe's movements with her fingers, pointing at the locations.

"He didn't drive," Maria turned toward me and started to shake. "'*Cop is driving*'…'*cop is driving*'…What's down that way?" she asked, pointing toward Utica Avenue.

"Lincoln Place, then St. John's Place," replied Mark. "There's also a police precinct down there, a newer 77 precinct. The old 77 was on Washington…"

"That's it!" Maria shouted. "They went that way! Abe was in the police car for a while. Why do I see him on the floor?" I can see the cop driving, but I can't see where he's going. Why is Abe on the floor?"

"Probably because they don't want anyone to see that Abe's in the car with them," Mark suggested. "They probably drove around to make sure no one was tailing them, and then went to wherever they're gonna go."

"I can feel the road underneath him," continued Maria. "He had money on him. Everything he had on him was taken. I see him paying people…he had money…but when he's on the floor he doesn't have any-

thing…they took all his personal items off him. Abe's car is still here…
this is the police car with the 69 on it. There is another well-dressed guy
sitting on the back seat, but Abe is on the floor. The backseat is huge!"

"Well, old Caddies and Buicks had huge back seats, big enough for
someone to lie on the floor," explained Mark.

"They drove to a building…like a warehouse type building…not a
busy street…oil barrels…. it drops into empty space, like it goes into water."

"I'm trying to think where there are warehouses," continued Mark.
"It's different if there's one warehouse or a block of them."

"I see oil drums, and they are going to a place under a bridge," Maria
described. "The police car is parked under a bridge."

"The place could be the Brooklyn Navy Yard, or it could be in Canarsie off Linden Boulevard. But, if you're saying water, then that would be
down at Atlantic and Penn toward the Belt Parkway. There's a whole area
that's industrial and warehouses, and they used to dump bodies there."

"Maria saw the words 'Atlantic' and 'Pennsylvania' in our last session,"
I interrupted.

"Atlantic and Penn are avenues that intersect," Mark replied. "You
make a right and go south, and at Atlantic and Penn you're on the edge
of the 69th precinct Canarsie area."

I raised my eyebrows in surprise. *The Avenues crossed? 69th precinct?
Incredible!*

"The next thing I see is Abe on his knees, hands tied behind him,
down against the police car. They are yelling at him…there were 4 or
5 cops there," Maria continued. "I just heard someone say, *'clean-up'…
'clean up.'*"

"It probably means *'clean up the scene'* after the murder," Mark suggested.

"We need to go to the church across the street," said Maria. "I want to
hear what White Carnation Man has to say before we take Abe's last ride."

We crossed Eastern Parkway to the front of St. Matthew's. The large,
gray stone church rose to a patinaed green dome. A residential rectory,
adjacent to the right of the church, was colored in a deep red brick tone.

Eric thought the gate Maria had seen in her vision might be somewhere at the church. Through Google's camera, the fencing appeared to be short and modern, not at all like the rusted gate Maria described.

We scanned the length of the fence, which recessed deep into the block, between the rectory and the bank. Instantaneously, Maria and I both saw it at the same time—a much older, obviously original, wrought-iron gate, about 100 feet back from the street. Its ancient iron had rusted to a reddish brown, with ornate speared ends broken off at the bottom. It was secured with three rusted padlocks, and trash was strewn underneath its disintegrated bottom spikes. This was it!

The gate was recessed far enough off the street to appear somewhat concealed. I faced it then turned back to look across the Parkway and was stunned to see it was a direct shot to the front of where Dubrow's had been. Abe could have seen Amen with his white carnation standing outside waiting for him, run across the parkway, and then moved to the seclusion of the alcoved gate for their meeting.

Maria stood next to the decrepit gate shivering. As she started speaking her visions, her shivers turning to a violent shaking. "Abe's talking to Amen…he gave him a list of 20 to 23 names. There were numbers next to those names…they had another meeting set for two weeks after this night…23 names on the list. Abe gave him a folded piece of paper…a copy not an original…ledger paper with holes on the side…he folded it into thirds, gave it to Amen and talked about meeting in two weeks."

Maria continued with her eyes closed, still shaking. "They parted ways. I can see two well-dressed cops standing over here," she pointed to the corner of Utica Avenue and Eastern Parkway to our right. "It's time to go down Utica Avenue and retrace their drive."

All of us quickly walked back toward the rental car. "It's so amazing to actually be here. Just imagine it's night, that it's 1:30 a.m., and it all just comes to life, doesn't it?" I said to Maria.

"Why 1:30 a.m.?" A troubled look came over her face.

"The eye witness report said that Abe was at the restaurant until about 1:30 a.m. His body was found around 6:30 a.m."

Maria stopped in her tracks and looked at me as if she'd been hit by a thunderbolt. She had been waking at 1:30 a.m. every night for the last two weeks, leading up to this New York visit, and couldn't go back to sleep until around 6 a.m. because of horrific, violent visions that filled her mind. "It all makes sense now. Shit!" She exclaimed, "I had no idea!"

We got in the car and headed down Utica Avenue. Maria was concentrating and I was hypothesizing.

"If they took Abe someplace, but his car is left on Eastern Parkway, how did his body and car end up on Empire Boulevard a few hours later?" I questioned.

"They put him in the trunk of the police car and brought him back to Eastern Parkway," Michael suggested.

"Then who drove his car?" I asked.

"What makes you think they drive back to Eastern Parkway to put his body in his own car?" Mark asked us. "How do we know that his car is even still there? They might have met up to move the body from one car to another."

"A cop moved Abe's car," Maria added. "The same officials who approached Abe when inside the restaurant. They 'watched' and 'followed.'"

"This whole scenario transcends robbery. This isn't about money Abe won in a crap game…this is about something much bigger." Mark said.

"So, the idea that they put Abe back in his own car, on a popular street like Empire Boulevard, was to make it known that Abe was dead." I added.

"That's right," agreed Mark. "The perps were sending a message, they wanted people to know this happened. They were making a statement: *'we are in control and we silenced him.'* I'll bet you the wiseguys of that time knew all about it."

The scenario was potentially complicated. "Zoo," the police's eyewitness had said two men got into Abe's car with him and drove off. Maria said the articles were contrived and she saw him being taken away in a police car. And, as Mark pointed out, you never know who was working on the inside.

We refocused on the drive at hand. Maria insisted on going down Utica Avenue, but didn't know why. She again described to Mark that she saw a warehouse on one side, the marked police car parked under a bridge, and the ground dropping off into water.

Traveling down Utica Avenue, the buildings became more and more run down as we left the Crown Heights district and made our way towards Brownsville. At Atlantic Avenue we turned right and found ourselves driving parallel to the elevated "El" train, nestled above the looming oxidized arches of the Long Island Railroad.

"There is a whole warehouse-industrial area here on Atlantic Avenue, crossing at Pennsylvania, where the above-ground trains intersect. This might be the bridge you are seeing."

Once in the Brownsville/Canarsie area, the neighborhood was littered with warehouses. Mark continued down Atlantic Avenue to the intersection with Pennsylvania Avenue. Warehouses were giving way to old brick buildings and storefronts sporting tire services, pawnshops, and liquor stores.

"Is there water near here?" Maria asked anxiously. Mark assured her there was a small waterway under the elevated tracks, and he had an idea where these elements intersected. Michael and I were listening in awe to the synergistic flow of information happening between Maria's visions and Mark's ability to figure out what she was seeing.

He turned the car onto Pennsylvania Avenue, then right onto Liberty Avenue, where the terrain again turned to warehouses. Down Liberty, I could see the elevated railroad in the distance, maybe seven blocks away. Mark was talking rapidly about how bad this area was, populated with junkies and prostitutes.

As we passed underneath the elevated train tracks Maria started to shake. "This is it!" she shouted. "THIS IS IT!" Her index finger feverishly banged against the car window, pointing down Van Sinderen Avenue. Behind tall metal fencing was a dirt road, directly beneath the elevated tracks, closed off to the public. "THIS IS IT! STOP!" Maria screamed.

"There is a gully down there," added Mark. "You used to be able to drive under the tracks very easily back in the day. You can't anymore, that fencing went up about 15 years ago." Maria was transfixed, continuing to bang her finger against the window.

"Can we back into the one-way road?" I asked.

"We can do anything, I'm the police," Mark winked at me. He sped down Van Sinderen Avenue in reverse, almost to Atlantic Avenue. The narrow one-way road was flanked by a brick warehouse with metal siding rising about 8 feet high. On the other side was the unpaved road following the length of the elevated train, dropping off to a gully, all of which was fenced off with signs for the Buckeye Pipeline Co.

"Awwww, Jesus!...this is awful," moaned Maria as she started to shake uncontrollably. "This is just awful!"

We jumped out of the car, leaving Mark and Michael inside, and crossed to the padlocked fence blocking the entrance to the unmarked road beneath the elevated tracks. The sound of rushing water was all around us. Wet gravel crunched beneath our shoes as we peered beyond the fence that separated us from the location where Abe's life had come to an end. Maria stood mesmerized before the fence, her face scrunched with pain, her body shaking.

"The police car was parked here...they threw Abe on the ground... they're beating him...my left ear is ringing...it's so loud...I can't hear." Maria stopped speaking, not sharing what she was seeing, except to say "It's so horrible...so very, very horrible what they did to Abe...I can't even tell you."

We clasped each other's hands tightly, gazing at the wet road before us in silence.

Back in the car, we were on the move again to 675 Empire Boulevard. *"25 feet east of Albany Avenue,"* was where the Medical Examiner had recorded Abe's Buick sedan and body were found at 6:55 a.m. Maria had no previous visions about this final place.

As we turned onto Empire Boulevard I immediately recognized the deep red brick of the apartment complex at 675. I had researched this spot and walked it on Google's Street-View. The boulevard was crowded with parked cars. Mark double-parked and Maria, Michael, and I got out.

This was the location of the crime scene photos I had. One image showed Abe's body lying on the pavement, police standing over him going through his pockets. I found myself searching the concrete for bloodstains that would have soaked into the ground some 73 years earlier. Of course, there were none. I'd never shown that particular image to Maria.

"I feel like I'm being pulled by the nape of my neck, dragged out onto the street. It's bad enough he was murdered, but then they just tossed him out of the car like a piece of meat." Maria was silent for several moments.

"I can feel the thud of Abe's body hitting the ground," Maria continued. "It's awful. There was just no regard for him. But, Abe's not here. Usually when someone dies the place holds their energy, but there's nothing here. He was dead by the time they brought him here. It was just a drop-off spot. Abe died under the train tracks."

We milled around the patch of gray sidewalk for several moments, mostly for my benefit, as Hassidic Jews walked by staring at us. Standing in the exact spot where the police had removed Abe's body, I wanted to just sit down on the pavement and cry. Half of my life I had spent trying to figure out this mystery, and now that I'd retraced the steps, I felt such great sadness—of the family's loss and the sheer terror of what my uncle must have endured.

"Someone is standing here," Maria's voice interrupted my thoughts. "Someone...I can't tell if he was a bystander or a cop...he's standing here watching all of it. And I want to say it is someone that Abe knew. He's saying '*They got him.*'"

We took one more look around, then stumbled back to the car to rejoin Mark.

●———●

Everyone was quiet as we drove back to Manhattan. Maria stared out the window at the passing Brooklyn scenery. "I'm sensing a very deep, deep sadness, and also a relief that something is finally being revealed with this case. I'm just overwhelmed…this city is crazy."

"There's a lot going on here—300 years of anything you can imagine," Mark replied with a smile. He and Michael were eager to get food. Maria and I were lost in our individual thoughts.

As the hour neared 5 p.m., we were back on the Upper West Side. After a well-deserved, liquor-saturated dinner, we went our separate ways. Maria came back to relax at the friend's apartment I was housesitting. She did not want to go to sleep before her early morning train back to Connecticut. She didn't want to revisit in dreams all the death she had seen earlier in the day.

"I can't tell you everything I saw during Abe's horrific death," Maria said softly. "What I saw was so awful. It hurt my heart." She started to cry. "It was so emotional…it was fucked…nobody had any regard for him and nobody understood who he was. I'm angry about that. I kept asking Abe, 'Why is this happening to you?'"

"I need to know what you saw on the road under the tracks," I probed.

"My God, I felt so frightened. I was scared because there was nothing I could do. I couldn't change it. There was utter chaos happening. The fear Abe and Frankie experienced was very real. I felt the deafening ring of their final moments…I can't even…I can't…when I do this work I want to spare people what it feels like…so I block it." Maria's voice rose to a high pitch and she started to cry again. "I don't want people to have to see or hear what I do."

"So, when you heard the ringing, was that Abe's last moment?"

Maria nodded and made two rapid low sounds. "Poof…poof…you don't hear the gun the way the victim does. They don't hear the pop… they feel a poof…Abe felt a pressure that knocked him forward, and then it bounced all through his brain and popped out on the right. He felt every ounce of that….and then a deathly coldness."

"Did you see anything before Abe's last moment? Any words spoken?"

"I felt Abe physically hit the ground. There were five men there—two men in front of him and three men behind him. Two were in cop uniforms…I see the others in long tweedy, texturized coats. White Fedora Man was also at the final location on Empire Blvd. He was in the mix. The only part I can't see clearly is how they got Abe's body back into his own car."

"A lot came together today," I whispered. "I wonder what the cops wanted so badly from Abe that they did this to him, and then tried to get it from Frankie three years later. What were they trying to find at Lincoln Place?" I shook my head. "Maybe we'll just never know."

"Or maybe we will," replied Maria, as we both drifted into a reluctant sleep.

25

The Silence of the Medical Examiner

Back home in California, the Medical Examiner's report on Uncle Abe's body was on my mind. Not only did his age and the spelling of his last name differ throughout the report, but curiously, his body was not examined for external marks, bruises, or cuts. The internal organs were examined during the autopsy and his brain tested negative for alcohol content, yet not recording the exterior body seemed like a huge oversight. I would not be able to substantiate if ligature marks were on his wrists, as Maria had envisioned.

The office of the Chief Medical Examiner recorded that Abe had light brown eyes and dark curly hair. He had been in America for 27 years, originating from Poland (it was Russia when he lived there), and was a restaurant owner. It gave the names of Abe's parents and noted that his brother Ike had identified his body at 10:30 a.m. on Thursday, September 25. I wondered how the police knew whom to call to identify the body. Supposedly only his driver's license was left on his person. I assumed they went to Great Grandma Anna's house, the address most probably on his license, and she called Ike. The report stated there had been no witnesses at the crime scene and the investigation was marked for the District Attorney's office.

The detailed description of the gunshot wounds was in medical language that was foreign to me, so I focused on sections of the report that included the police memo and details of his clothing. There were bloodstains on the front of his pink shirt, but his white undershirt was "markedly" bloodstained only on the back. How could that be? If he had died in his car, propped up on the passenger side of the sedan, the blood pattern didn't make sense, even to a novice like me. It should have just pooled on the backside of his shirt. The report also noted there was vomit on the right shoulder of his coat. If he was shot in the head, when did he have time to vomit? There was no mention of eyeglasses found on him either, and we know "Goggie" needed them. I didn't fully understand the report, but I knew something wasn't right here.

Mark had gone away on vacation, so I called upon two friends from the 7-Point Star Group in Northern California for help in understanding the report. Consultants Julie Marin and Patrick Callahan had extensive homicide investigation and criminology backgrounds, and Julie was also an expert at crime scene re-creation.

They asked to see the photos that accompanied the ME's report. I had none, but Julie was sure that ME's were photographing bodies as far back as the 1940s, and there should be at least a drawing. If they existed, the Municipal Archives did not have them in their files.

Despite the lack of photos, Julie and Patrick were able to analyze the recorded facts and shared some interesting information. We met at my house. They came with graphs, drawings, a "blue" gun (a demonstration, non-firing gun) and other items to recreate the crime scene.

We started with the gunshot wounds. The report said that the first gunshot, on the left side of the neck, was surrounded by a contusion collar, two inches from the ear and one inch below it. The bullet traveled at a 45-degree angle upward through the head, and exited on the upper right side of the skull.

Julie raised the blue gun to the left side of Patrick's head, behind the ear at the exact angle the shot would have been fired in order to enter the skull as described. Patrick translated the term "contusion collar" to mean the wound was a close-up shot and had caused bruising from the barrel of the gun being placed against the head. "Gases and projectile coming out of the barrel enter the body causing the bruising. This means that Abe had to have been alive for a few moments so the body would start producing histamines to heal itself, forming a contusion."

The second bullet, directly behind the left ear, entered at a 30-degree angle, passing into the cranial cavity and lodging in the posterior fossa, or bottom rear of the skull. "It was also a close shot," explained Patrick. "I can tell this because it is described as 'smudged' and because of the angle of the shot."

Smudging means there is not a clear edge to the wound—it's softened, smeared—the pressure of the gas from the gun enters the wound and presses things out. "Smudging tells me for sure that the gun was right against his head," continued Patrick. "If Abe was sitting with his head straight up you could only get the first bullet's 45-degree angle if you were up close. His head had to be tipped down in order for the second bullet to enter the skull at the reported 30-degree angle. He could have been either sitting or in a kneeling position.

"Let's say the shooting took place in the car," Patrick hypothesized. "The assailant would have had to be behind him from the left, tilting the gun. That would have been difficult for someone if they were driving or next to him. So, if the shooter was in the back seat, he'd have to be a left-handed shooter."

Patrick stated that if Abe was seated in the car when he was killed, he would have bled out of the lowest wound—the bottom part of the back of his skull—onto the shoulder and down the back, the blood pooling where he was seated. "But, the pooling in the report doesn't support that he was seated in the car. There's also no blood splatter reported.

What wasn't recorded on the report was the time difference between the two shots. "The ME should have been able to estimate how much time transpired before the second shot was fired. I believe there was a period of time where Abe was critically, fatally wounded but he was still breathing."

"Yes, he would have been frantically breathing and that would be part of the vomiting," added Julie. "A major head or brain injury will do that. For a contusion to appear there had to be blood pumping in order to start healing the wound, so death was not instantaneous. With the second shot, there should be no sign of life, but the report states it was also surrounded by a contusion collar, which suggests he was still alive and breathing after the second shot."

"The perp probably thought Abe wasn't dead yet, because there was most definitely a death rattle and vomit, so he put a second round into him. Abe could have been conscious at some level and may have been able to hear. Hearing is the last sense we lose, but the report is not clear on this." Patrick concluded, "His head would have been forward, hence the 30-degree angle of the second shot. He was most probably shot in a kneeling position, with the triggerman squatting down near him, placing the gun against his head. This would be too difficult to do in the car."

This led to the theory that Abe was killed somewhere other than in his sedan, where he was found. Julie brought to my attention that the report said "found dead" because they didn't know where he died. Overall, there was little information about the crime scene. A police report should have more details.

From the press images we had, Patrick and Julie didn't see any blood splatter or brain matter in the car's interior that would indicate he was killed in the car. "We can see there is no blood on the door or windshield of the car," explained Patrick. "The bullet from a .32 is so small that it may have gone through the roof of the car, split the fabric, and closed itself up again. All that would be in a police report. Furthermore, Abe's hat is in place. Was the hat on him when he was shot? There should be a bullet hole through the hat if the body hadn't been moved. If there is no bullet hole in the hat, then it was placed on him afterwards. There is no mention of that in the clothing descriptions."

"With the kind of exit wound they are describing, it would have at least knocked the hat off," added Julie. "Furthermore, you mentioned he had a driver that night whom he sent home, so why is he in the passenger seat? He should have been driving himself home. It's his car. I believe he was moved after he was murdered and there are a couple of reasons for that. Namely, there's blood on the front exterior of the shirt, but not on the front of the undershirt. That transfer of blood had to come from a third party—another person."

"That's fascinating!" I exclaimed. "That means someone had to pick him up and carry him."

"They probably did," replied Julie. "The transfer of blood to the front of the shirt would have happened when the perpetrator picked Abe up and moved him—hence the blood from Abe's back smeared onto the front of the perp's clothing. Then, when they repositioned Abe in the car, they were probably facing him and the blood on the perp's shirt front would have transferred to the front of Abe's shirt."

"Yes," agreed Patrick. "And his heart had to be pumping in order for the blood to be pooling in the places that it was. It all points to a scenario that he was killed elsewhere, put in the car, driven to the final location, and the perp walked away. The photo shows Abe's hands folded in his lap, his pockets turned inside out, and the hat has no hole in it. That all adds credence to the idea that the body was staged."

It had been a gruesome yet informative evening. They confirmed my suspicions, added some surprises, and even verified Maria's visions: he was still alive after the first shot, the bullet had exited the right side of his head, the trajectory of the bullets demonstrated that he may have been kneeling when he was shot, and the body had been moved and staged.

"There's so much that wasn't said in the report that it seems to have been done in hurry," summarized Patrick. "There were standards, even in the 1940s, that had to be met. This report is not a thorough post-mortem. There's no description of the outside of the body—nothing about what may have been under his nails, condition of his knuckles, dirt on his shoes, etc. Someone wanted this done fast—get it over with and buried."

Julie and Patrick surmised that the records were sanitized, especially since no police report could be found and there were no witnesses.

When Mark returned from vacation I asked his opinion of the report as well. Over Skype, we hashed out the details again, and overall, he agreed with Julie and Patrick's findings, particularly in regard to the moving and staging of Abe's body.

"There doesn't seem to be a crime scene report," Mark said. "Something had to be written because it was a big news story—required documents and notes had to be taken and preserved. It's interesting that there is none of that in Abe's case. The ME is very detailed about the internal organs, which have no bearing on the murder. So, where's the drawing of the body? 1941 ain't that long ago. It's not like it this happened in 1841!" Mark snickered. "Look at it this way—the perps got Abe into their car, and it's never easy to abduct a guy, no matter how small he is. Wouldn't Abe have put up a fight? Was his clothing ripped? If the ME were really trying to solve a homicide he'd have documented the things that were lacking or unremarkable, but there's no description of his body. It's weird there's nothing else in the report—that the ME wouldn't even make a comment to support the negative—such as saying, '*I found no other markings of note*,' etc.,—in order to say that he did his job accurately."

Mark agreed with Patrick. "When something smells rotten it usually is. If the ME purposely left information out, it was for a reason." The bigger question was why the cover up?

26

O Brother, Where Art Thou?

Following our Brooklyn adventure, Maria was continually waking up in the middle of night with visions. "When I got home from New York," she shared in a late night Skype call, "I had three days of crying fits because of what I experienced about Abe's death under the train tracks, and Frankie's beating at Lincoln Place. It was overwhelming." Maria paused thoughtful, then added, "I can't stop thinking about Lincoln Place."

As we continued to talk, the conversation turned into an impromptu session, where Frankie and Abe came through and told Maria that the information we needed was near the dumbwaiter, in the large storage area of the Lincoln Place basement. We were to look for a "false floor," near a "tarp," where it was wedged into a "crevice."

"What's there?" I asked.

Maria bowed her head and swayed back and forth. "I got the word 'answers'...he's showing me paper, I can't see what's on it, but it's paper... not the ledger book, but paper...in the satchel." Maria also received information from Frankie that the mysterious "Jonesy" was someone that Police Commissioner Wallander had hired to gather information on their operation. Frankie had trusted him, but he was "double crossed" and revealed more images of where he was buried—a brick tunnel that flowed into water—and Maria drew an image showing a 7 next to a reverse 7.

I asked where we go from here with our sessions. "There's important information Frankie needs us to find. I really think we should go back to Lincoln Place."

Go back? I was intrigued but felt satisfied with the trip we had made. Over the next few weeks Maria became more and more adamant about returning to the headquarters. She felt there was unfinished business there and that Frankie's spirit needed a clearing. She wanted to conduct an evening séance at the old headquarters.

I had no idea how I might afford a second trip, but Maria's insistence inspired me to find a way. Who was I to say no to the spirit of Uncle Frankie? If we did go back I felt it would be an opportunity to document the locations by bringing a videographer with us. Determined, I launched an online crowd-funding campaign, and along with some very generous donations from friends and family, raised the needed funds within a month.

With a proposed date for late summer, the team was getting ready to go back to Brooklyn. But there were other logistics to figure out. The only way we could access the building at Lincoln Place again was through Jason, the tenant of the basement apartment. I was hoping he would help us. I sent him several voice messages and emails, but there was no response. I had to find another way to get us back into the basement.

Eric finally found contact information for the landlords—but if they said no, that would be the end of it. I didn't want to take that risk. My only other resource was Jason's roommate Tina, whom he'd mentioned when we had met. Luckily her last name was captured on my audio recording, but I didn't know how to spell it correctly and couldn't locate her. I put Mark on the trail.

Overnight he tracked down her information. I left Tina a voice message and sent emails, but there was no reply. I was starting to panic, but Eric reminded me that no young folks answer their phones these days, they text.

I gave texting a try and Tina immediately responded, which led to a phone conversation. Jason had told her all about our visit and she was happy to accommodate us in August. Problem solved.

In May, I followed-up with Detective Stradford of the Cold Case Squad to see if he'd made any progress in finding the murder investigation report. He had nothing. He explained there was no single department that looked for old report requests. There was just one person, who traveled to the Hoboken or Long Island warehouses and found what they could. Stradford had made thirteen requests for cold case files in the last six months and only received back two. "A case from 1941 will not be a priority."

It was becoming clear why Abe had never been mentioned in any of the gangster histories—there was no information. The Municipal Archives and the John Jay College of Criminal Justice archives had nothing. The Police investigation on his murder was nowhere to be found. Record clerks at the court houses and police departments were just not interested in helping find old records, or I was told, they were not able to release them, which seemed odd since the case was so old. The files were shrouded and inaccessible. I would have to continue to put my hopes on Detective Stradford. It would be worth the wait if something ever surfaced.

I was spending much of my time looking for Frankie's arrest records— any clue that might help lead to more information about his last years— but there was nothing I could get my hands on. The Muncipal Archives did not have Felony Court files by name, only by case numbers. *How was I supposed to find a case number from 70 years ago?* The Archives lacked an accessible, cross-referenced filing system for researchers.

I returned to searching the *Brooklyn Daily Eagle* online, hoping I might find a corresponding news article for one of his arrests. I tried all the different name combinations for the family in the newspaper database with no luck, until I extended the dates of the search parameters. Suddenly I found something: a legal notice in small type, buried in a long, narrow column in the back of the classified section on April 1, 1953:

> To FRANK BABCHOOK, also known as Frank Balzack, if living, and if dead to his widow, if any, his heirs at law, next of kin, distributes, successors in interest, legal representatives, if any, and any and all unknown persons who may be proper and necessary parties in this proceeding, all

of whose name or names and whose place or places or residence are unknown and cannot after diligence be ascertained, SEND GREETING.

WHEREAS, DAVID BABCHOOK, etc., who resides at 874 Saratoga
Avenue...has presented his account as executor of ANNA BABCHOOK,
also known as Anna Balzack, deceased, and a petition praying that the
account may be judicially settled and for the determination of the claim
of LARRY SIEGEL.

NOW, THEREFORE you and each of you are hereby cited to show
cause before our surrogate Court of the County of Kings, to be in the
courtroom at the Hall of Records on the 1st day of June, 1953, at 9:30
o'clock in the forenoon, why such settlement should not be had.

This was baffling. It seemed Great Grandma Anna possessed something Grandma Rae's fourth husband wanted, years after Anna's death.
She had been a poor Russian immigrant who couldn't speak English. She
owned the home at 9214 Avenue B that Great Grandpa built, but I had
heard from family members that the house had been foreclosed because
youngest son, Ike, never paid the taxes.

The Siegel aspect of this court notice was as mysterious as the Frankie
angle. I couldn't fathom why Siegel would be suing the family four years
after his divorce from Grandma Rae had been finalized. Frankie was obviously gone by 1953—vanished into thin air—but the courts were asking that Frankie, if alive, chime in about the case brought up by Siegel.

As I re-read the notice it stated at the top "Supplemental citation affi-
davits as to persons in the military service (Soldiers Relief Act of 1940)
require that the people of the state of New York send greetings to Frank
Babchook/Balzack." Did this mean he had been in the military? I was
confused by the jargon, but it looked like I was finally getting a break—
the legal notice listed a file number.

I wasn't sure what Surrogate Court encompassed. It sounded fami-
ly-ish, so I was hoping that Rae's divorce information from Siegel might
be there as well. I called Brooklyn's Surrogate Court records department,
where a very patient man explained that Surrogate Court was for estates
and probate. He also explained that what used to be known as Felony

Court in the old days, was currently called Criminal Court. Divorce records were in Civil Court.

I gave the friendly clerk the case number from the newspaper notice and he put me on hold. Ten minutes later he came back on the line, shocked by how large the file was. He said he could make a copy, for a substantial fee, but if someone came to the office, they could use the copy machine for much less. I thanked him and then called my sister, who agreed to the task.

The following day, Valerie texted: "This thing is over 100 pages! I've been xeroxing for three hours! Will send in the mail tomorrow."

I texted back: "Anything juicy jump out at you?"

She sent a cell phone photograph of two pages. It seemed the estate lawyer was desperately trying to find Frankie and there was a list of his arrest records and his aliases: Frank Gold, Frank Goldstein, Frank Blake and John Doe. The document also stated Frankie was paroled in April of 1944 from his long jail sentence at Riker's Island. This was valuable information that could potentially shed further light on his story.

●———●

Great Grandma Anna died on December 20, 1946, of a heart ailment at the age of 69. But I was sure she died of a broken heart. Her husband Morris had passed away on September 24, 1930. Eleven years later—to the day—her son Abe was murdered. Her son Frankie, according to family lore, had disappeared around 1945. Her brothers and sisters had been murdered in a mass shooting by the Nazis and Ukrainian collaborationists in her hometown of Ludvipol during World War II. And, her youngest daughter, Rae, was in an abusive marriage with Siegel. I imagined that my Great Grandma must have felt overwhelming grief and helplessness.

The huge document Valerie retrieved was Anna's last will and testament, which named Abe executor, and in his absence oldest brother Dave was to become the head of her estate. Each of her living children had signed a waiver and consent to submit the will to probate. Uncle Frankie signed his waiver in an inky scroll on February 28, 1947. *What!?!? Wait a minute! I thought Frankie had disappeared earlier!* This extended my timeline of his life by two years.

Anna didn't have much. Just the house in Brooklyn and a modest bank account. Although all the children were to receive a 1/5 interest in the house, Bertha, Dave, and Rae signed a waiver that their shares be turned over to youngest brother Ike. But, two unexpected things happened by the time the will went through probate in 1948: Rae's current husband Larry Siegel sued the family while also in the middle of their "scandalous" divorce, and Frankie went missing.

At first, Siegel claimed he had paid for Anna's burial costs and wanted to be reimbursed. The court said no. Then he petitioned for interest in the Avenue B property. The court said no. However, it took seven years to settle. On the Siegel side of the probate case, there were two items I found curious:

1. Siegel had recorded his address as the house in Harrison, New York. He had managed to stay at the property, which Rae had bought, after their divorce was finalized in 1949.
2. Siegel made statements to the court about the missing Uncle Frankie.

The other side of the probate case was that a tremendous search had taken place for over a year to find Frankie. The court needed to disperse Frankie's inheritance before they could close the proceedings, which by 1953 everyone involved was anxious to do. All the family members were contacted by a court-appointed Special Guardian named Bertha Skolnick, to discuss what they might know about Frankie's whereabouts. Brother Dave said he hadn't seen Frankie since 1947; Sister Bertha and brother Ike never responded; Rae reported she thought Frankie was dead.

On November 20, 1952, Special Guardian Skolnick visited Frankie's last known residence at 418 East 52nd Street in Brooklyn. The super of the building told her Frankie had moved away and left no forwarding address.

Skolnick then wrote to extended family and friends about Frankie's whereabouts. Larry Siegel replied that Frankie had a record and thought "he might be roaming the country."[1]

Learning that Frankie had a record, Skolnick went on to contact Frankie's parole officer, the police, and even the FBI during her year-long search. Frankie had been released from Riker's in 1944, and released from parole in 1945. There were no more arrests for him after that, anywhere in the country.

The FBI ultimately responded with a letter from J. Edgar Hoover himself, stating they had no information on Frankie. Interestingly, Hoover's letter came three weeks after an FBI special agent from the New York office replied to Skolnick that the Bureau could not give her information from their files because they were confidential. Hoover wrote that they *did* perform a search through their Identification Division in Washington for Frankie, but "regret to inform you that this search resulted negatively."[2]

The Special Guardian then tried to locate the men who had been arrested with Frankie. She found Sydney Lewow, who claimed he had seen Frankie a few years back, and that he was known to hang out at a deli on Ralph Avenue and Lincoln Place, off Pitkin Avenue. Lewow said "someone" had seen him as recently as a few months ago, and volunteered to go down to the deli and spread the word that Frankie's family was looking for him—this was the same deli off Pitkin Avenue where Frankie had met with Mudsy before his disappearance.

Skolnick decided to go to the deli herself. She found a note on the door that the establishment was closed for the day, and if necessary the owner could be found at home, at 375 Vermont Avenue. Skolnick went to the single family home, where the deli owner's wife, Mrs. Kreitner, answered the door. When asked if she knew where Frankie was, the woman replied, "He's hard to locate. He roams around."[3] Skolnick was keenly aware that one of Frankie's last known addresses was the same as the deli owner's home. Did he live there? Mrs. Kreitner replied no—the address had been a cover. Mrs. Kreitner had used the exact same descriptive phrase—"roaming around"—that Siegel had used. When Skolnick informed Rae about the deli sightings, Rae decided to go see for herself. Oddly, upon Rae's return from the deli she changed her story, stating that she now felt Frankie was alive, but had not seen him.

Skolnick tried contacting Mudsy several times, but to no avail. Finally, Uncle Leo called the Special Guardian. "My father is too ill to reply to you. He doesn't know where Frankie is, but heard he might have been in Spring Valley, New York, at some point."[4] Skolnick checked with the police in Spring Valley, but it was another fruitless search.

Citations were then placed in the back pages of the Brooklyn Daily Eagle in April and May requesting Frankie contact the family or show up in court on June 1, 1953. No response.

By November 24, 1953, Special Guardian Skolnick concluded her report, believing that Frankie was alive—somewhere. No death certificate was ever located under any of his many aliases and she had the curious statements of Lewow, Siegel, and the deli owner that he was "roaming."

The Surrogate case was finally closed two years later in 1955, when Siegel's continued claims for money were refused by the judge and dropped. Skolnick instructed that any monies owed to Frankie from the estate should be placed for him and his heirs in the City Treasury.

The court papers had revealed a strange twist in the case of Uncle Frankie. Was he killed as we suspected, or was he in hiding? The answer could lie in whether his inheritance was ever picked up. I wrote to the City Treasury and filed a Freedom of Information Act request to see if the money had been picked up. I had to wait—up to eight weeks—for an answer.

27

My Cousin Jared

July 2015

It was time to touch base with cousins again, this time to find out if they knew anything about the Surrogate Court case involving Larry Siegel and Uncle Frankie. I was also curious if the family did indeed spell their name Babchook at some point.

Cousin Selma, Dave's daughter, was now 87-years-old. She had many childhood memories of Frankie, but knew nothing about a court case. Her sister Terry had no memories either, but interestingly, she had heard that when Frankie was killed his body was thrown into water. That was intriguing, as Maria had said the same thing. But Cousin Terry couldn't recall how she knew this information.

I hadn't been in contact with Uncle Leo's daughter Debbie in decades. Although I had sent emails over the years, I never got a response. There had been that ruckus about Rae's damn fur coat 30-years earlier, and I thought Debbie might have been avoiding me because of Rae's bad behavior. It was time to reconnect, so I contacted her mother—Uncle Leo's widow, Miriam. She had never really spoken to me before, but seemed happy to hear from me and gave me Debbie's phone number.

Debbie was a delight and held no grudge—or memory—about Rae's fur coat. Her Brooklyn accent had a musical quality, as she called me "dear" every other sentence. We caught up on our lives and were both deeply moved recalling the lasting bond our fathers shared. Mort had looked up to Leo as the brother he never had. They ate their way through

Brooklyn, played basketball, and cruised in Leo's car singing along to Vic Damone or Frankie Laine. "Tough, aggressive, but always jokingly good-natured…he was brimming with energy and humor,"[1] was how Mort remembered Debbie's father. That was the Leo I remembered as well. They both were gifted storytellers, and I'm sure that's where Dad picked up the art.

Debbie didn't know about the surrogate case, so I asked if she remembered any of her father's stories. Sadly, she responded that she never really paid attention. Most of the cousins thought Leo exaggerated, telling the sort of pulpish tales of old New York that only "The Shadow" would know if true. Debbie suggested I contact her son Jared, insisting he knew all Leo's stories, as they had been very close.

When I hung up the phone I felt despondent. I missed Dad and Leo terribly. They had been the solid, exuberant men of the family that my generation grew up with. It was a harsh reminder of how important it is to appreciate family and friends when we are with them. The times we take for granted don't last forever. I felt it was a gift that Debbie and I had reconnected. Everything happens when it is supposed to. I had to keep believing that on this journey.

●————●

I hadn't seen or heard about Jared since he was eight-years-old, running around Grandma Rae's house at the 1988 dinner party.

"So, who have you become?" I asked him on the phone. Now 35-years-old, Jared was more than willing to launch into his life story. The years had been hard on him, and I was a bit surprised at how easily he divulged his history to a cousin he barely knew. As he spoke of his troubled youth—running with the wrong crowd and suffering PTSD from surviving the 9/11 attacks—his story came around to Mort. "My grandfather Leo talked about your father all the time. I felt like I knew him," Jared said in a thick, baritone tough-guy accent. He had read all of Dad's books, including the lengthy literary memoir, and resonated with the connection between Mort's troubled youth and his own—hoping he would somehow find himself as an adult, the way Mort had.

As a kid, Jared loved gangster movies. But that celluloid world morphed into reality when Leo told him the saga of the great uncles. Although the elders of the family had taken an oath of silence, somehow Leo managed to sprinkle his tales with anecdotes of the uncles and old Brooklyn lore.

Although some took what Leo rattled-on about with a grain of salt, it was Jared who was listening. "I didn't understand till later in life that Abe and Frankie were gangsters," he said. Jared had researched some of the old newspaper articles about the murder and was fascinated with Abe and Frankie. He felt it was an important part of our family history and it kept him connected to the memory of his grandfather—just as it had kept me connected to Dad.

Leo had taken young Jared around Brooklyn, in much the same way he had taken young Mort around—having "guy" adventures. "Grandpa Leo was outspoken and bold," remembered Jared with a bassoon laugh. "He definitely marched to his own drum." On their tour, Leo showed Jared places where Abe and Frankie hung-out. These included the Lincoln Place headquarters, Rae's house on Eastern Parkway near the Botanical Gardens, and Dubrow's Cafeteria Restaurant.

Leo had also taken Jared to see the location of Midnight Rose's candy store in Brownsville. Leo had revealed to Jared that Frankie had been summoned to the infamous Murder, Inc. headquarters the last day he was seen alive.

Aunt Carol and Dad had told me years ago that Frankie made his last call from a candy store. Jared was now confirming it was the murder-for-hire mob's homebase. This was a huge piece of the puzzle. Yet, it was also strange. Murder, Inc. was dissolved by the end of 1941, after Reles and the Brownsville Boys had either met their deaths or were in prison. Who was operating out of Midnight Rose's in 1947? Or, could it have just been a nostalgic place Frankie felt comfortable returning to, only to meet up with the wrong crowd?

"I wish I had asked him more questions at the time," Jared concluded. "Leo knew stuff."

Leo had known stuff—more than anyone realized or was willing to believe. He knew that Abe's body had been moved, that Attorney General Thomas Dewey, the DA's office, and a police captain had been stalking him. Jared and I hypothesized that Leo's knowledge of the uncles' deaths might be the reason Leo went into the army in March of 1943. His parents, Bertha and Mudsy, may have insisted he get out of town, to keep him from harm's way.

Jared and I shifted from wondering about the uncles to wondering about Leo—he knew too many facts to not be more involved in the whole family racket. Mort had once recalled that Leo was collecting money and running numbers—possibly for Uncle Frankie.

Jared was anxious to help me research. "As you uncover more about them, their stories are bigger than any of those gangster movies I watched as a kid." We had work to do. We needed to look up Leo's military records and find out when he returned from the war to corroborate Mort's story, now that we knew Frankie was alive at least until 1947.

I was enjoying my rediscovered cousin. Jared was kind and inquisitive, and we had a mutual desire to get to the truth about our family history. I wanted Jared to come on the next Brooklyn adventure as part of the team. But, a month out from the excursion, every cousin in the New York area—whether related to the uncles or not—wanted to come to Brooklyn with me. Jared's mother Debbie was even willing to pay to come along and hear what Maria had to say. I explained this was not like buying a ticket to a show. We would be filming a documentary and I had responsibilities—I had Maria to think about. She didn't want a lot of excess energy on the excursion which could easily sidetrack her. And, there was limited space in the rented SVU with all the gear. I had to say no to everyone. But I felt Jared should be with us. This was as important to him as it was to me.

I asked Maria how she felt about a new cousin tagging along. She thought for a long moment and then replied, "I'm sensing this cousin is an important part of this journey. He should definitely be with us. Bring him!"

I invited Jared to join our group and he was ecstatic. I let him know the psychic had requested his presence. "Oh, shit," he replied with a rich laugh. We agreed to meet in Brooklyn, on Eastern Parkway—our first stop being Dubrow's Cafeteria Restaurant.

"Tell me what you look like so I can spot you."

"Well don't be shocked," he warned me. "I'm a big guy and I have a lot of tattoos."

28

New York Noir, Redux

New York, August 2015

We were returning to Brooklyn. The on-the-ground team for this new adventure consisted of Mark, Maria, Cousin Jared, Eric, and Emery—a videographer. Although the return was prompted by Maria's insistence that the satchel and Abe's list of authorities on the take were located at Lincoln Place—I saw it as an opportunity to document the locations we had visited five months earlier. I hired Emery, a talented young videographer from the Bay Area who had worked on the crew that filmed Dad's TV show. He was honored to film our family story, and his humble and heartfelt expression of that sentiment meant a lot to me.

Mark was taking care of minor details like the car rental. Maria was finishing up her cross-country summer ghostbusting tour and meeting us in New York. Emery and Eric accompanied me on a 6 a.m. flight from San Francisco to JFK.

There was a lot of anticipation around returning to Lincoln Place. Previously, we hadn't had a chance to really look through the basement for the supposed satchel/paperwork or for the objects on the adjacent lot. Maria was now feeling very confident where the missing paperwork was located—somewhere around the ancient dumbwaiter. Eric and I were prepared for rummaging through the dank recesses of the toxic storage room. We packed elbow-length gloves, facemasks, and headlamps for the team. If there was something to find, we were determined to find it.

On the plane, Emery and I were absorbed in plotting our location shoot schedule. Eric was excitedly bouncing and twisting to disco songs on his iPod two rows behind us. He was quick-witted, intelligent, and very high energy always cracking jokes and singing songs. He had been extremely helpful in my research and knew Maria from the New Orleans adventure many years ago. I was thrilled he was coming along.

Emery was thoughtful and fun loving, and he knew how to be present and ingratiating with strangers—an essential function for a documentarian. He was excellent at staying focused, as well as blending in with whomever he was talking to at the time. He quickly took up smoking cigarettes in order to join Eric and me during our "time-out escapes."

We decided to return to Lincoln Place in the early evening hours to film our search through the basement. We chose the evening for several reasons: The temperature would be cooler, most of the tenants would be out and about on a Saturday night, and Maria felt the spirits were more active during those hours. Mostly, I wanted to make sure we had a break during the day—we were covering a lot of locations and it was the hottest time of the year.

August 22, 2015

Maria arrived at our Upper West Side AirBnB at 9:00 a.m. She was dressed in T-shirt and jeans for a day in the stagnant heat. Her layers of silver jewelry accentuated her tattooed tan skin and wisps of soft gray hair peeked out of a camouflage cap. She knocked on Eric's bedroom door, winked at me, and slipped into the room to surprise him. I knew Eric was excited to see her. It had been twenty years, almost to the day, that we had a very different paranormal experience with Maria in New Orleans. It had been life-changing for Eric. He had learned on that trip that he was sensitive to spirit activity, and although he didn't utilize or understand that part of himself, he did regularly pick up feelings about places. Maria had helped him through an emotional event with a spirit at Le Petit Théâtre, recorded in Katherine Ramsland's book *Ghost*.

By 10 a.m., Emery had wired Maria with a lavalier microphone pack for the day's filming and Mark was waiting in front of our building with the SUV humming. Mark was always the driver on these excursions, navigating the streets. We purposely planned not to go down the West Side Highway, taking a route to the East Side and eventually over the Manhattan Bridge to Brooklyn. We didn't want to risk Maria having another episode near the Twin Towers location.

Emery filmed out the window of the passenger seat while Mark told stories of old Brooklyn. Maria excused herself and put on headphones, blasting Heavy Metal music to block out psychic interference, shielding herself for the first location.

We planned to visit the same places that we'd gone to on the March trip so that Emery could capture them on video, as well as anything new that Maria might channel. Thanks to Cousin Jared's revelation about Midnight Rose's candy store in Brownsville, we would be visiting that historic site as well. Maria didn't want to be told anything about this new location before we got there. She said it helped to keep her visions pure. I was eager to see what she might pick up about Uncle Frankie.

As we made our way across East 79th Street, Maria suddenly removed her headphones and asked the group, "Are we going to another place where business was conducted? There is a lot of physical pain associated with this place. The building is very old." She started to grunt and make painful noises. "I'm also picking up a name...sounds like '*Rachelle-lee-o.*'" She put her headphones back on, saying she'd let us know if she got another hit.

It was crowded and muggy on the Parkway as we neared Utica Avenue in Brooklyn. The small storefront shops were packed close together—beauty supply stores, express food stops, candy and smoke shops, and discount clothing stores. As we neared the Dubrow's location, Maria recognized the neighborhood from our last visit and removed her headphones. She announced that she was starting to get a headache and other physical symptoms which meant Abe and Frankie were present. She was confused as to why she was sensing Frankie here as opposed to Lincoln Place.

Mark parked and stayed near the SUV, watching the street. Eric was on the lookout for Cousin Jared. Emery and I followed Maria to the front of the discount clothing store that once was Dubrow's Cafeteria Restaurant.

Maria repeated what she had seen on our initial visit so Emery could record it. Her version of what happened never changed, but small details were added. When she finished recapping Abe's talk with Amen in front of St. Matthews Church, she sat down in the shade of a tree in front of the church's entrance.

As I turned to follow her, I noticed a big guy standing with Eric watching us—six feet tall, buzzed hair and sunglasses, wearing long, red board shorts and a black t-shirt. It was Cousin Jared. I stared at him for the longest moment—he looked exactly like the photograph I had of young Uncle Frankie. I went to greet him and then introduced him to Maria, who was also struck by the uncanny resemblance.

"I said I wasn't going to get sidetracked today, but there is someone standing with you," Maria said as she shook Jared's hand. I hadn't told Maria anything about Jared other than he was a cousin, but she immediately picked up his backstory.

"You are a record keeper. You have information about the mystery location we are going to today. I'm seeing Frankie…he's talking to you about this location, there's a knowledge that you have…stories…from this location."

Jared stood motionless, listening to Maria as she bowed her head and started rotating her fingers in circles. "I keep seeing a name that looks like 'Rachelle-lee-o'…Frankie is here, he's poking me in the ribs and talking about the new location we are visiting. Frankie has a kinship with you…there's a male figure walking with you who knows Frankie…I keep hearing something about a business…not that you are in the family business, but there is a kinship to this business…a lot of information is flying back and forth between you, Frankie, and the figure walking with you…it's like old home week with them right now."

"Who's standing with Jared?" I asked.

"It's a mix of the Cousin Michael side and the Frankie side…it's a melding of the two. He's paternal…a father…no, a grandfather. I see him taking you by the hand and guiding you…you are walking with your grandfather. This is an important part of your life and you're supposed to carry on the story…but…you look like your ancestor—I'm seeing you as your ancestor. Your mannerism and speech are like Frankie. It's like he has come back to tell the story." Maria looked up at Jared. "This is an honor. Let me stay connected to you, because I'll probably get more information as the day goes along."

"I'm interested in hearing," Jared replied.

"You walk with people who guide and support you. I keep getting the name 'Rachelle-lee-o'...it's like two names in one...I'm getting two people standing with you."

"Rachel?" asked Eric, knowing that was Grandma Rae's birth name.

"Yes!...Rachel!" Maria acknowledged. "And then Leo...the "L's" are intertwined...."

Jared was shocked by the acknowledgment of Leo. Maria started to choke-up. "There was a very special bond between Rachel and Leo. It's beautiful...they are walking with Jared...the temperature in this area is cold...you can feel it."

I reached my hand out to feel the air near Maria, as she wiped tears from her eyes. It was cooler near her—a sign of spirit activity—than the hot summer air around the rest of us.

"We have to go now," motioned Maria. "We need to go to the place connected with Jared."

Midnight Rose's Candy Store, 779 Saratoga Avenue

Everyone squeezed into the SUV and we made our way to the "mystery location"—the old headquarters of Murder, Inc. The corner of Saratoga and Livonia Avenues lay in the shadow of the elevated 3 train. Mark warned this would be the most dangerous area we would visit and not to let our guard down. We were the only Caucasian people in this run-down area of Brownsville.

What had once been Midnight Rose's candy store was now a market/bodega. Mark parked directly in front of the graffiti-laden building on Livonia. The intersection was swarming with cars leaving trails of loud rap music in their wake, motorcycles zinging past, and the deafening clack of the train. The two-story building included two street-level establishments: the market and a Jamaican hole-in-the-wall eatery called Stumpy's Spot.

The location was causing Maria to feel sick and she didn't want to get out of the car, afraid that she might pass out. We opened the hatchback, so she could stay in the safety of the SUV's cargo area, yet still see the building which was ten feet away.

"We don't like this building," she said, her hand nervously covering her mouth. "I see some strange textured façade on it from the old days, with bullet holes in it." Maria was correct. Back in the 1940s the building had a rough detailed brick exterior, which currently had a muted brick-colored paint.

Jared stayed close to Maria holding a digital recorder while Emery and I circled around her with cameras. Eric disappeared from my view, walking around the outskirts of the building. Mark patrolled the corner, chatting up the locals, who stopped to stare at Emery's filming, pointing and shouting, "Look, it's HBO!"

"There's a panic inside this building," said Maria. "I don't want to go inside. It feels dirty and painful here…a lot of death and frenetic energy…I'm seeing Frankie here and I don't understand why…your people don't belong here."

Maria was seeing two different stories: a little boy hiding behind a man's leg, peeking out watching a fight, and also a swarthy, greasy man with a pock-marked face named Shapiro. "Whatever happened here, there's a lot of death and radiating pain."

Maria saw Frankie go into the building and up to a second level where she said there was an office. "Then I see Frankie coming out of the building and the Shapiro guy follows him…he's a low-life who has visions of taking over. He's saying *just you wait, this is going to be mine.*' He gets into an altercation with Frankie and beats him. Upstairs in the building there is another person of higher rank who's in control and connected to the history of this building from back in the day…Frankie went up to the office, wasn't there for too long, then Frankie comes out and I feel all his pain…the same physical pain I felt at Lincoln Place."

Maria closed her eyes and was quiet for several minutes. Jared and I kept exchanging glances, knowing what we did about Frankie and the location.

"Frankie was tenacious...a real fighter...he didn't back down. I keep hearing the name Leo here as well. Leo witnessed a lot of stuff here he shouldn't have seen. It feels like he was here when Frankie was here... and he shouldn't have been. The second floor makes me sick, it smells bad. Frankie was beaten here...I don't know if he then dragged himself to Lincoln place or was taken there...I don't understand it all yet."

Eric appeared from around the corner. His lips were quivering and his eyes red. He went over to Maria in the open hatchback of the car. "Oh God!" he said with panic in his voice, then whispered that he had experienced an overwhelming sense of pain associated with the building and visions of people screaming "No!"

"You need to sit down," Maria directed Eric, waving a smudge stick over him to clear the energy. "There was some kind massacre here," said Maria. "There's a lot of blood and bullet holes everywhere...there's blood on the street...something upstairs isn't right either. I don't know why this area had such an appeal for murder, but it did. It makes me sick."

"Are you picking up stuff too?" I asked Eric.

"Oh, girl..." he sighed, shaking as he huddled near Maria.

"Why is your family here?" Maria asked again. "They shouldn't be at this location. There's a piece to this whole thing that's missing." Maria went into a trance again, sitting motionless with her legs crossed indian-style; the humid summer air engulfed us as we anxiously waited for her next message.

"I'm being told to tell you 'Goldstein' and 'Philly'...it has to do with Frankie. I was told that Frankie was in hiding at some point and I see an image of three row houses with pointy A-frame roofs on a cobblestone street...and a plaque with the word 'fishtown' on it. I don't know what it all means, but it appears that there was some 'business' taking place there. There's a lot of fear and anxiety associated with this 'fishtown.'"

Eric pulled out his cell phone and immediately Googled Fishtown. "It's a neighborhood bordering on the Delaware River in Philadelphia...

and look...," He thrust the phone toward me showing images of a Fishtown area with cobblestone streets and row houses.

"Jesus," I said and turned toward Maria. "I just recently learned that Goldstein was one of Frankie's aliases and Abe did have territory in Philly."

"Oh, Shit!" Maria responded, rocking backwards. "It seems that Frankie went to Fishtown to do business, but I still see his beatings in New York and then his body in water."

"With the recent information I found in the court papers, it makes sense that Frankie may have been in hiding in Philly for a while, then came back to New York."

"It would seem we have a new angle on the Frankie scenario," Jared responded in amazement.

Mark and Emery joined us, gathering around the hatchback of the SUV. "Let's tell Maria where we are," I said, and then recounted the history of Murder, Inc., how the building had been their headquarters, and their office had been on the second floor of the building.

"Leo told me that Frankie received a call to show up here and then was never heard from again," Jared continued. "Leo always said that if you got called to this place for any reason, you weren't coming home that night."

"The big question is who was hanging out at Midnight Rose's in 1947?" I asked our group.

"It felt like they were lower-level street scum, trying to be something they weren't," Maria said.

She again described feeling the same physical sensations of her nose and lungs filling with fluid, and the taste of blood and dirty water in her mouth. She kept seeing a slanted wall, like a reservoir. "I see him in a dark, cold place when he actually died...dark green-black water in a brick tunnel. I can't breathe there."

"Oh," I said. "You drew me a picture a few months ago of the tunnel you saw Frankie in—It looked like a 7 and a reverse 7."

"Where's the nearest body of water to here?" asked Eric.

"It could be the border of Canarsie and Pennsylvania Avenue," Mark replied. "There used to be marshes there, where bodies were dumped in the old days. When they were building the housing project at Starrett City, off the Fresh Creek Basin in East New York, they told the workers to just keep bulldozing no matter what they found."

"So, Frankie gets called here, but there's also the scenario of the cops beating him at Lincoln Place. Did this happen on the same day?" Eric questioned.

Maria nodded. "I see injuries here to Frankie, then a *'hurry up before he expires so we get the information.'* They couldn't do any more to him. With the amount of pain Frankie felt I don't know how he survived getting to Lincoln Place, but he did. Something horrible happened here, and there, then I see him in a dark, cold brick tunnel with water."

"It makes more sense that they called Frankie here and then took him to Lincoln place," suggested Mark. "The closest water to Lincoln Place would be the Gowanus Canal, which is another place where bodies were dumped."

"Let's put this all together," I interrupted. "The Surrogate Court papers exposed a clear timeline for Frankie. We now know that he was released from Riker's Island in 1944. He attended his brother's wedding and was released from parole by June of 1945."

"Then he probably went to Fishtown in Philly to keep the family out of his line of fire," added Jared. "He may have had some numbers action going there as well."

"Then his mother, Anna, dies in 1946 and he returns to New York," I continued. "Leo's back from the war and goes to work for him—maybe even going between Philly and New York for the rackets. In 1947, Frankie signs the probate consent, but things are starting to get heated and the cops are pressing in on him, trying to find the ledger of names from the headquarters—probably because they were all under indictment at that time for their extortion of policy racketeers."

"If Frankie knew who was responsible for Abe's death he may have been threatening them or vice versa," said Jared.

"Yes, Frankie's getting nervous," I said. "He meets with Mudsy at the Ralph Avenue Deli, and according to Aunt Carol he is worried about something at the old headquarters. Shortly after that he's summoned here, to Midnight Rose's candy store, where he places his last call to Aunt Bertha that he is coming over for dinner within the hour."

"Then I see Frankie being beaten by the swarthy man named Shapiro," added Maria.

"And it's Shapiro who then delivers Frankie to the cops who are waiting for him at Lincoln Place," I suggested. "Wallander, Heffernan, and the cop Jonesy try to get Frankie to find the paperwork at the old headquarters, and then they kill him, dumping his body in a canal."

Incredibly, it seemed Frankie's story was revealed. Still, I felt I had to verify if his inheritance had been picked up at some point. I was still waiting to hear from the New York State Comptroller's office for an answer.

"They are telling me *'on to the next location,'*" stated Maria.

Later, when I researched the Gowanus Canal, I discovered that there were brick-lined tunnels at the head of the canal, built in the 1880s to flush the sewage out, that had been used until the mid 1960s. There are multi-level tunnels in the Gowanus, and the water is a chemical-laden green-black. It has been referred to as "the only body of water in the world that is 90% guns,"[1] as well as being one of the most polluted bodies of water in the United States.

Van Sinderen Avenue

On our last trip to the Van Sinderen Avenue location of Abe's death, the fencing had been padlocked and the road below the El train inaccessible. This time the fence was open.

As we approached the entrance to the long dirt road, Maria declared, "I'm walkin' it," and headed down the garbage-strewn gravel stretch. The rest of us gave her space, milling about near the entrance.

At the halfway point, Maria knelt down, peering at the remaining length of road. The echoes of children playing from the high-rise on the other side of the gulley were intermittently silenced by the train's deafening clack as it roared overhead.

I went to join her, and she pointed to the left. "This isn't right. There is a body buried over there...it has nothing to do with Abe, but it's disturbing...and distracting me." I looked in the direction of her gesture and saw the bottom of a sneaker that was so deeply imbedded into the ground it had become part of the road. "This is a popular spot for mayhem," she added, standing up from her crouched position, walking to the edge of the road, then kneeling down again and bowing her head in concentration.

"I'm having horrific pain and ringing in my ears...I'm getting a message...*'you should have listened'*...*'you shouldn't have'*...," Maria looked up at me abruptly. "Oh! There's someone standing behind you right now...he looks like the White Fedora Man."

Everything seemed to suddenly turn to slow motion as I met her gaze. The air was suddenly still and a strange sound started to build—a howl of wind—coming out of nowhere. There was no other noise, just the two of us alone, in the dead heat. "What the fuck?" Maria exclaimed.

We heard it again. It reverberated like wind through a microphone. "This is off the hook! It's White Fedora Man. He's trying to communicate!" Maria shouted with excitement. "An ice-cold breeze just came through here!" she cried out, then started rocking back and forth, staying close to the ground. I stood completely still, freaked-out by the strange sound.

"*'Fighting'*...*'last'*...the cops were fighting at the end of Abe's life... White Fedora Man is telling me his side of the story...I got the word *'hassle'*...first off, thank you for being here," Maria said to the spirit.

"White Fedora Man is showing me a big argument happening, through his eyes...I hear a bunch of different people...there was a mistake made with Abe's car...the argument is surrounding Abe's car...everyone is talking at once...I'm trying to pull words from the white noise I'm hearing."

Maria was shown a chaotic scene under the train tracks when Abe was shot. "The whole situation with Abe's car was a debacle...someone made a mistake...the arguing is crazy...it looks like five people around Abe...one in the back, three around him and then someone over to the left…the energy spinning around this scene is nauseating…Abe is on the ground…there's a lot of yelling and finger pointing…they are saying *'what the hell is this?'*…and there are uniformed and non-uniformed people there…they are going in Abe's pocket and then shaking their heads… *'see!'…'I bet you'*…it's a bit of a sentence, and then they said something about going *'back to the desk'*…they have to go back to the precinct to do something at a desk…the argument is all heated and full of blame."

"Who drove Abe's car to Empire Boulevard?" I asked.

"*'Escort'…'left with'*…they are showing me two cars, one following the other…but I can't hold the image…*'two cars leaving.'*" She continued rocking back and forth, repeating, "*'You should have listened,'*…Abe responds *'I know, I know.'*"

Eric and Emery approached us, curious as to why we looked so shaken. "The police officers are talking about *'erasing'* the rest of the *'family'*…and something about relocation," Maria said between deep breaths. "I just heard someone whisper *'I'm sorry'*…it's White Fedora Man…he has regrets…*'I'm sorry.'*"

Eric and I looked at each other with surprise. We had spent most of the previous week speculating about what Abe had requested of Amen that he found "too extreme." The newspapers had reported Abe was negotiating his terms to testify. Eric and I felt it had to be about relocating the family, and now Maria was channeling it.

"*'Time to leave, can't stay'…'time to leave'*…," she repeated several times. "It could be the police talking…or it could be Abe, knowing it's his time to go."

Mark and Jared had gathered behind Eric and Emery as Maria slowly rose and then stumbled backwards. "I'm trying to protect myself from his death experience…shit, I can barely stand up." Her breathing turned heavy and she started sniffing her hands. "I smell fire and something chalky on my hands."

"Gun powder and sulfur," Mark said as he went to assist her. "That's the smell of a fired gun."

Maria nodded in agreement as Mark and Eric helped her slowly walk back towards the car.

Jared and I remained, absorbing the location. The surrounding sounds of distant children were prominent again, and rather dizzying. For Maria, all the sounds—natural and unnatural—must have been completely overwhelming.

"This is crazy," Jared said. I was still in shock from the experience and unable to speak. "It's amazing to be down here," he continued. "This is a part of New York that hasn't changed over the decades. I'm so honored to be part of this journey." He put his arm around my shoulder and we walked back toward the car.

Lincoln Place

At 7:30 p.m., Mark and I were investigating the backyard area of Lincoln Place, looking for the key that Tina, the basement tenant, had hidden for us. Maria was hyperventilating in front of the building, not yet ready to go inside. She stood on the street with Eric, who was keeping a lookout for Jared who was arriving separately. Mark had warned us that we would need to leave immediately if anyone questioned us. We didn't want to get arrested for breaking and entering because Tina wasn't home to vouch for us. We needed to keep a low profile and all agreed to silence cell phones and keep noise to a bare minimum.

Once Jared arrived, we entered the basement from the narrow alleyway, one by one, and immediately got busy. The key only opened the main basement door. Once in the entryway across from the laundry room, we had to jimmy the lock of the inner basement door to access the large storage area where the dumbwaiter was located. Donning long rubber gloves and holding flashlights, we moved through the inner door and down the hallway, passing a small alcove to our left which housed a security camera system monitoring the front and rear doors of the building. This system had not been there five months earlier and surprised all of us. "The cameras are active and working. We need to stay quiet," whispered Mark. We all nodded in agreement.

We entered the large, cluttered storage area of the basement. Mark and I started moving boxes and broken objects that were piled in front of the dumbwaiter. Emery and Eric were dealing with video tech stuff. Maria was getting hit with psychic energy and appeared to be in a state of paralyzing bewilderment. She nervously entered the smaller storage area across from the laundry room, where she had seen Frankie's beating.

"Holy shit!" she hollered, opening the door to the small room. She claimed it swung back at her. "Something is trying to keep me out. Okay...I'm coming in." As she opened the door again, she stood frozen in the archway, "Damn, there's a huge shadow figure in here." Maria carefully ventured in, followed by Emery and Eric with cameras. "There's a shadow man standing right here," she pointed straight ahead in astonishment. "He's big and looks like he's about to lose his shit, he's so mad we're here."

Suddenly Jared's cell phone went off, startling all of us. The ringtone sounded like an old-fashioned phone and echoed throughout the basement. "Damn," whispered Mark, rolling his eyes.

Emery asked if the overhead light could be turned on for filming, but Maria wanted darkness. To add some light, we put on headlamps, looking like miners in a cave. Maria took two large, rusted vintage keys from her belted fanny-pack. She explained she often used them to contact spirits during a séance. We were assessing all the new junk that had accumulated since our last visit in the smaller room, when suddenly Maria yelped in pain several times and bent over holding her side. "The shadow man is punching me in the ribs." She dropped to her knees. "There's another man here also, with a gray fedora...he has a huge head...it's Heffernan." Maria started panting with pain, announcing that her ears were ringing. Then she started calling out directions about where to look for the hidden documentation.

"Look behind the dumbwaiter...look behind the dumbwaiter."

I went down the hallway to the larger room and reported what Maria had said. The dumbwaiter shaft was sealed shut with nails. Mark and Jared were searching through the room's junk for something to pry open the shaft.

In the smaller room, Maria was bent over in a crouched position, dry-heaving. "I'm getting kicked in the ribs over and over again, and Frankie is saying *I don't have more to give*...they're saying something like *'money key'*...there's another space behind the dumbwaiter...I don't know if it's a room or a space...but there's something behind it."

Mark and Jared were trying to open the dumbwaiter's front cover with a makeshift screw driver. "We need a better tool for this," Mark whispered.

Eric was searching the wall-length ledge of strewn garbage, adjacent to the dumbwaiter, for anything that resembled a satchel or the paper we were seeking. I kept moving between the two rooms, delivering Maria's instructions.

"*'Tell the boy with the numbers...there's a false floor.'*" Maria rhythmically banged the rusted keys on the concrete floor in a trance-like state. The small room's dark four-foot crawl space had a door laid across it like a walkway, where the actual ground was below, the concrete broken. Emery and I tried to lift it, but found dead rats underneath and dropped it back into place.

Mark could hear the residents directly above the basement. The rotting ceiling boards over the dumbwaiter had small pinholes that peered through the apartment floor above. It was not enough to see anything, but we could hear the muffled conversation of a woman and a man, which meant they could probably hear us as well.

I peered down the hallway to see that Maria had exited the smaller room and was now sitting by the basement entryway, Indian-style on the floor, with her head down, muttering repeatedly, "*Why is he back...you with the numbers, why are you back?*"

As I walked toward her, she instructed me not to go back into the small room. "The spirits are angry and might start flinging objects at us." I closed the door of the small room. "Someone is coming...a living person is coming."

I reached behind Maria and bolted the main entrance shut from the inside. She slowly picked herself up and relocated to the security camera room, tumbling to the floor like a rag doll, and doubling over in pain. "It feels like something is coming out of my ribs," she started to sob. "My ribs feel like they are splitting in two...it's hard to breathe...they keep saying *'you with the numbers why are you back'*...they are talking about Jared...they think he's Frankie!"

Back at the dumbwaiter, the guys were getting nervous about being discovered and pointed to the ceiling, where the conversation in the apartment above was getting louder, and footsteps could be heard, shuffling back and forth. Jared shined his flashlight through the ceiling area of the dumbwaiter to show me where he and Mark were exploring the recessed spaces between the beams. He had found papers, but they were just garbage. I warned them that Maria thought someone was coming.

Suddenly, Maria screamed from down the hall, "Something's wrong!" Mark and I went to her side. "It feels like something is coming out of my ribs!" She lifted the side of her T-shirt revealing red splotches across her rib cage. They were hot to the touch. She started sobbing again. Mark helped her rise to her feet, and we moved into the main room with the others. Maria couldn't stand and sat down on the floor holding her ribs, repeating, "It's a *'money key'* or a large wallet...there's a folded letter in what looks like a long leather wallet...tucked into a crevice of the dumbwaiter."

"I think they called it a money-grip," said Mark. "I'd love to get the dumbwaiter open, but we can't get more than four of the screws out. We need a tool...and we need to go *very* soon." He disappeared down the hallway to check the security cameras, and then returned. "Someone is ringing Tina's bell, obviously to see what's going on down here. We can't do this much longer."

Maria told Jared that the message "the boy with the numbers" was for him, and he would know what to do with the letter when we found it. "You know something about numbers. It's like a register that you would understand." She raised herself slowly to a standing position, bracing her body against the wall. "That's it...I can't do this anymore...my body can't take this excruciating pain."

Jared and I looked at each other with frustration. We were going to have to call it a night before we could find the supposed evidence. "Let me take one last look," I insisted, stepping onto a stack of dry cement bags to heighten my view through the broken ceiling beams above the dumbwaiter, debris falling around me.

Suddenly, footsteps could be heard coming down the outside steps to the main basement entrance, followed by the rattle of keys. All six of us froze.

Eric reached for the hallway light switch and flicked it off. We were all standing in the dark, listening to the main door jiggle. I had bolted it, so I knew no one was coming in. When the person was unsuccessful, we heard their footsteps climbing the outside stairs to the street.

"We need to get the hell out of here!" Mark declared, switching the lights back on.

Eric, eager to be the first one out, unbolted the entryway door as the rest of us quickly gathered our belongings. Just then, footsteps could be heard descending the outside steps again.

Eric flicked off the lights for a second time and ran to my side. We were standing in the dark holding our breath. A million versions of what I might say when that door opened were racing through my mind. I nudged Eric to flick the lights back on. I had no excuse for standing in darkness with five other people.

The next thing we heard was a key being inserted into the door—this time it wasn't locked from the inside. It was the longest turn of a handle, as the door slowly opened. A Rastafarian man carrying a basket of laundry walked in. He didn't seem phased whatsoever to see us. "Hey," he nodded in our direction. We were still as statues.

"Hey," I responded back.

The man quickly turned into the laundry room. Our group exchanged glances and then bolted out the door, up the steps, through the black gate, and ran down St. Charles Place to our SUV parked near the corner of St. Johns.

Maria crawled into the backseat of the car and lay down. The rest of us stood on the corner of St. Johns Place, under the yellow glow of a street lamp, smoking cigarettes and excitedly rehashing what had just happened—and where the leather clutch could possibly be. Mark and

Eric sensed that the disintegrating ceiling boards opened up behind the dumbwaiter shaft, but they couldn't reach it.

We were so close to the locating the documentation that I hated to leave, and even toyed with the idea of going back in 15 minutes. Mark shook his head at me. "We're lucky they didn't call the cops and have us arrested." We all looked at each other, then burst into laughter at the ridiculousness of it all.

"Why did Maria call you *'the boy with the numbers,'*" I asked Jared. He shared that he had been a commodities broker at the World Trade Center before 9/11 and explained that the stock market was not regulated back in the old days as it is now. "If you showed up with $100k in your pocket back then, they didn't ask questions. You just dumped your money into the market for a few weeks, took it out, and you had a legit reason to have that money in your hands—it was money washing. Today that would send up red flags. What Maria saw could be a money grip with a brokerage slip in it, hiding the money they were making. Or it could be Abe's list of names."

Now that Maria knew exactly where the money grip and paper was, Jared was anxious to find it. "I'll come back tomorrow if I have to," he said with determination.

"You have to check this with Tina first," said Mark. "I wouldn't take the chance coming on your own. It's one thing to be in there, it's another to be in there with a crowbar breaking something open."

29

The Racket Buster

Santa Cruz, Autumn 2015

The second Brooklyn adventure had been a fast trip, but we had learned a lot. Maria had uncovered Frankie's story and I was feeling confident that it was most probably what had happened. I still wanted to verify if he had picked up his inheritance. That would be the final piece of his story, and I was still waiting for those documents.

The movements of Abe's final night were clear, as was a deeper meaning for the murder—the list of authorities he possessed had held deadly consequences.

I still needed to polish my list of culprits and had a few post-Brooklyn questions for Maria, which included trying to make contact with John Harlan Amen. If any spirit had answers to Abe's murder it would be the "Racket Buster" himself.

When we connected for a video session, she immediately described having "discombobulated dreams" about the family, and was given the words "rose," "gold," and "twist."

"Maria, you are amazing!" I laughed out loud.

"I don't know what the words mean or what they have to do with anything." She shook her head.

I told her it was a name. Rose Gold was a real person who worked with "Kid Twist."

"But it doesn't feel real," Maria replied. "They are words with no body attached to them…it's Rose *and* Gold…like it's a cover…a con. I don't know how else to describe it."

In the last week, Eric and I had been doing extensive research on Rose Gold, the owner of Midnight Rose's candy store. We were trying to figure out who was operating out of that location in the mid-1940s when Frankie would have returned there. It had been difficult to find information on Rose Gold after her arrest in 1939 for running Murder, Inc.'s books and a prostitution ring.

"Maybe I was picking up on you and Eric," Maria said thoughtfully. "But, the name gives me a weird feeling…it feels pretend."

"She's real," I replied for the second time. "She owned the candy store where Murder, Inc. hung out—where we went in Brooklyn."

"No," insisted Maria. "Her name was used by someone…it's a cover."

I didn't understand what she was getting at, but jotted some notes, and we moved on.

"When I read your request to talk with Amen, right before we started, he immediately came through and hasn't stopped talking, so I never got to the rest of your list," Maria chuckled. "He said, *'there were 70'*…when I saw Abe's ledger there were 20 to 23 names on it, but Amen's saying there was another list with 50 or more names of people who were involved in the Abe issue…I got the last name of *'Connor.'*"

Maria had given me this name before, in an earlier session naming the men responsible for the hit on Abe—all of whom were recorded in Amen's Grand Jury report.

"Connor relates to the *'shamus'* in the restaurant that night with Abe," Maria continued. "I saw the shamus with a big head, and Connor has an even bigger head. But I don't know who he is…but there are pictures of him…Amen's showing me film, like 35mm film, that looks like surveillance pictures on a film strip."

I retrieved my copy of Amen's report from my files and turned to the page where I had written down the names Maria had been given. Robert E. Connor was a police officer Amen indicted and the report did contain surveillance footage stills of several different cops taking bribes from bookies. But there was no photo of Connor. "Is he in uniform or regular clothes?" I asked.

"A uniform," Maria responded, after which I held up the filmstrip surveillance evidence from the report. "Yes! That's what it looks like!"

"This is from Amen's actual report," I told her.

"Whooaa!" she responded, and started vigorously fanning herself. "He keeps saying *'there were 70'*…I don't know what it means…Amen is here…it's difficult for him to come through, so he's showing me numbers and names on paper and these surveillance photographs. He's saying *'70'* and *'spent'*…ask him questions."

"I've been trying to find Amen's personal papers that correspond with his investigation, such as the hundreds of tips he received from the public about Abe's death. Can he tell us about those?"

"That's what he's showing me…papers are blowing away or being thrown away…*'70 spent.'* He's saying *'the higher-ups did it'*…and to *'look at the list of names.'*" Maria started drawing with her finger in the air. "The second list of people has titles under their names. They aren't officers…they range from high-ranking officials to clerk names…and they have to do with the blocking of—or taking of—funds."

"Can Amen verify that he spoke to Abe that last night by the old gate on Eastern Parkway?" I asked.

"I heard three words…*'victory seemed nice'*…it seems that he thought everything was going to be ok…keep talking to Amen so we can get info from him while he's here."

"Who does he feel was responsible for killing Abe?" I asked.

"I see the pages flying away again, and he said…*'two'*…when you asked who killed Abe he showed me two…he's saying *'surrounded'*…*'the original source'*…Abe was ambushed, more people were involved…I'm getting a name like *'Levine'*…Levine, Connor, and two others orchestrated this…he's talking very fast, like he's frantic."

"Who ordered the hit? Who had the most to hide?" I asked.

"Very loud and clearly he said, *'all of them'*…he's showing the list with the names of higher officials that evidently weren't caught…this list had the ability to alter things…he keeps saying *'they had boats and things they shouldn't have had.'*"

That was in the report! Amen had written that officers had boats, took lavish vacations, and had large bank accounts that didn't match their wages.

"...he's saying that officials were going round and round with him, and wouldn't give him the info he wanted. The list that didn't make it to public view named people who had a lot to hide...and again he's giving me the number 70...I don't know if it's 70 pages or 70 people."

Yes!—DA Clerk James Moran had hidden the paperwork from Amen on the waterfront rackets! "Did Abe's death keep Amen from prosecuting certain people?" I asked.

Maria nodded her head with a definite yes. "He's showing me something that's type-written...it looks like a report with names and occupations. He's telling me they all worked together...I heard *'District Attorney'*...something about the Police Commissioner isn't boding well either...*'Heffernan'*...all were in cahoots...*'Harry'*.... a Harry has something to do with this...he is a *'final visitor'*...Amen's walking through an office, and there is lots of *'handing off'* happening...the guys who did the hit, including White Fedora Man, did not order it...they did it for someone else...they did it for everyone above them."

I asked Maria if Abe was killed for more than just the list of names.

"Amen's saying Abe *'was smart'*...he had a lot of information and he was a smart man...he saw what was going on, and if he had been in a situation of safety this would have been one of the most infamous cases of dirty officials that would have shaken the City...*'he knew about it all.'* Amen's showing me the candy store we went to...Abe had a lot of information about that place...he had a lot of info on the cops and more."

Maria was silent for a moment then blurted, "Holy shit!" She started fanning herself again, rocking back and forth. "He has more to tell you...he's saying *'research and review'*...*'look at the island'*...do you have something laying around?...maybe look at a map...he's saying *'look at the tower'*...he's telling me, to tell you, to go to a tower...I don't understand what he means."

I didn't understand either. The only map in my office was of Brooklyn, pinned onto the large crime board I had created. I got up from my chair to examine it, disappearing from Maria's view on the video call.

"A Harry Walsh is on my crime board, he was a 2nd Assistant DA," I yelled to Maria, removing the pushpin from the news article on

O'Dwyer's cabinet and reviewing it more closely. "There's also an Edward Levine listed as an Assistant DA as well."

"Oh, crap!" Maria hollered, fanning herself faster.

The two news articles on my crime board that I was reviewing were about the police Amen took down—and they were directly behind the tower of my wireless router. The 'tower' was my router!

Suddenly my chest started to hurt, and a wave of nausea swept over me. "You're experiencing symptoms...welcome to my crazy," Maria smirked. "When the spirits come in hard and fast you have no control over it." She suggested I burn the Palo Santo wood she had given me to clear my space. "Hold on, there's more...He keeps saying 'tower' and something about a citizen came and met with him...Jesus, I don't know this kind of language...'citizen met in the original state'...he's talking up a storm...Amen keeps saying 'state of review'...'keep reviewing.'"

Then, as quickly as Amen's spirit had come through, it disappeared. The messages seemed to explained why I couldn't find Amen's personal papers, the stalling of his investigation into corrupt officials by the DA's office, and verification of the names of those we thought had orchestrated Abe's death.

"Go back to reviewing your crime board," Maria instructed me. "He is going to help you research."

Several times Maria was given the names Connor, Beine (phonetic spelling, Be-hin-e), Jeffrey, Kelly, and Sweeney, as the culprits who fulfilled the hit. In Amen's final investigation, that made it to public viewing, the following men were listed:

- Robert E. Connor—plainclothes duty for the 14th division. Retired during Amen's investigation to keep from testifying. Denied appeal to retire with benefits in 1942.
- Lawrence J. Beine—plainclothes duty for the PC squad. Retired during Amen's investigation to keep from testifying.
- Charles W. Jeffrey—plainclothes patrol for the 12th division. Charged with negligence and grafting.
- John E. Kelly—plainclothes duty for the 10th division and later became a lieutenant at the 70th precinct. Retired during Amen's inves-

tigation and ultimately was dismissed from the department in May of 1941. Kelly refused to sign a waiver of immunity before the Grand Jury.

- John Sweeney—First grade detective, once considered a hero in the narcotics squad.

The list appeared to neatly wrap-up those responsible. But there were a couple of discrepancies when matching up these men with the names Maria was given.

Although Robert E. Connor is mentioned in the Amen Report, and had caused a ruckus by refusing to sign a legal waiver of immunity and then quickly retired to escape testimony before Amen's grand jury, he doesn't quite match Maria's description. She saw Connor as a "bulldog of a man with a big head" whose image was captured on surveillance footage. Amen's final report does not contain surveillance images of Robert Connor.

But, Amen's report does include a patrolman named Patrick J. Connolly, who matches Maria's physical description, and there is footage of Connolly taking bribe money from bookie Teddy Levine (another name Maria was given) at 93 Grafton Street, just a few blocks from Midnight Rose's candy store. Connolly worked out of the 73rd precinct and was charged with misconduct, negligence, and grafting.

As I had discovered earlier, Maria's information sometimes needed the slightest bit of decoding. Maybe Patrick Connolly have been the Connor that Maria mentioned.

The other discrepancy with Maria's names was Beine. One of Amen's earliest investigations was into Lieutenant Cuthbert Behan, who was charged with stealing, mutilating, and destroying 7200 pages of police records from the Brooklyn Police Headquarters in regard to his involvement in the bail bond racket. Racketeer Abe Frosch, who took over Uncle Abe's territory after his murder, testified for Amen against Behan.

Behan had a long history of getting into departmental trouble beginning in 1921—everything from stealing from citizens to violating magistrate orders when at the Canarsie precinct. In 1940, after being indicted by Amen and serving a stint in jail, he was acquitted at a departmental trial, but ultimately ousted from the force—just 17 days before he was eligible for retirement. He went on to open a bar at Court and State streets which was well known for brawls and prostitutes from the waterfront crowd. There was often so much trouble there that an officer was assigned the detail of watching the bar. Behan had also worked closely with Chief John McGowan in the past, and I might add, he had a huge head! Could Cuthbert Behan have been complicit in the murder to help his old pals at the 69th precinct dispose of Uncle Abe? Or, was the name that Maria channeled the Lawrence Beine who was also in the Amen report?

The two new names Maria gave me—2nd assistant DA Harry Walsh and DA Edward H. Levine—along with Edward Heffernan, were members of the corrupt and often investigated DA's office under the direction of William Geoghan. When William O'Dwyer became DA in 1940, he kept the three men on as assistants. Heffernan was assigned to homicide cases, and Walsh and Levine were in the appeals division. Interestingly, Levine was one of the prosecuting DA's on Sam Kovner's appeal case (my fall guy), making sure Kovner was put away.

I wasn't sure what to do with all this new information—I'd never be able to prove any of these men were involved in Abe's killing—but if Amen were supposedly telling me to pay attention, I'd bet it would probably be a good idea to listen to him.

30

Scandal Royale

Returning home from an afternoon walk—a warm September breeze helping to clear my mind of all the new recent developments—I noticed the postman trying to cram something into my mailbox. He had a package for me.

I had received a bound copy of the FBI file on "Kid Twist" Reles, which I'd sent for a couple of months earlier. I ripped open the package, hoping there might be something in the file about his association with Uncle Abe. Unfortunately, much of the FBI file was nothing more than a lot of interoffice correspondence that had been redacted. *So much for the Freedom of Information Act.*

As I flipped through the pages, I came to the last section of the file, which contained a copy of a 25-cent paperback book copyrighted 1949 by E. E. Rice, simply titled *Murder, Inc.* Its cover tagline read, "The Hair-Raising Story in Pictures of America's Bloodiest Crime Ring." The small penny dreadful started with the famous Rosenthal murder case and then showcased tidbits on famous mob bosses Al Capone, Arnold Rothstein, and a summation of Special Prosecutor Thomas Dewey's early fight against the rackets. Why it was named a book on Murder, Inc. I couldn't understand.

Toward the back I came upon a short section on Lucky Luciano, leader of the syndicate, and his famous vice trial of 1936. Often tax evasion was the only charge authorities could get to stick on the big crime leaders. Special Prosecutor Thomas Dewey took another approach and vigorously pursued Luciano for his illicit enterprises—drug importing, numbers, industrial rackets—and finally nailed him for running houses of prostitution.

Luciano was picked up in Hot Springs, Arkansas and returned to New York. On January 31, 1936, Dewey staged a series of raids on Luciano's houses of ill repute and arrested hundreds of madams and girls, bringing them in for questioning. They would become the witnesses that would put Luciano away and ultimately have him deported back to Italy.

Dewey would not allow the women testifying at the trial to be photographed—only drawn by court sketch artists—and he had their names changed to protect them. As I turned the page, I came to a drawing of a woman. The caption simply stated she had testified against Luciano in court.

I was speechless—the drawing was a dead ringer for Grandma Rae. This woman, in a tailored jacket, had chin length dark hair and facial features similar to Rae's—full lips, rounded eyebrows, and a comparable nose. She wore a very distinctive pixie-ish hat that flipped up on one side with a long quail feather jutting off the brim.

The hat seemed vaguely familiar to me. I started combing through Rae's photo collection and finally found what was gnawing at me: a photo of Grandma from the late 1930s, early 1940s, wearing the exact same hat and jacket, dancing with her gangster boyfriend "Red Bill," whose name had been handwritten on the back of the photo.

Could this be the final piece of evidence proving that Rae really had been a call girl? In January of 1936, Rae would have been four-weeks pregnant with Dad and married to Max. Could it be possible she had testified against Luciano?

I scanned the drawing and emailed it to my mother and sister, asking them who the picture resembled—not stating where it came from. Without hesitation they both answered Rae. I also emailed it to Cousin Michael and his sister Sheila. Response: Absolutely Rae! My heart was racing as I started an online search about the trial.

One of the definitive writings on the case was Ellen Poulsen's *The Case Against Lucky Luciano*. Her book on the trial focused on the experiences of the witnesses—the syndicate madams and prostitutes from

1933 to 1936 who were held as material witnesses in the case. Her website had several drawings of women who testified during the trial. I found contact information and wrote Poulsen a letter of inquiry about the trial drawings. We had several exchanges, and Ellen was surprised that she had never seen the drawing from the FBI file that resembled Rae. She, too, felt the drawing was of Rae, although she noted that the mouth was different—Rae was smiling in the photograph and the drawing showed a woman "understandably nervous and despondent," wrote Poulsen. "You can just never be too sure."

This was a bombshell! I had tried to put Aunt Carol's story about Rae's secret life out of my mind many years ago, but here was yet another sign that the suspicions might be true. I wondered if any living relatives knew about this and said nothing out of respect. It seemed my Grandmother's life may have been classified for a very good reason.

Like tossing a pebble into a still lake, there was ripple after ripple, expanding and breaking the surface of silence. Looking for information about Abe and Frankie seemed to be continually leading to deeper family mysteries.

31

The Man Who
Knew Too Much

Cousin Jared and I were in constant communication. Although we were disappointed that the missing documentation at Lincoln Place wasn't found, we had turned our investigation to Leo, trying to piece together how it was that he knew so many details about the uncles. "Look, there's none better than you and me to get to the bottom of all this," Jared declared.

Our questions started a frenzied dialogue among the cousins. Initially, I felt guilty that I hadn't connected with many of them before this year, but I became keenly aware that it wasn't just I who hadn't connected. Several were estranged from one another, yet gathering the family's stories into one solid picture seemed to be bringing a few of us together.

The cousins were all abuzz to help us find information that would connect the dots between Leo's life and Uncle Frankie's last days. Cousin Sheila was talking to Cousin Debbie, Debbie was talking to her mother Miriam, I was talking to Cousin Terry, Cousin Michael was only talking to me, and Jared was talking to anyone who would listen.

"Jared is driving everyone nuts with questions," said his mother Debbie, on the phone to me one afternoon. She mentioned that her mother Miriam seemed reluctant to talk, but having found Leo's military records online, combined with stories collected over the years from Dad, Carol, and other relatives, we learned that Leo was a true survivor in many ways.

As a teenager Leo had his own group of pals, but he also enjoyed family dinners with "Kid Twist" Reles and the perks of being Frankie's favorite nephew—including taking joy rides around the neighborhood in his car and learning to use his pistol. Leo was the new generation of male blood in the family. In the fateful Fall of 1941, Leo found himself the man of the house when his father Mudsy was sent to jail, and he must have felt a deep sense of responsibility, forgoing his dreams of becoming a singer. But the family wanted him out of town—they couldn't have another man in the family fall victim to the streets or the corrupt police. On March 23, 1943, he got as far away as he could. He joined the army.

Initially stationed in Arkansas, where he was known to sing up a storm for his fellow troops, Leo became part of the 66th Infantry Division of the U.S. Army—nicknamed the Black Panther Division—and was aboard the U.S.S. Leopoldville when it was hit by a German torpedo on Christmas Eve of 1944, near Cherbourg, France. Leo was one of the survivors of that famous disaster which took the lives of over 800 American men. After the disaster, and following assignments in France, the Division sailed home on October 27, 1945 and was deactivated on November 8.

Leo returned to New York in early 1946 as a 21-year-old with survival skills under his belt. That left a year-long window in which he may have worked for Frankie running numbers, as Dad had suspected. If that were the case, it would explain how he knew the details of Frankie's disappearance.

These were also the years Dad and Leo bonded. Rae was married to Larry Siegel (husband #4) and he had adopted 10-year-old Mort, who was at home, enjoying a short-lived stint of "perfect family life" in Harrison, New York.

These were also very lean years for the Babchicks. By 1948, all the breadwinners were dead, in jail, or missing. Leo did what was needed to get by and support the family. But the money collecting eventually got him beaten up and thrown from a second-floor window.

After recovering from the fall in the hospital, Leo went on to night school and then, on the insistence of his mother, went into his father's "other" trade as a butcher. It seemed Leo's life sailed a steady course after that point—he married his English girlfriend Miriam and they had two daughters. At the height of Leo's career as a butcher, he was the meat department manager for Key Food supermarkets.

As I created a timeline of Leo's life, Jared told me that Leo had confessed, on his deathbed, that he had worked for Paul Castellano, running several meat departments across Long Island.

Who was Paul Castellano?

Hook-nosed, thin-lipped Castellano or "Big Paulie" had succeeded Carlo Gambino as the head of the Gambino crime family in 1976. Castellano, who considered himself a savvy businessman first and foremost, learned the butcher trade from his father as a young man. One of his earliest businesses was Dial Poultry, a meat and poultry distribution company. Castellano and his sons had a coveted corner on the wholesale chicken market by the late 1960s, distributing to over 300 butchers in New York City.

He was also a vicious murderer. It is alleged, in Mafia lore, that in 1975 Castellano had ordered the murder of Vito Borelli, his daughter's boyfriend, for comparing him to Frank Perdue, which Castellano considered an insult because of Perdue's balding, elderly appearance and his comically awkward mannerisms in his television commercials for Perdue Farms. John Gotti, as a show of allegiance to Castellano, murdered Borelli. All the chicken stuff aside, these were dangerous men.

Dial Poultry was the sole distributor of poultry and meat to Key Foods. Could it have been that Leo, minding his own business, crossed paths with Castellano, who said, "You want chickens? You have to buy from us." Or, who's to say Leo wasn't remembered as the nephew of Abe "Jew Murphy" Babchick. Everyone in the underworld was connected. Castellano was a cousin of Carlo Gambino, and Gambino in his youth had been a member of the Italian and Jewish gang, the Young Turks, which included such members as Frank Costello, Albert Anastasia, Vito Genovese, Meyer Lansky, Bugsy Siegel and others.

We have no way of knowing if Leo was on Dial Poultry's payroll, and saying he "worked" for Castellano may be too heavy-handed. It really doesn't matter. What's telling is that a crime element ran through the family into Leo's generation, on both his mother and father's side.

After 20-years at Key Foods, Leo was laid-off and became a summons server at the age of 59. It was a rough and often scary profession for a man of his age, but Leo never complained. He was one of the most lovable and memorable of the Babchick men. With an incomparable zest for life, he had a wonderful sense of humor and an even deeper sense of honor. In no way did Jared and I want to tarnish his memory, or judge him. Leo was a good man, but underworld involvement may have been the only way he knew to survive and support his family during hard times. It was what he'd grown-up with—running numbers and collecting money for Abe, Frankie, and his own father, Mudsy.

Despite Leo's verve for telling tales about the uncles, a fear permeated the family for decades following Abe's death and Frankie's disappearance. As Leo's children grew up, he remained nervous about past threats to the family. Even 25-years after the fact, Leo sent his daughters to summer camp in the Catskills to get them out of the City. No Babchick descendant should be just hanging around Brooklyn if it wasn't necessary.

Jared had several leads he wanted to follow: he wanted to look through Leo's old papers at his grandmother's house and he wanted to open a large free-standing safe that hadn't been opened in some 30 years. It was stored in the basement of her apartment building. Unfortunately, he found out the super of the building had cleared out the old clutter, and with permission, had tossed the safe. Miriam insisted there was nothing to find in Leo's old paperwork. So, Jared wasn't shown anything, if indeed something still existed.

Cousin Michael didn't believe Leo's connection to Castellano was real. "Leo never ran several meat counters, just one. I think Jared is making this up because he thinks all this gangster stuff is cool."

Needless to say, information continued to come forward. Miriam had confided to a nephew, on her side of the family, that she and Leo had been invited to Castellano's home for dinner. The Gambino crime boss had been courting Leo, positioning him to run the poultry racket in Puerto Rico. Supposedly, Miriam refused to move there and that was the end of it. I believe that Leo was too smart to take the offer. At that point he knew better than to get involved with men of Castellano's ilk.

At Christmas, when some family members gathered at Debbie's house, Cousin Sheila took the opportunity to sit with 86-year-old Miriam and ask her more questions about Leo.

"Miriam didn't want to talk much about the past," Sheila observed when she called me the next day. But Miriam did add to the time line of events, albeit not in the way any of us were expecting.

In 1948, at the age of 18, only a year after arriving in the U.S. from England, Miriam had met Leo, whom she described as "charming, outgoing, and good looking, too!"

Miriam divulged that while engaged to Leo, in 1949, Larry Siegel (Rae's husband #4) had tracked her down, cornering her in a train station. Miriam had no idea who Siegel was or how he had found her. He angrily warned Miriam what kind of family she was about to marry into and showed her newspaper articles about Abe's death.

What the hell was going on? Siegel was seemingly more and more of a nefarious character. From the Surrogate Court papers I knew that Siegel had tried to sue the family during, and years after, his divorce from Rae was finalized. And oddly, those same court papers showed that Siegel was still living in Rae's home in Harrison, Westchester County, long after the marriage had dissolved. I also couldn't forget Mort's story that Rae had Leo bury money on the estate grounds to hide it from Siegel during the divorce. This had been verified by cousins.

Sheila suggested I write to Miriam and ask her questions directly, as her hearing was fading and phone calls often didn't work well. As 2015 came to a close, I wrote Miriam an email asking her more questions about the Siegel incident and if she knew who Leo worked for when he came home from the war in 1946.

An hour after I hit the "send" button, Miriam responded: "I will say this, and I regret to say it to you because you are descended from the

Babchicks—I think that much of what Larry Siegel told me that day was true. For whatever reasons I have, I have removed myself emotionally from the Babchicks so please don't ask me any more."

She ended her letter with: "I now believe that because of the family history, the past was hush-hush. I remember when you were born and your parents moved from New York to California. Leo loved Morton and they were very close. I think in some way it was your father's way of getting away from the past. I wish you luck and I'm sorry to say I can't help any further."

Miriam had shut me down. There were only two elders remaining in that family—Miriam and Cousin Selma—and Selma had already told me all that she could remember. By the tone of Miriam's letter I had no doubt that she knew something she wasn't saying. The cousins and I were just trying to get to the truth. Whatever it might be, it was the past and I wasn't judging the family for their past actions. I immediately wrote Miriam back, beseeching her to change her mind—or at least write her knowledge down for a future time, after she was gone.

The next morning Miriam replied with a lengthy explanation of her position. She felt Leo had put the Babchick clan before her, and their marriage was not always a happy one. "That family was part of the reason we separated [at one time] because he always put them before me." Miriam claimed the Babchicks did not like her, stating that Rae was especially cruel.

"Regarding my meeting with Larry Siegel, he no doubt wanted me to break up with Leo just to hurt him," wrote Miriam. "He obviously had a bitter grudge against your grandmother and her family, but at the tender age of barely 19, I wasn't remotely interested. I remember that he showed me news articles about the family and a full-page photo of Rae in lacy black underwear under the headline *Sex for Money*."

Miriam said the article reported that Rae had extorted money from Siegel in exchange for sleeping with him. Miriam believed that Siegel's warning to her about the family's criminal past had been true—and Rae had been involved in the sex trade.

"I wouldn't have told you this but you are so determined to push it," Miriam concluded. "By cornering me in the subway, Siegel had wanted to hurt Leo, and I feared he had been trailing us both."

Here were yet more clues about Rae's torrid past. It was starting to add up to be much more than just idle remarks, and I was very conflicted about facing them.

On the other side of this, why would Siegel be so angry with Leo? Aside from burying money, maybe Leo had intervened on Rae's behalf during the divorce. If his beloved Aunt Rae said she needed help with an abusive husband, perhaps Leo had shown up with his buddies and roughed Siegel up.

My father had distinctly remembered the day Leo picked him up from summer camp in 1948, to stay with him, Carol, and Aunt Bertha in Brooklyn. Leo grimly revealed to Mort that Rae was leaving Siegel and the family was worried that Siegel would either kidnap Mort or sway him to speak against his mother during court proceedings. Kidnapping sounded serious, but Larry had adopted Mort in 1946 and was legally his father for three years. Mort remembered that after a highly publicized divorce, the judge ruled in Rae's favor, annulled the marriage, and the adoption was reversed. Siegel—who Dad remembered drugging Rae and having her sign away her money and the property—continued to harass her for up to five years after their divorce. That seemed counter to me, if Siegel had already gotten what he wanted from her.

The research on Leo had morphed into a Rae-Siegel puzzle. Every new piece of information I gathered seemed to lead to yet another conundrum in the Babchick clan history.

I needed to find the divorce trial transcripts. I called both the Brooklyn and Westchester Civil Courts, but was informed that divorce records were sealed for 100 years in the state of New York. That meant I couldn't review Rae's divorce proceedings until I was 87-years-old.

●———●

I dug through Rae's papers again. I was looking for the divorce decree. I knew it was in her vast files somewhere, and hopefully I had just overlooked a trial case number or a trial date—both of which would help me locate that elusive news article on the divorce.

This time, I found something intriguing that I hadn't noticed in her papers before. There was a letter of confirmation from lawyer Maurice Edelbaum to Rae, dated June 1, 1951. Edelbaum was confirming receipt of stocks and bonds from Rae—with series numbers and values—amounting to over $40,000.

I studied the typed glassine page which gave no explanation for the payment. In Grandma's typical fashion, she had saved the letter all those years to remember what her stocks had been. She loved to keep lists of her belongings.

I typed the lawyer's name into a Google search. Maurice Edelbaum had been a top New York Criminal Lawyer working out of Brooklyn, renowned in the 1950s, 60s and 70s for many highly publicized cases. Among his clientele were Mafioso, including Vinnie "The Chin" Gigante, who was charged with attempting to rub out Frank Costello in 1957 and later became the #3 man in the Genovese crime family. To add an even thicker layer of the bizarre to all this, Edelbaum had represented Sam Kovner (my fall guy) during his appeal trial in 1943 against DA Edward H. Levine, for the bookie robbery that sent Kovner to Sing Sing for 15 years.

I couldn't understand why Rae needed a criminal lawyer in 1951, especially one of such magnitude as Edelbaum. $40,000 was a huge amount of money for a single woman in that era to be paying a lawyer. Was someone in the family in trouble? The divorce from Siegel was over by 1949 and the divorce decree showed that Bernard Miesel had been Rae's lawyer in that case, not Edelbaum. Dad was 15-years-old and in a private school upstate—he was not in any trouble. The Surrogate Court case in which Siegel was suing the family was taking place during that time, but she didn't need a lawyer for that. Could the lawyer have been for Rae herself?

I found a second letter, dated October 22, 1952—a year and a half later—addressed to Edelbaum from a huffy lawyer who represented an undeclared party. The lawyer was annoyed about the "silence" in regard to a query of stock for the Scranton Electric Company in both Mort and Siegel's name, which "Rae should have claim to, being Mort's guardian."

Could Rae have possibly been trying to settle some dispute with Siegel to make him go away, even after the divorce was final? By today's standards that $40,000 would have the buying power of $370,543.

I tracked down Edelbaum's daughter, a lawyer herself, who was kind enough to tell me that her father's files were gone, and even though he had some famous cases, client-attorney privilege did not allow his papers to reside at any archive like the John Jay College of Criminal Justice.

I felt exasperated. This whole thing was a mess. Everyone appeared connected in one way or another. I didn't know if Rae's payout to Edelbaum had actually been for a court case or something that was settled out-of-court. There was no way to track the origin of the letter, but something was bubbling under the surface about Grandma Rae that I had to resolve.

32

Winds of Winter

Santa Cruz, Spring 2016

The questions about my grandmother's secretive past seemed to be rising like a tsunami. There was the divorce from Siegel and the scandalous news coverage that accompanied it. There was the mysterious money she paid out to criminal attorney Maurice Edelbaum. There was Aunt Carol's story that she was a call girl, backed-up by Leo's widow, Miriam. And, there was that drawing which resembled her from the Lucky Luciano trial. Going down this path of investigation felt dark. Did I really want to unearth Grandma's secrets? I feared the answers could mean I would have to reexamine how I felt about her and our entire relationship.

I called my sister to talk it through. Valerie had very distinct memories of Rae that I had forgotten. We laughed as we remembered some of her old sayings like, "Don't take any wooden nickels," or "You can love a rich man as easily as a poor man." But the seriousness of the memories lay in what Rae had mistakenly communicated in her conversations.

Valerie recalled how she would often make jokes about hookers. When lounging in her negligee having a lazy day, she would declare, "I've been in bed all day just like an old whore!" At the time it had just seemed to be part of her quirky sense of humor. There was another cousin who had a whole story that when she was young, Rae had taught her how to seduce men, and then set her up with an escort service somewhere downtown. Neither Valerie or I believed that story. But, interestingly, Miriam's nephew had told me their family believed Rae had been a madam. What I did know was that men loved Rae. She had a very disarming charm.

To get to the bottom of all this meant returning to the New York Public Library and the Municipal Archives, where the Lucky Luciano trial papers were held. I needed time to be in New York to do extended research—alone this time. I started to make plans to return for the entire month of June.

Rae's House in Harrison

Cousin Michael emailed me a photograph of Grandma Rae's estate in Harrison. He had driven by it recently, prowling tag sales for his antiques business, and had taken a snapshot.

As long as I had known Michael he had always been fascinated by Rae's wealth and taste, and several times had mentioned her country home. I was surprised that he knew which house it was—the infamous home of Dad's short-lived childhood memories, Rae's sinister marriage to Siegel, and the place where Leo had buried the money during the divorce. Michael also knew the story about the money, but in reverse—Leo had dug-up the money after the divorce. It might be interesting to visit the house on my upcoming East Coast trip. The estate was roughly a 20-minute drive from Michael's home in Greenwich, Connecticut, and it would be a great reason to visit him and his partner as well. I made the suggestion and he invited me to come out to the country for a weekend.

Michael didn't know the exact address of the house, but knew how to get there and suggested we just go. That didn't satisfy the researcher in me. Besides, I wanted to contact the current owner and ask permission to pay them a visit beforehand.

I accessed the Harrison County Clerk records, but there were no addresses listed on the grantor/grantee records. In the countryside of Westchester County, land was based on its bordering roads. The Clerk suggested I trace back the records to see who had bought the house over the years, and then she could identify the exact address. I was able to discern that Rae and Siegel had bought the house on June 5, 1946. Although the purchase was in both their names, I knew it was Rae's money that had bought the property. The land records showed that Larry Siegel moved the house into the name of the Irving B. Lydecker Trust in May of 1949, six months before their divorce was final. That seemed odd. Regardless, I obtained the address on Taylor Lane in Harrison.

Once I had the address, I returned to the current land records and found the name of the present owner, Mr. Armstrong. Easily finding his phone number online, I left a message that my grandmother owned the house in the 1940s and I hoped he might allow me to visit in June.

Mr. Armstrong returned my call the next day. The elderly man was a bit skeptical at first—not sure if I was a scam artist or not—but slowly he opened up, appreciating my forthright answers to his questions. He told me that he bought the house from the Siegels nearly 40 years ago. He didn't know Larry Siegel, only a Gertrude Siegel. He acknowledged the house had been in a trust, but it was a Siegel family trust. He said he would tell me more when we met.

The old man would be happy to walk the grounds with me, but was curious as to what I hoped to find. I dispelled his doubts, letting him know that I just wanted to see where my father had grown-up and the locale of many family stories. I did mention the legend of the buried money and he loved that, laughing aloud and commenting, "I assure you we have never found anything!" Then he asked if Larry was related to Bugsy Siegel. That caught me off guard, but the old man was still chuckling, finding it all very humorous. We set a date for a June visit.

I was curious how the Siegels still owned my grandmother's house in the 1980s, and why Larry had moved the house into a trust in the middle of their divorce. I went online and discovered Irving B. Lydecker was a well-known lawyer in White Plains.

In Dad's biography he recalled Siegel befriending an attorney who gave young Mort a dog he named Nosey. He wrote that he had a crush on the lawyer's daughter, with whom he attended grade school for a short time. Dad had also written that the same lawyer became Siegel's lawyer in the divorce—but Lydecker was not Larry's divorce lawyer. The divorce decree listed Minot & Zasoff as his council.

Who was Gertrude Siegel? I wondered if she might be Larry's sister, since it was a family trust. I wasn't clear what was going on here, but it seemed shady. With everything I was learning I questioned who the hell Larry really was.

$$\bullet\!\!-\!\!-\!\!-\!\!\bullet$$

As I prepared for my month-long stay in New York, Maria called via video to wish me well on the final leg of my journey. We hadn't connected in several months and it was nice to catch up. The real purpose of her call was to let me know she had received a "message" for me from Rae about a man whose name, she said, "was like the famous catalogue—Spiegel." Grandma's message was that she had been "backed into a corner" by this "shiesty catalogue guy." Maria's physical description of the man fit Siegel, but she was concerned that something was off about him.

"You are waiting on a piece of information that you can't get access to," said Maria. "You will find it…and it seems someone wasn't divorced…or a marriage wasn't real…I got a weird feeling about it all, like Rae had to pay someone off…it was all very bribe-ish…her spirit said to *'check the record'*…the catalogue guy has a correlation to Frankie as well."

The message was eerily about Siegel, but only the part about Frankie made sense to me—when Siegel had told the Surrogate Court Guardian that Frankie was "roaming around." I made some notes and filed them away.

33

Winter is Here & It's 90 Degrees in the Shade

New York, June 2016

I landed in New York for my month of research and was greeted by a hotter than average June. The first stop on my agenda was the New York Public Library. I was hoping *The Daily News*, often referred to as the "picture paper of the day," would have the article on Rae's divorce from Siegel. I had to find it. I needed to know more about Siegel and the whole scenario about naming Rae a prostitute during their divorce. The trouble was I didn't know when the divorce hearing took place, only that it was final in November of 1949. With the divorce transcripts sealed by the state for 100 years, the newspapers would be my only printed resource about the scandal.

My simple plan of attack was to start with January 1, 1949 and look through *The Daily News* till I found something. Unfortunately, the paper had several daily editions, and I spent eight hours scanning through microfilm for only two months of 1949.

I returned to the library the next day with a fresh plan of attack: I would look for the article in a different paper that was published only once a day, and then go back to the *Daily News* with the actual date.

I tried *The Post*, but it was not as picture heavy in the 1940s as I had hoped. After three hours I found myself lost in thought, staring blankly at the microfilm monitor. This wasn't working. I looked in the Westchester County papers, where the divorce proceedings actually took place, but no luck there either. Three people had seen this article and distinctly remembered the photos and sensational headline. It existed, but I didn't know where. I needed a break—literally and figuratively.

I went outside to the front of the library on Fifth Avenue, and sat in the shade of a giant stone lion that guarded one side of the massive staircase leading to the library's entrance. I dragged on my cigarette and stared at the throngs of people scurrying about. I knew the article had to be in a picture-heavy paper, but, it also had to be in a paper that ran the kind of stories that were chock full of gossip and scandal. I started to re-play in my mind the many articles on Abe I had collected over the years. Some of them had been laden with descriptions of his character, rather than about the murder itself. Then it dawned on me that the first article I ever found about Abe, in Grandma's secret drawer, was like that—very personalized—and it had been in the *New York Daily Mirror*. That had to be it!

The *Daily Mirror*, which had been stored on 12th Avenue years ago, was now located in the basement of the library. I requested the year 1949, and also the September 1941 issues. I wanted to see what else they had printed about Abe's murder.

When the microfilm arrived I anxiously put it into the viewing con-traption and discovered they had a section called "the day in pictures"— and news articles that were character-driven. I decided to start with the time period surrounding Abe's murder.

I discovered that journalist Arnold Prince wrote about Abe for five consecutive days, reporting that his career had been as "fabulous" as Arnold Rothstein. "A cigarette dangling from his lips, it was 'nothing' for the reputed millionaire policy king to lose as much as $60,000 in a dice game and win back $100,000 the next night, according to his asso-ciates."[1] I was dazzled by the amount of money reported. This was the 1930s and would be considered a huge amount of money even now. Back then it would have been equal to over a million dollars that Abe was staking on his gambling bets.

In one of Uncle Leo's many stories, he had mentioned that when his father Mudsy and other key men of Abe's operation were arrested at the headquarters after the murder, their photos had appeared in the papers as they left the police station 24 hours later. I'd never seen that article until now. Although the quality was horrible, *The Daily Mirror* had run the photo of Mudsy and Meyer Rabinowitz exiting the police station, arms up, trying to cover their faces from the camera flashes and crowd of reporters. This demonstrated just how significant the story of Abe's death had been. Journalists were hounding the family everywhere they went. It also verified that the family read the *Daily Mirror*. The article on Rae's divorce had to be in this paper, but I couldn't get past the articles on Abe. They were filled with fascinating details not covered elsewhere. There were even three separate articles in one day, in different sections of the September 26 edition.

Prince had interviewed friends and acquaintances of Abe's in the Brownsville/Crown Heights neighborhood and gathered some interesting information, the most curious being the reiteration that Abe's power in the gambling/policy/loanshark business spread beyond Brooklyn into Manhattan, North Jersey, and West Philadelphia. The article went on to state that Brooklyn Homicide Chief John J. McGowan and three NYPD detectives flew to Philadelphia four days after the murder to confer with the Philly PD about their mutual in-depth investigations into Abe's illegal rackets. The articles said the police "refused to state the nature of the new lead," and that "several politicians" in the Jersey and Philadelphia areas "were on [Abe's] payroll as protectors."[2]

I was curious what the NYPD hoped to discover in Philly. Maybe they were conferring with bigwigs in that city who also had an interest in assuring Abe never uttered their names to John Harlan Amen or anyone else. I hoped there would be some Philly records I could look through, since the NYPD files had been wiped clean.

I spent the rest of the afternoon reviewing new details about Abe's case. I thought about Maria's messages about "Goldstein," "Philly," and "Fishtown." All roads seemed to lead to Philadelphia. If Frankie was "roaming around," it made sense he would go to a place where he knew people *and* could get a piece of some action if needed, or start up his own.

Mark and Patrick from the 7-Point Star Group had connections at the Philly P.D. They inquired about old records for me, but the replies they received from sergeants were that Philly kept no records before the 1960s. I called the Philadelphia archives. They had no police or DA files. I found it baffling that the oldest police department in the country had no archived records.

I did manage to work my way through half of 1949 in the *Daily Mirror*, looking for Rae's divorce trial article, but never found it. It was time to move on to other research for the moment.

A Day in Harrison

It was a humid day in New York when I happily walked into the air-conditioned Grand Central Station to board a train to Greenwich, Connecticut, to visit Cousin Michael. The 40-minute train ride zoomed past the heat haze of brick high-rises in Harlem, quickly fading to the thick greenery of the countryside. Michael picked me up at the station and we spent the afternoon touring around the town.

The following day we arrived by noon at what had once been Rae's home on Taylor Lane. The sprawling white two-story house was accented with deep red shutters and shaded by flowering bushes and tall trees. The long driveway paralleled a blanket of green lawn and wrapped around to the rear of the house.

The heat and tranquility of the afternoon was almost dreamlike as Michael and I followed the footpath to the front door and rang the bell. The elderly Mr. Armstrong answered with a smile. He and his wife Mary were very hospitable, yet a strange sense of reserve permeated. I tried to walk slowly through the entrance of the house and take in the interior, but he ushered us to the backyard immediately. I could understand his position—he didn't know us—he was guarded, and that put me on guard.

The backside of the house, lined with flagstone paths along the perimeter, segued into an acre of velvet lawns and lush shrubs with dense trees opening to a small, magical forest. It was just as my father had described—venturing through the woods with his dog Nosey by his side, almost 70 years earlier.

Armstrong walked us around the large grounds, explaining the architectural structure of the house and lands. Michael was paying attention, he loved that stuff, but I lagged behind taking snapshots with my iPhone. As we strolled, the old man pointed out that the grounds had once included several acres leading into the forest area, but those had been sold years ago and were now populated by two other homes.

As we wove through the property, I asked Michael where he thought Uncle Leo might have buried the money. Armstrong overheard me. "I've been thinking about that since you mentioned it on the phone. I have an idea." He walked us over to a large grouping of shrubs in a back wooded area and started clearing ivy nestled at the base of a tall tree. Hidden under the overgrowth was a large rusted circular top on the ground's surface, about 24 inches in diameter. He opened it and a rusted black shaft appeared that went deep into the ground. It looked like an old mini oil drum, perfectly concealed. It must have been the spot.

The old man surprised me that he'd copied the land records and wanted to share them with us over cake and coffee. He seemed to feel more at ease, thanks to Michael's excellent job of talking to him about housing prices and Westchester life. He invited us into the solarium and his wife appeared with a platter of pastries and a coffee pot. It was lovely in the sun-speckled glass room, looking over the grounds as we ate and talked. The couple stated again that they had never met Larry Siegel, only Gertrude, who lived in the home with her three sons when they bought the place in 1981. The Armstrongs were certain they had been Larry's wife and children. It seemed Gertrude was not Larry's sister, as I had suspected. Perhaps she was Siegel's new wife and he had adopted her children the way he had adopted Mort?

The land records stated that Siegel had put the house solely in his name in 1949, and then changed it to a trust a few months later. Armstrong looked to me for answers. I explained that Siegel had been abusing Rae and had her sign the deed of the property over to him. "I'm sorry to hear that," the old man said sincerely. Trying to lighten the tone he gestured toward the grounds outside the solarium's sun-washed exterior wall. "Just think, you are looking at exactly what your grandmother saw when she would sit here. We haven't changed a thing."

As we prepared to leave, he showed us his wood-paneled office, which had once been Siegel's, and the front sitting room with a large white fireplace. Since we were sharing old stories, I mentioned my father had memories of the kitchen—though not saying he had been thrown across the room while trying to stop Siegel from striking Rae during one of his rages. I hoped Armstrong would show us more of the house, but he didn't. He walked us to the foyer, pointing out the crystal chandelier, which was original to the house.

We thanked them for their hospitality and shook hands. I looked around, taking it all in one last time, a sense of melancholy pervading. Then I walked out, leaving the ghosts of the past behind.

●———————●

Back in the City, I logged on to Ancestry.com to figure out who Gertrude and these Siegel children were. Research revealed that she married Larry around 1924 and they had three sons. She had been his first wife! They were living on Ocean Parkway in Brooklyn when the 1940 census came out. At the time Larry was 46-years-old. That would make the swarthy Romanian 52-years-old when he married Rae, who would have been only 40.

The story that I was able to piece together was that Siegel and Rae began seeing each other around 1944, and ran off to be married in Reno, Nevada, in December of 1945. The Harrison estate was bought in June of 1946. In 1950, six months after the divorce was final, Siegel moved his first wife and children from Brooklyn into the Harrison house, changing the land record from the Lydecker Trust into Gertrude's name. Larry lived there with his first family, claiming the address as his residence on the Surrogate Court papers when suing the family for Great Grandma Anna's estate in 1952.

Rae would never have relinquished the house willingly. He had certainly stolen it from her. Larry might have gotten back together with his ex-wife after his divorce from Rae, but what woman would move herself and her children into a home bought by the woman she was left for? There had to be more to the story.

I decided to investigate if any of Siegel's children were still alive. Mr. Armstrong had dropped some leads, but I found that all the children had passed away. I did, however, locate the widow of one of Siegel's sons in Connecticut and gave her a call. She was very helpful and spoke with me at length. Siegel's youngest son had not been close with his father. She divulged that Siegel had quite a bit of money later in life. He left the garment trade and started the Hamilton Sterling Corporation in the Bronx, which manufactured fancy perfume bottles, silver trays, and the like. Siegel died around 1960 and left the company to his middle son.

The jaw-dropping moment of the conversation was when the woman said Gertrude and Larry had never divorced and she had never heard of my grandmother.

Was Larry a bigamist? A scam artist? Had he illegally married and purposely taken advantage of Rae for money? Maybe that's why Larry had them marry in Reno, so the two women would never know about each other.

The Siegel scenario was mind-boggling. He obviously wooed Rae—the dashing suitor she had always dreamed of, but he turned out to be the devil himself.

Still, I needed verification of what Siegel's daughter-in-law told me. I knew the divorce transcripts would be confidential till the year 2049, but I called the Brooklyn County Clerk's office to inquire anyway. After being transferred to several different people, I was instructed to send a written request along with a research fee to have them confirm whether a divorce had happened. It would take a couple weeks to hear back.

Frankie's Inheritance

For the majority of my June stay I was residing in a friend's duplex in the West Village. I was on the lower floor, which opened into a large, gorgeous jungle of a garden. A young art conservationist was staying on the upper floor while on an internship with the Whitney Museum.

It was serendipitous that one of her friends was a researcher for a lawyer who found missing heirs. I told her Frankie's story and how I was trying to determine if his inheritance in the City Treasury had ever been picked up. She was anxious to try and help, and called me the following week with useful information.

Any monies that sit in the treasury unclaimed for over five years are moved to the New York State Comptroller's office of Unclaimed Funds. Nothing there was listed under Frank Balzack, his official name on the Surrogate Court papers. Because of this, her office assumed the funds were picked up.

Further information revealed that in order for funds to be picked-up, a petition would have to be made to remove the funds, which meant going to court and having a kinship hearing. Even if Frankie himself had tried to get the funds, he'd have to go to court in Brooklyn and prove who he was. I was told the transcript of a kinship hearing should be filed in the Surrogate Court papers, but there was no hearing recorded in the paper work I had. That would mean the inheritance wasn't picked up. The woman was stumped and had no answer.

There were two simple questions to be answered: Were the funds ever claimed? If so, where is the record of who received the funds and on what date?

The Comptroller's office finally got back to me, replying that they had nothing, claimed or unclaimed, under Frankie's name and were "unable to answer questions."

The Department of Finance had an attorney reply to my Freedom of Information request: "Please be advised that your request has been researched and neither Finance nor our warehouse has any documents responsive to your request. Finance no longer retains the records from the time period you have requested."

Once again, I was left with my questions unanswered. It didn't make sense that issues involving money had no paper trail. If the funds were never picked-up then why weren't they at the Comptroller's office? No one had said there was a statute of limitations on unclaimed funds. I was back to square one. Initially I hadn't cared about the sum of money involved—but now I did want to know where the money was.

I located the name and contact information for a Senior Advisor for Intergovernmental and Community Affairs at the Department of Finance. He returned my call and spoke as fast as an auctioneer. He rattled on that Unclaimed Funds had records going back to the 1940s, but there was nothing under Frankie Balzack or Bebchook—claimed or unclaimed. The Department of Finance, he said, did not have information going back that far, i.e., no paper trail of what may have happened to a disbursement. He suggested I go back to the Brooklyn Surrogate Court for information on guardianship disbursement of funds.

Back in the phone queue of the court I was passed around several times to the Guardianship Department, the Probate Department, Estate Proceedings Department, and finally to the Chief Clerk of the Court, who had no answer for me. I still found it suspicious that there was no record of a money transaction.

Everything was about tying up loose ends at this point, which meant it was also time to check in with Detective Stradford of the Cold Case Squad. He'd had over a year to find the police investigation into Abe's murder. When I called he was talkative, always taking the time to speak with me, but his news was not good.

Abe's murder evidence and paperwork were thought to be in a warehouse location that had been flooded during Hurricane Sandy back in 2012. The City was in a lawsuit with the government to shut it down, but the Feds wouldn't let them. "Many important cases were housed in there," Stratford told me. The City wanted the warehouse destroyed because it had become a breeding ground of pathogens, carcinogens, and rodents. No one was allowed access without a special court order. If by some small chance you were granted access, you would have to wear a hazmat suit, and nothing could be removed. Bottom line: there were still no official records to be accessed about the murder. This had been my last hope to find the police report, and it was now gone.

Luck of the Draw

My last two weeks in New York were spent at the New York City Municipal Archives. I needed to prove—or hopefully disprove—what was suspected of Glamour Granny Rae's past, which was looking less and less glamorous at this point.

It was my third research trip to the Archives in 15 months and everyone knew me at this point. I had written the Director, Ken Cobb, in advance for what I sought and he was ready for me. Nothing moved without him greasing the wheels. Ken assigned Dwayne to supervise my needs. The gangly, 60-year-old ex-basketball player was spunky and humorous, but he talked to himself all day long, which was a big distraction. He didn't really know where anything was, despite the fact he'd worked there for 12 years—his excuse being that there was a conspiracy to keep the data from him—but he was my partner in crime for the next two weeks.

The heat was oppressive. There was no air conditioning in the large book-laden reading room—just a dirty old desk fan attempting to circulate the stagnant air. As a matter of fact, there was no one in the reading room the first week but me. Only the employees milled about complaining of the temperature.

Barbara, who ran the marriage, birth, and death records room, was a wunderkind. She was bright, efficient, and knew where everything was located. With her help, Dwayne and I found Grandma Rae's early marriage certificates and looked through the building tax assessment records, which contained photos of New York City buildings in 1938. They were gems. An old photo of the Lincoln Place headquarters showed a beautiful old Buick sedan in front of the building. I like to think it was Abe or Frankie's, as the photo was taken during the height of their wealth and power. We also found a photo of the family home at 9214

Avenue B. It was three lots in a row, one of which held a large brick house with a steep staircase leading to the front door. It was much fancier than I had expected it to be. It wasn't the 4-room "shack" as described in one of the newspaper articles.

I spent the next six days with Lucky Luciano. Each morning in the sweltering reading room, Dwayne would place the large archival cartons onto a rolling rack for me, ten at a time. Thomas Dewey, Special Prosecutor on the Luciano case, had his staff meticulously detail every iota of information leading up to, and including, the court trail of 1936. There were 66 boxes, each containing 10 to 20 file folders that I needed to look through to prove whether Grandma Rae had actually been part of the Luciano trial or not. I felt the real crime here was no air conditioning in a New York summer.

The Charles "Lucky" Luciano vice trial was the biggest case against a mobster at that time. Thomas Dewey was desperate to nab Luciano, finding the only way to do this was through his vice rings—houses of prostitution. They wire-tapped, interrogated, and hunted these women for over a year, but it wasn't the prostitutes or madams that Dewey and his men wanted. They needed the bookers of the prostitutes, who would then lead them to the higher ranking members, and ultimately to Luciano—the man behind the combination and the mob controlling it.

There were hundreds of prostitutes and madams listed. They were followed, arrested, and interviewed. Fortunately, the files secured their real names as well as their "working" names, so I was looking for anything that would signal it might be Rae. I didn't know what that would be—I just kept reading, and drinking a lot of water to stay hydrated. I read through some "charming" citizen tips to Dewey about vice in various neighborhoods, such as, *"There's an ugly woman named Frenchy, who's running a joint with girls at 345 East 31st Street, and they pay bond money."* These amusing tidbits read like a pulp novel.

Toward the end of day four with Luciano I was feeling pretty sure— and rather relieved—that Rae was not part of this. There were dozens of lists of witnesses that gave statements and ultimately testified, and none of them had descriptions or names—whether real or pseudonyms—that could have been Grandma. I wondered if it was worth my time to keep searching through the endless boxes.

Then, just as I was about to call it quits for the day, I came across a folder of interview notes in the "Trial and Related Materials" box for a Max Pincovitch. I pulled the file merely out of curiosity, due to the similarity to my grandfather's name, Pincus Max Marcus (who was married to Rae at the time of this inquisition).

Paperwork in the file stated that Max Pincovitch worked for a madam in Brooklyn named Rae Sharp. Rae was not a common name for women, especially with that spelling in that era. To make matters even stranger, Rae Sharp's booker was a fellow named David Miller, a.k.a., David Marcus. David Marcus and his wife Ruth's entire history were in the file, and knowing what I did of the Marcuses, there was no relation. Max Pincovitch also had nothing to do with Grandpa Max as I read his background file.

As I shuffled through the papers I came across file folder "111" filled with typed glassine pages of subpoenas that were to be served to over 70 women. Special instructions were attached for the subpoena servers. There, I found a note for serving Rae Sharp. It read:

Memorandum to Process Server—Feb. 3, 1936
Concerning Rae Sharp:

- Rae had a chauffeur and probably still has named Jake Resnick or Jake Weber.
- They drove a Plymouth car, late 1934 model, with license #6L7918.
- Rae Sharp is a madam of several houses of prostitution.
- Rae can be found at Driggs Avenue and South 4th Street in an apartment house; we do not know under what name. She had her stationery printed at the Jaffee Press, 368 Rodney Street near Grand Street Extension. She may have used on the stationery the names of Rose & Gold, Robert Gold, or some combination with the letters R and G.[3]

I felt the pit of my stomach drop. This felt like a sign.

Information on Rae Sharp was recorded in Max Pincovitch's statement, and a few others. Pincovitch was to be a witness against David Miller (a.k.a. Marcus), Rae's booker and a higher-up in the combination being indicted along with Luciano. Pincovitch, a 23-year-old alien who was later sent to Ellis Island to await deportation, had been employed for $7 a week to be Rae Sharp's doorman and take care of various repair jobs at her prostitution houses in Brooklyn. The girls also tipped him a few dollars a week to make sure the guys he let in were "okay."

Pincovitch stated to police that Rae moved houses every few months to avoid being "pinched" by the cops, and had a lawyer named Markowitz who took care of her. According to Pincovitch, the house was making close to $300 a week—a girl charging $1.50 for her services. The girls kept half of what they made, but Rae charged them $25 a week for board, $10 a week for bond insurance, and $8 a week for a doctor who visited the houses. Rae's girls included women named Babe, German Helen, Manhattan Helen, Tiny Mary and Rose Anita.

Pincovitch divulged that in 1935, Rae Sharp had houses at 45 Nostrand Avenue, 141 Hopkins Street and 434 Bedford Avenue. David Miller would supply Rae with girls and then collect 5–10% of their weekly earnings, depending on the receipts. Pincovitch had witnessed Rae pay off David Miller and other bookies, and negotiate percentage terms for her girls. Rae would call Miller to arrange for new girls, or whatever else she wanted. She had 50 to 100 clients a week, and a black book with close to 1000 names in it—all of whom received business cards when her floating houses moved. The printed cards announced that a certain haberdashery firm had moved to a new address. The firm always included the letters "R" and "G," usually "Rose & Gold."

Even more curious, the file contained a page of handwritten notes by the police interrogator that hadn't made it into the final typed report. The scribbles read, "Leo Goldberg or Gold, introduced Pincovitch to Rae at a candy store."[4]

Candy store? Rose & Gold? Could this be the Murder, Inc. headquarters known as Midnight Rose's, run by Rose Gold? It was 1935, and the Brownsville Boys occupied the store as their headquarters during that time, and Rose was their bail bondsman and ran a prostitution ring for the syndicate. The police had no idea who the Brownsville Boys were… yet. It would be close to four more years before they would discover the murder-for-hire ring. Could the calling card be a hint to prospective clients that Rae's establishment was protected by the Brownsville Boys and bail would be supplied by Rose Gold if needed? Could this be a connection between Uncle Abe and Rae's exploits? Suddenly it hit me: Maria had said, "Rose and Gold feels like a cover, not a real person." I didn't understand what she meant at the time, but now it made sense!

Leo Goldberg was not a far cry from Frankie's other aliases. As a matter of fact, I knew the uncles used family name combinations as aliases. Uncle Leo had been Frankie's favorite—could Leo Goldberg have been Frankie introducing Pincovitch to Rae?

Here's what I knew for certain:

- The courtroom drawing found in the Reles FBI File from the Luciano trial looked strikingly like Rae in a unique hat.
- I had a photo of Rae wearing the same style hat as in the drawing, dancing with an underworld character named "Red Bill," circa late 1930s/early1940s.
- Rae Sharp was the only person named "Rae" involved in the Luciano trail.
- Grandma changed her last name several times (not legally) between marriages, but always kept her first name intact (Rae Marks, Rae Shields, etc.).
- Grandma always had a life centered in Brooklyn, having dated or married men associated with her gangster brothers until 1935, when she married Max Marcus and moved to Manhattan.
- In 1934, Grandma had a fancy chauffeur-driven car when she was engaged, and later married, to Max.
- Rae often bragged that she returned to Brooklyn several times a week to care for her mother. Maybe that was her cover.
- Family members, and others, were sure Rae was in the escort business, and some thought possibly a madam.
- Siegel had used the "sex for money" scenario as the lead reason for their divorce.
- A cousin claimed Rae set her up with an escort service in the 1970s.

- Rae knew a lot about sex and how to charm men. It had been her live-lihood—at least in terms of her many marriages.
- Rae had an instructional manual on sex that she kept for 70-plus years. Perhaps it was the text she used to instruct her girls.

By the early 1930s, Abe and Frankie were at the height of their inter-ests, making money and living the high life. Grandma was very close to both of them. Wouldn't she have wanted part of that financial freedom as well? She was ambitious, but with little education what could she do other than marry well. It made sense that she would take advantage of her brothers' connections to get a piece of the action.

I recalled how Grandma always fancied herself a savvy businesswom-an. But what business had she ever been in? The years I knew her—from the age of 65 on—she had started a small dress business out of her apart-ment to supplement her income after her marriage to husband #5 ended. I remembered how she loved business cards and collected them. She would pass out her own card, "Rae Marcus, Distinctive Dresses," often telling me how important it was to have a good calling card for your associates. That was the only job she had ever held—that the family knew about.

If she was Rae Sharp, I had other questions as well:

Would she have continued her "profession" once married to Max? She certainly didn't need the money. Or did she? Max was known to gamble at such high stakes that he often borrowed money from family members when he lost, to get back in the game. Maybe she wanted to keep her independent income flow.

Did Max know about this profession? Or did she only work from time to time, opening and closing her doors, as some madams did? I was pretty sure at this point that Grandma had actually met Max through Abe, i.e., the mutual gambling connection. But, maybe she had met him through this "other" profession.

Pincovitch's testimony included descriptions of the men and wom-en who worked with Rae Sharp. There were descriptions of other mad-ams in the trial files. But, there was no description of Sharp anywhere. I couldn't verify her age or if she physically resembled my Grandmother.

What bothered me most of all was that Rae Sharp had given no actual testimony herself. She was subpoenaed, and was mentioned in others' testimonies, but there was no actual statement from her. She clearly was successful—more successful than other madams recorded in the files—and connected to many of the characters Dewey was trying to nail. Yet, somehow she had been able to avoid giving a statement during the Luciano investigation. Grandma would have been 7-weeks pregnant in early February of 1936. Maybe her pregnancy had been the excuse for not testifying at the trial come June of that year.

If Rae Sharp was Grandma, was she able to evade arrest due to her brothers and their connection to Murder, Inc. and the larger syndicate? Did she pay off the police? Rae Sharp was never arrested, never served time at the Women's House of Detention at Greenwich and 10th streets as 68 other women who had been rounded-up in her profession. She wasn't even on the witness list for the trial. How did she escape this?

I called Mark. How could a subpoena be served to someone, yet there's no testimony? Mark gave several scenarios: She could refuse the subpoena. She might run away, in which case a warrant for her arrest would be served. She could show-up in court and plead the 5th amendment, or, if there were a lot of witnesses—as was the case in the Luciano trial—they may not have gotten to her, or canceled her testimony altogether.

"But I have a drawing with a caption that states that she was a witness who took the stand," I explained.

"Did she?" Mark questioned. "In the drawing do you see her on the witness stand?"

"Well no, it's just from the shoulders up. And it's in a different style than other drawings from the trial that I have seen."

"Ok, so you don't know if she was on the stand. Usually court artists use pencil, and artists from the press use heavy charcoal. She may have been sitting in the courtroom and someone drew her image," Mark suggested, giving me a different perspective.

"Yes! It's like a heavy charcoal drawing!" I exclaimed. "I never understood why Ellen Poulsen, who wrote the definitive book on the trial, had never seen this drawing before. How did it end up in a book about Murder, Inc., buried in Reles' FBI file?"

The origin of the drawing may actually be the bigger mystery here. Was it in Reles' file because they knew she was Abe "Jew Murphy's" sister and a well-known madam?

"Look, you may not know for sure if Rae Sharp was your grandmother or not," Mark concluded, "But when you put on your detective hat you have to weigh the clues. If countless similarities are leaning toward a possible answer, you have to follow it as your best hunch."

I knew Mark was right. There were too many things leaning toward this actually being Grandma. I continued to look through the Luciano papers for another three days, but there was nothing else about Rae Sharp.

34

Where the Sidewalk Ends

"We have other stuff," one of the archivists said to me, as my research was coming to a close at the Municipal Archives.

"What stuff? Other investigation reports?" I asked.

"No, we have objects," the archivist replied with a mischievous grin.

No objects were listed in the Murder, Inc. collection inventory, but my pals at the Archives shared that they had "Kid Twist" Reles' suitcase, which contained the blanket and bedsheets the police claimed he used to climb out the window to a 40-foot drop.

Did I want to see them? *You bet!*

Two days later, waiting for me on a table in the reading room, was Reles' suitcase wrapped tightly in white archival paper. I had brought along my friend Kevin Baker, who had written a fictional version of the Reles murder in his book *The Big Crowd*, and was a New York history aficionado. We stared in awe for several moments at the large white package as if it were a sacred object, a monumental piece of history, the holy grail of mob lore.

Together, we carefully unwrapped the thick paper until the suitcase was revealed. String was wrapped around the disintegrating leather, holding it together—its corners crumbling in our cotton-gloved hands. Faded stickers of the Cunard White Star to Europe emblazoned one side reading "Tourist Class." Inside, the case was lined in forest-green plaid fabric. A divider separated the deeply stained wool blanket imprinted with the words *American Hotel Corporation* from the bed sheets (which were a deep rust color from the FBI testing kit). There was also a thick, white cotton weave blanket with pink trim, that had been ripped and tied together as a makeshift rope. We lifted them out, one by one, and examined them. Actually touching objects and documents, realizing that they represented real people and real events, is what makes this kind of research so rich. I couldn't help but wonder if Reles had really tied them together himself or if it had been part of a staged crime scene.

Kevin and I rehashed our theories about Reles' death. District Attorney Burton Turkus pointed out in his retelling of the case in his famous book, *Murder, Inc.—The Story of the Syndicate,* that most of the common theories didn't pan out. It was clear that Reles had been murdered—not falling while trying to escape, as the most popular theory claimed. We agreed the murder had to have been committed by someone who had enough clout to walk past the downstairs and upstairs police details, threaten the guards if they happened to wake-up or catch a glimpse of him, and have enough muscle to throw Reles out the window.

Homicide Chief John McGowan appeared the most likely suspect. He had the title, the brawn, and the power to threaten the detectives. And, McGowan had never preserved the crime scene, collected evidence, or conducted interviews with the guards or hotel staff. Considering the reputation McGowan once had as an investigator, why else would he have done such a negligent job if it weren't to cover for himself…or someone else?

McGowan had initially concocted the theory that Reles was trying to escape, but that theory was bogus. Everyone involved knew that Reles was terrified of Mob retaliation if he were to be out in the open, and he was nervous even in the protected sealed suite. McGowan's theory then morphed into the story that Reles had been trying to play a prank on the guards by lowering himself to the room below and planning to come up the stairs to surprise them—but he fell instead. McGowan came up with this new theory after the hotel manager went to inspect the room directly below Reles' and discovered that the window was open, the screen was torn, and there were several black scuffmarks on the sill.

As blameworthy as McGowan appeared—and who Kevin felt was the culprit—I took the theory one step further. DA Chief Clerk James J. Moran had the ultimate authority to have committed the Reles crime—or at least make sure it happened. He was O'Dwyer's right hand man and in charge of Reles at the Half Moon Hotel, having assigned Captains Bals and his detail to protect him. Moran had even greater power than McGowan—he might have sauntered into the suite at any time. Police Sergeant Elwood Divvers, who ran the Reles detail under Captain Bals, had testified during the 1945 Grand Jury inquisition that "the general feeling in the DA's office was that Mr. Moran was practically the spokesman for the District Attorney, and the police officers took their orders from the Chief Clerk."[1]

It had been Moran who told Bals to call McGowan the morning Reles' body was found, to help him and DA Edward Heffernan with the crime scene. Moran even admitted during the second investigation in 1951, that he had removed items from Reles' room early that morning.

And, as I had learned, Moran was the link between the DA's office and the underworld bosses.

Moran, along with McGowan, Bals, and Heffernan, was deeply indebted to O'Dwyer for his career path. They were all loyal to O'Dwyer—and to each other. In the end they all may have thought they were making decisions to protect their comrades, but it is more likely that McGowan and Moran, who had the ability to make people and documents disappear, were orchestrating commands given by the Mob itself.

Most likely it was Moran, as Mob liaison, who orchestrated the hit for two reasons: to stop Reles' testimony against Cosa Nostra boss Anastasia, and also, to get the last of the lower level Jewish gangsters out of the picture. When Reles turned state's evidence, and "Lepke" Buchalter and many of the Murder, Inc. members were headed for the electric chair, they had all become a doomed commodity to be connected to the Mafia, and had to be eliminated.

Moran was also known to extort money from racketeers, being "a cynical grafter of unbounded greed." He was tough, insensitive, and a "thoroughly corrupt politician who relentlessly hounded subordinates suspected of holding out on him."[2] He, McGowan, and Heffernan had long, documented histories of corruption. These men were either directly involved, or inexplicably linked, to every corrupt police investigation I had read about from 1932 to 1946—and they were directly in charge of Uncle Abe's murder investigation.

On the night of September 24, 1941, following Abe's murder, McGowan raided Abe's policy headquarters on Lincoln Place, along with two detectives who later would be on the Reles detail. McGowan created the story that Abe's murder was a robbery gone wrong—just as he had concocted the Reles theory. He made sure that Sam Kovner was arrested, and even testified against him at his robbery trial—and probably made sure that "The Killer" Beitler was permanently quieted in the Times Square shoot-out, to become the easy fall guy in several cases.

Moran and McGowan could have been covering their own tracks in regard to Abe's murder, protecting their names from going public on Uncle Abe's "list." But the "list" included names going even higher in rank than the DA and Police Commissioner's offices, directly to Mafioso and politicians Abe paid homage to—just like Reles.

With Reles' death just seven weeks after Uncle Abe's, I was convinced there was a powerful connection between the two cases.

The old saying "third time's a charm" was the hope when Cousin Jared suggested we go back to Lincoln Place one more time, before my stay in New York was over. On the first trip we hadn't stayed long enough to search through the basement. On the second trip we came close to unearthing where the satchel and paperwork were located that Maria envisioned, but couldn't open the ancient dumbwaiter door before the neighbors became suspicious.

Jared still believed the evidence was there. So did Maria. She remained certain of its location. When Valerie and her son Zach, now 12-years-old, jumped at the chance to go to the old racket headquarters, I agreed we should give it one last attempt.

I decided to call the landlord this time, making the visit legitimate. At this point we had nothing to lose if he said no. Much to my surprise, he loved the idea of an old mystery in the building and was happy to let us in. "Have at it!" he suggested enthusiastically. He gave us permission to do what we wanted in the basement, "...as long as you take responsibility if you tear out a wall or something." *I wasn't planning to tear down any walls.*

I spoke with Maria at length and drew maps of exactly where she said to look. She planned to join us via video call on location to help navigate—which was probably best, since she had such violent reactions when there.

●———————●

Accompanied by Mark, Jared, Valerie, and Zach, I met up with the landlord's handyman, Freddy, in front of Lincoln Place. He was there to supervise and help if needed. Small birds were chirping and flittering through the empty lot next to the building. Without Maria's psychic attacks happening, the area seemed peaceful in the morning sun.

Freddy, a thick-accented Latino, unlocked the black gate and led us down the steps. Dozens of flies buzzed over open garbage cans lining the narrow alleyway to the basement door. Everything was filthy, and combined with the summer heat, it reeked. Inside, we passed the laundry room to the left, and Freddy opened the locked doors to the separate storage areas. He thought the dumbwaiter was located in the security camera room, covered by sheetrock.

"That's the dumbwaiter," I said, pointing further down the hallway. It had a giant "A" painted on its cover. That's when it struck all of us that there were probably two dumbwaiters to service the building in the old days. Dumbwaiter "A" was for the front of the building. There was obviously a dumbwaiter "B" someplace. Nonetheless, our group planned to search where Maria had directed us to go.

We decided to divide and conquer. The guys started on the empty lot, searching with a metal detector where Maria had mapped the location of a ring or watch that belonged to the uncles.

Valerie and I put on masks and long gloves, and ventured into the small storage room to the right of the entrance, where Frankie had been beaten. We called Maria via Facetime. She directed us to the back corner of the room, where a large rusted sewage pipe was protruding and ran the length of the wall. There were many cracks and openings between the crumbling mortar and bricks.

Valerie started to carefully chip away where Maria instructed. She was filled with determination. She scraped, picked, and dug at the bricks and mortar, brushing away the dust by the light of our headlamps and a small LED pen. We used a camera scope, that connected to my laptop, and jammed it into the crevices to see what was between the bricks. We were excavating like archeologists on an ancient dig. Bricks were crumbling, dust flying, the thick stench of mold filling the air.

Maria saw an apparition of Frankie standing near us, disheveled and exhausted, and started to feel nauseous from what she sensed was a foul smell. Thirty seconds later, Valerie and I smelled gas. My fully charged phone battery drained to nothing—a sign of spirit activity—and Maria's transmission was abruptly disconnected.

Freddy, watching soap operas on his smart phone in the laundry room, came in to check for a gas leak. As we waited for his inspection to conclude, we leaned against the interior wall which was parallel to the outside steps. Although it was brick, we noticed it had a different sound when we knocked on it. It was hollow! Excitedly, we started knocking up and down the length of the perimeter wall and agreed that this must be the "false floor" or sublevel leading to the empty lot that Maria had channeled from the very beginning.

The handyman gave the okay that there was no gas leak and we continued to dig, pecking away at the hollow wall and trying to find an opening for the scope. We found only old newspapers that had been stuffed between the bricks for insulation. The area had obviously been rebricked and something could have been behind it, but unless the building was demolished we were never going to see in back of it.

Over an hour had passed and the guys had dug with shovels through a ten square foot area on the empty lot. They found lots of stuff—keys, Atlantic City tokens, a toy police badge—but nothing of prominence.

With our spirit of adventure still high, we all moved to the back storage room, the guys donning masks and gloves to finally open the dumbwaiter.

Our flashlights streaked across piles of junk—broken glass, doors and window frames strewn about, rusted paint cans, mildewed cardboard boxes atop each other—there was trash in every square inch of the place. Carefully we stepped across the garbage, cobwebs whipping our faces as we cleared a path to the dumbwaiter door.

The decaying ceiling above the dumbwaiter had large gaping holes leading into darkness. Old wooden boards and rusted pipes jutted out in all directions. We poked through the ceiling holes with the camera scope, but found only shredded pieces of garbage and rodent droppings leading into a vast void.

We removed junk from the adjacent brick shelf that lined the back wall and Valerie crawled up on it, looking for crevices around the dumbwaiter. There were no openings. The area was sealed with cement. As rack and ruin as the place was, there were few crevices in the walls of this area.

Jared and Mark used crowbars to yank the dumbwaiter's front door off its hinges—a cloud of dust particles and tumbling bricks crashed down as the metal door swung open. A long decrepit rope, that once wheeled the contraption up and down, unraveled like a snake. Mark hoisted the dumbwaiter several inches from its stationary position while Jared shone a light to look underneath.

"I see something! I see something like paper!" Jared exclaimed, reaching down into the darkness of the shaft. His arms were covered in black soot as he lifted out old candy wrappers. He reached into the blackness again with the camera scope, Zach navigating its path on the laptop, but there were only large cockroaches scurrying about. Mark let the dumbwaiter go and it crashed back into position within its metal and wood structure.

Crawling into the narrow shaft, Mark searched the crevices above and behind with the camera scope, but it was too dark to see. Exasperated, Mark started tearing apart the structure piece by piece with sheer force, his headlamp bobbing through a heavy fog of dust.

"Be careful. Maria warned someone might get hurt trying to remove it," Valerie heeded.

"Yeah, yeah...enough already," Mark declared, and continued ripping the wood frame of the dumbwaiter out of its casing.

"I've waited for over a year to see what's back there," Jared chuckled with glee. Through buffeting clouds of gray ash, they both yanked and tugged—heaving the bottom out first, then the metal sidings, and finally dismantling the entire casing until the brick wall of the shaft was exposed.

The shaft rose one story and then was sealed with cement. There was no mysterious paper waiting for us. No crevices. No leather clutch. Nothing.

"This is so disappointing," Jared sighed.

"Well, at least we can say we gave it our all," replied Mark, shaking a thick layer of powder from his clothes.

Everyone was feeling rather crestfallen as we prepared to leave. As I watched them pack up a different feeling come over me—one of pride and deep satisfaction. We were all together. Jared, Valerie, and I were the generation that had pried open the secret story of our ancestors. Our day of digging through the rubble really wasn't about whether we found something or not—it had been about being together, in the place where this chapter in our family history had started some 80 years earlier. Zach, the new generation, would always remember this day at Lincoln Place. For me, that was almost reward enough. We were the storytellers who would carry this adventure into the future. It was a circle that somehow felt complete.

"Maybe at one time something was here. Even Leo had thought something was here," Jared hypothesized as we walked toward the car.

"Well, it's gone with the ages at this point," I replied, looking back at the building one last time. I knew I would not be returning to this place of enormous family history again.

We decide to lunch in the neighborhood, and gathered around a large table at a Mediterranean eatery on Franklin Avenue.

"So, who was Uncle Abe and what really happened in that building?" asked Zach. He wasn't aware of the extensive hunt that had taken place over the last two years.

Jared leaned across the table toward him. "Your Great Great Uncles, Abe and Frankie, were very smart men who made a lot of money to support the family when they came to America. They were what's called racketeers. They were Jewish gangsters."

"Whoa…," Zach slid down in his seat, his eyes becoming large as Jared explained a numbers policy, who Abe Reles was, how the headquarters were used to count and stash money, and hold records—like what we had been looking for that morning.

"One night, Abe won a huge amount of money gambling at a crap game," Jared continued. "He hid his winnings, then went to have a late supper with his men at a restaurant right near here." Jared looked to me to pick up the story.

"Abe was wanted by the Attorney General for questioning about who he was paying off to keep his illegal gambling ring going. We believe that he met with Attorney General John Harlan Amen that night and gave him a list of names—from cops to politicians. It was a list that ultimately led to his demise."

"Why? What happened?" Zach asked eagerly. He was mesmerized by the story in much the same way that Valerie and I had been when listening to Dad's stories.

"The police were afraid Abe would give them up," Mark jumped in. "So they followed Abe that night and kidnapped him. They probably didn't realize that he had already given their names to the AG before they snatched him."

"I'm pretty confident at this point who abducted him," I continued. "Most probably Homicide Chief John McGowan, Edward Heffernan of the DA's office—ordered by Clerk James Moran –and cops named Connor and Beine. They threw Abe into a police car and took him to an abandoned area, that we discovered off Van Sinderen Avenue on the outskirts of Brownsville, where they interrogated and then killed him."

"The cops then staged a crime scene a few miles away," Mark continued. "Putting Abe's body back into his own car, positioning him on the passenger seat, and then drove him to Empire Boulevard and left him there. There were no cell phones back then. A car radio would have only been in the police car, so the whole thing had to have been planned out beforehand."

The storytelling quickly turned to theorizing, as Jared suggested, "I think they left Abe and his car on Empire Boulevard because it was down the street from the 71st precinct. They were going to be the cover for the 69th. We know detectives from other precincts worked together, especially to cover something up."

"The cops left Abe's body and car on Empire Boulevard because they were sending a message to anyone who might rat them out – '*keep your mouth shut or this will happen to you, too.*'" Mark said.

"It's clear that law enforcement at the highest levels was involved with the Mafia, which meant Uncle Abe and 'Kid Twist' Reles were aware of the authorities who were taking bribes and possibly doing the bidding of the Mob," I concluded. "Patrolmen may have taken the bribes from local bookies, but the payments were going all the way to the top of the food chain. If Amen needed Abe to testify against high-ranking officials, such as the DA's office, the Police Commissioner's Squad, or even higher, they would do whatever was necessary to conceal themselves."

"Yes," agreed Mark. "Since Abe worked with Reles, they must have known the same incriminating information. Think about it—'Lepke' Buchalter was on trial. Reles was in custody. Abe was out there on his own—the partner who got away with everything. For the cops it was too dangerous having him on the streets."

"That's why he was killed?" Zach asked anxiously.

"The motive was more than just the list of names Abe had—it was for all the knowledge he possessed of who was doing what," I answered. "Abe's death may have been a warning to Reles to keep his mouth shut from testifying against Cosa Nostra Albert Anastasia. Or, perhaps, the authorities were sending a message to John Harlan Amen, blocking his investigation by taking out his two most important witnesses. Amen was too close to the truth, and the authorities were letting him know they were willing to kill the two Abes and anyone else who could trace the DA's association back to Anastasia and mob boss Frank Costello."

"That's the key—and the link is Reles," said Mark, nodding his head. "Their deaths were signs of just how far the authorities were willing to go to stay clear of Amen's investigation. It was a warning to everyone."

"And let's not forget that Frank Costello was reorganizing Tammany Hall," I interjected. "He had Senator Michael J. Kennedy elected leader of the Democratic organization, who in turn made sure O'Dwyer was elected mayor. During the Kefauver Committee Hearings, it came out that O'Dwyer placed gangsters in city jobs...hell, O'Dwyer was publicly fighting the mob as a cover for Anastasia and Costello. Everyone was interconnected. And that's what Uncle Frankie knew as well. Uncle Abe's 'list' had been a deadly possession—a secret that held fatal consequences for anyone who knew its contents."

Mark agreed. "It's important to remember that underworld activities can only exist with the participation of corrupt officials at the highest levels."

I looked at Zach, "...and their deaths officially remain unsolved murders to this day...but we did a pretty good job of unraveling it, uh?"

"That's the story," Jared nodded. "Leo had hinted at this, and now we know why the family was so scared—they had nowhere to seek protection from the authorities."

"This is crazy!" exclaimed Zach. "This is for real?"

"This is part of our legacy, kiddo," Valerie responded, putting her arm around him. "Great Uncle Frankie, the cowboy, was really Abe's enforcer. Being the older of the two brothers, Frankie may have been entrenched in the whole underworld architecture long before Abe."

"He sure loved the family though," added Jared. "I find the most amazing part of his story was that he fearlessly pursued Abe's killers and then vanished."

"The whole thing is tragic," I responded with a long exhale. "We'll never really know if Frankie ended up at the bottom of the Gowanus Canal or not."

Swept up in a tornado of corruption, the Babchick brothers and Reles had known too much—about everyone. The family's code of silence was finally broken and the scenario was as complete as we could make it at this point. Although we never found the missing documentation or satchel at Lincoln Place, the "list" had been the final, lethal piece of information that had ended their lives and erased them from the history books.

We were all quiet for a moment as the massive weight of it all sank in. I put my arm around Mark and kissed his cheek, then reached out to the others, squeezing their hands. "I can never thank you all enough for your help on this."

35

The Departed

The next day, I received a reply from the Brooklyn County Clerk. It was a notarized copy of a microfilm document that read at the top, "Gertrude Siegel vs. Laurence L. Siegel." The original 1940s handwriting was in shorthand and full of illegible words. I couldn't discern what it was saying, but I didn't see the word "divorce" anywhere.

I called the County Clerk for a translation. When the gruff manager came on the phone he declared, "Oh, you're that researcher from California, right?" My reputation had preceded me at this point. I said I needed help deciphering the document they had sent. He didn't have access to 1940s files nearby, so I emailed a photo of it to him while we were on the phone. He was silent as he retrieved the document from his email. Then, with emphatic New York attitude, he replied, "You should have never received this document, Lady, it's confidential. Sealed for 100 years from the date."

I explained that I understood I couldn't see a divorce transcript, I only wanted a "yes" or "no" answer if a divorce had taken place. He let out several long sighs as he weighed what to do. "Well the damage is done," he finally answered. "Let's see what it says."

The document was a copy of the Clerk's minutes during proceedings between Gertrude and Siegel. On April 13, 1945, Gertrude filed for alimony. On three other occasions that year the Siegels met in court. On May 7, an affidavit was ordered denying motion to re-argue the alimony. On May 16, Siegel appealed the motion. On July 9, it seems the Appellate Court ordered that alimony be paid to Gertrude. I knew that Siegel then married Rae five months later, in December of 1945.

Nothing else was recorded on the docket until six years later—November 2, 1951—when an affidavit and order for permission to reexamine the whole case was listed. There was no mention of a divorce.

The clerk told me that one could receive spousal support without a divorce. I asked if this was the only record on file for Gertrude and Larry—could there be a divorce listed anywhere else? "This is it," he answered. "It appears that they started a procedure and stopped it. There is no record or mention of a divorce having ever been granted."

The official answer: Siegel was a bigamist.

Usually in cases of bigamy the second marriage is considered illegal and invalid, yet Rae and Siegel were in divorce court. I may not have learned what the $40,000 in stocks to attorney Edelbaum was for, but I now knew the startling truth: the "scandal" wasn't about Rae being a prostitute. It was that Siegel had another wife and family. No wonder Max Marcus went to the trouble to appear in court to testify on Rae's behalf. I believe that Siegel, who had officially adopted Mort in 1945, was using his guardianship as a means to threaten Rae. That may have been the reason for $40,000 in stocks to flow through Edelbaum—to pay Siegel to reverse the adoption. The second letter from the attorney in Grandma's papers back-up that theory.

All of this brought me back to the message that Maria gave me before I left for New York: "Either someone wasn't divorced or the marriage wasn't real." Once again, Maria had been correct before I even knew what she meant. I still wondered why Gertrude would move in to a home Larry had lived in, and bought, with an illegal wife. Either she never knew about Rae, or it was a scam they were both part of from the beginning.

My Grandmother Rae. What a baffling and convoluted life she led. Rae used men all her life, and the one man she had truly loved used her. It was a bitter irony.

Her life once seemed so idyllic in old photographs. When I was young I thought I knew her so well—a tough, Yiddish-spewing socialite of Central Park South. But I hadn't known her at all.

Learning the truth behind her relationship with Siegel was disturbing, yet also enlightening. Her jaded ways and distrust of everyone, which had most probably originated from the murder of her brothers, had been cemented with the horrible betrayal and extortion she experienced in her marriage to Siegel. Then again, because of her mistrust, she had attracted the betrayal she feared the most. Now I could understand that her overprotective and judgmental behavior toward me was her way of shielding me from the evils of the world as she had known them—but it had come across as erratic and punitive. Still, this new information didn't forgive the horrible things she had done over the years to me and to other members of the family.

Rae had been a charismatic narcissist, much like my grandfather Max. In many ways they were perfect for each other. They both sought money and status above all else, living extraordinary lives and making selfish choices. Desperately searching for a way into the American establishment, they bulldozed anything that got in their paths, which included "correct" established values and the law. However, the price of their actions came at the cost of those who loved them, especially their children.

Was she the Madam Rae Sharp? All roads lead to that conclusion. At first I thought I should be ashamed. But then I realized that women had very few options in the 1920s and 30s to establish themselves independently—you either married well, became a teacher or a nurse, went into domestic service, or worked at a factory. Working women, who were a very small portion of the population, only made half of what men did back in those days, with an average pay of about $500 per year. Then there were the illegal jobs like prostitution, which were a thriving industry. During the depression people were desperate for work and family roles were changing, which gave women a certain power. Rae wanted a piece of the good life, saw what her brothers had achieved and wanted in. They would never have let her be a call girl, but she certainly had the chutzpah and drive to manage a stable of call girls. Financial freedom was paramount to her. Never again would she be that barefoot girl playing on the railroad tracks of a dusty Ukrainian village.

Rae's temperament had softened in her old age, trying to make up for those lost years with Mort, and she attempted to be present and caring.

Although the Rae I knew was a difficult woman, I can't forget or lessen the fact that she did have a great sense of humor and could be wildly fun at times. We had just as many laughing fits together as we did arguments. Whatever her life had been, she was my grandmother and I loved her. And I wanted to be loved by her.

My journey into the family history had started with Rae, and it seemed it was ending with her. She was the sun that every story revolved around. With my 21st century lens I've tried to see all the family for who they were, foibles and all. Rae, Abe, Frankie, Leo—they all did what they thought was necessary to have a better life. There was collateral damage, but every decision they made—from the tenements of Brownsville to Central Park South—became the life I have today.

Many truths had been revealed on this trip, and I realized that what hadn't been found might never be known. I had taken this hunt as far as I could. It was time to go home…to California.

I had never forgotten the old tale Valerie had recalled, that mysterious red roses were left on Abe's grave weekly, for several years after his death. Before I left New York I felt it was important to mark the end of my journey by returning to Abe's resting place to pay my respects, and in many ways, say goodbye. I decided to purchase a dozen red roses from a flower stand in Manhattan and then boarded the Long Island Railroad to visit the old Montefiore Cemetery. It was a workday for everyone in the family, so I asked Mark to join me.

I settled in for the 20-minute ride, the increasing rhythmic churn of the train wheels becoming hypnotic as I stared out the window. It had been heartbreaking to lose my father before this quest was completed— he would have loved the adventure—but the greatest gift Maria had given me was the assurance that Dad's spirit was guiding me the entire time.

Abe, the well-dressed policy mobster breaking the bank at Chinatown crap games, was reflected in my mind's eye like Sky Masterson from *Guys and Dolls*—all fancy suits, wads of cash, and flirtatious grins. Frankie, a lovable tough-guy who took the kids to Coney Island for pony rides and drove a convertible through Brooklyn whistling a tune, was his Nathan Detroit.

But in reality, a gangster's life is tumultuous, filled with paranoia and a gritty sense of survival-of-the-fittest. What I most respected about the uncles—unlike Rae and Max—is that they never pretended to be anything other than what they were. Abe and Frankie didn't fool themselves into believing their way was righteous. They knew their lives were dangerous, and maybe that danger was a thrill unto itself. They were now on the other side of the guns. They had been the victims in the old country, but in the New World, they were in charge of their own lives—living fully in the moment by their own rules and taking care of those they loved. Although the uncles were not angels, to me they were the true family heroes.

Formal documentation will never be found as to who pulled the trigger that ended Abe's life or who was responsible for Frankie's disappearance. Almost every trace of the brothers had been erased—records destroyed or conveniently lost—and I will have to live with that. And while there can be no going back in time to bring to justice those who deserved to be held responsible, I had to remember that we all face the consequences of our decisions and actions, and maybe, just maybe, justice is naturally meted out in the end. Irrefutable facts of what happened 75 years ago probably don't matter anymore. Dad used to tell me that part of being alive is the search for answers, trying to solve unanswerable mysteries. My journey has been the experience, not the conclusion.

I felt deeply connected to this side of the family in a way I never expected. Now I understood them and held in my heart an appreciation for who they were.

As the elevated train clacked into the Locust Manor station in Jamaica, Queens, Mark was waiting for me at the end of the platform under a gray, overcast sky. It was a perfect day to visit a graveyard.

"This is not a good neighborhood," he warned me in his usual, protective fashion, scanning the surrounding area below the elevated train stop.

It was rather hectic getting to the cemetery location. I felt a bit guilty at first, dragging Mark along this crazy route, but he shook his head at me. "I've been on this journey with you for so long, I need to say goodbye to Abe as well."

The wind was picking up as we walked under the large arched brick entrance to the necropolis. It had been almost ten years since I'd visited the Babchick plot at Montefiore. That trip, with Dad and Valerie, had revealed a neglected old burial ground, sad and forgotten, with ramshackle dry brush and weeds. As Mark and I walked through the cemetery it was now green and fertile with flowering cherry blossoms and burgeoning shrubs. Thousands of black headstones were shoved firmly together, tipped left and right, with intricate engravings of stars, birds, hearts, etched Hebrew writing, and eternal flames reaching to the heavens.

As we made our way to the family plot location, Mark tapped my shoulder. "Look at that," he pointed toward a row to the left. "It looks similar to your family name."

A headstone with an elaborately scored curtain and tassels on the top portion, followed by Hebrew writing and a large Star of David, read "Morris Bobechook—Died Sept 26, 1930, age 57 years—Husband, Father." It was my great grandfather's grave. I had never been able to locate it, and now I knew why—The family name, once again, was spelled differently. And the date was wrong. Morris's death certificate had recorded September 24 as his death date—the same day as Abe's, but eleven years earlier.

The Babchick Monument, where Great Grandma Anna and Uncle Abe's footstones lay in its shadow, was one row over from Morris's headstone. Anna's grave covering was bare, with only small patches of grass. But much to my surprise, a thick green bed of ivy and plants was thriving on the full length of Abe's plot. Ten years ago this plot had been parched and dry. The current abundance of greenery seemed to indicate a contented acknowledgment, as if Abe's spirit was saying thank you.

I've learned that the dead do talk…if you listen. They reach out to tell their stories. Abe and Frankie had taken me on a journey to discover their stories, and it had become akin to a spiritual pilgrimage, a quest that had spanned half of my lifetime. Now that journey was coming to an end.

The surprising flood of emotion I felt left me weak as I knelt next to Abe's footstone and tears welled up in my eyes. I unwrapped the red roses and placed them on the hard, pale stone. I didn't want to say good-bye—neither to Abe, or the connection with my father that this journey had helped keep alive.

Mark was investigating the hidden scripture at the base of the monument, moving the ivy back and reading aloud, "The stars may fade, the sun grow dim, but you shall always be remembered."

As I ran my hand across Abe's name carved on the stone, I felt a merging of the past and present. The family's history had become a microcosm of human history. In the beginning, I had questioned if my great grandparents' journey from the Old World to the New stopped with them or continued through me. I could now see that I had not been just a relentless researcher, but an active participant in their ongoing story, carrying into the future their hopes and dreams. Each step I had taken was recognition, and also a memorial, for those who were no longer here. No, I didn't have to say goodbye, "…for whatever lives in them of me, the dream begins right here,"[1] my father had written in a poem to me and Valerie. Yes, they were each a part of me and always would be. They are my line of blood.

We took photographs and slowly walked through the tranquil cemetery. Trying to lift my melancholy state, Mark suggested we go back to the city for drinks.

Later, sitting at a crowded bar, we ordered Manhattans. There was an empty seat to my right, yet somehow I felt compressed, elbowed in my seat. We were not alone. Abe, Frankie, Leo, Mort and Rae—they were all present. I could feel them and for a moment thought that I could see them sitting across from us, their sleeves rolled up, laughing, drinking, and kibitzing.

Mark handed me a glass. The entire city seemed to be floating on the surface of the heavy red liquid, buoying back and forth. He smiled, with that familiar gleam in his eye. "Here's to Abe, Frankie, and the whole family."

Uncle Abe

By Morton Marcus

1.

By silent agreement, no one in the family
is allowed to speak his name—
this uncle, short and nondescript
with round face and rubbery nose,
who lived with them in 1941.
His handsome suits—dark brown
and banker's gray—though elegant
did not attract the young boy's gaze
as did the metal eyeglass frames
flashing from behind his ears
and circling his pale blue eyes
in channeled streams of gold.

Each day he shaved with the boy.
Without his gold-rimmed glasses,
he squinted at the bathroom mirror
as if trying to discern the shape
that lumbered toward him
through the steam. The boy's razor
was empty, a gift from this uncle
against the day when he became a man.
But the uncle's razor cut both ways,
and he left one day with a jaunty wave,
never to return, hauling his hand
and everyone's memory of him
out the door.

Six years later,
when the boy is twelve, he dreams this uncle
stealing through the bedroom window,
less a prowler than a Santa Claus.
"There was this man," he tells his aunt.
"He wore glasses made of gold
which flashed in the dark…"

But he gets no further than that,
for his aunt staggers against the icebox
and clutches her heart. Even the big uncles,
who never look down but stride past shops
with everyone staring at their backs,
twitch when he mentions the name,
as if they were punched in the chest,
and weep as they walk down the street
without wiping the tears away.

2.

"Yes," says Cousin Leo at the handball court,
"but never mention him to your mom,"
and he brings the shaving memories back
when he tells the boy the story.
By silent agreement, no one in the family
is allowed to speak this uncle's name:
he was Abe, just Abe, the name shortened
in America, no longer biblical,
no longer recalling the patriarch
who must sacrifice his son
until an angel sent by God
at the last moment intercedes
and proclaims a covenant
by which Abraham's descendants
shall be as numerous as the stars
and the nations of the earth
shall consider themselves blessed
to have his heirs as citizens.

Abe's angel, it turns out, was Irish
or Italian, and interceded

with two bullets in the back of the head
to separate him from his life
and from the one hundred thousand
he was carrying from a poker game.
Abe, "the policy king of Brooklyn,"
ran a numbers racket on his own,
employing more than two hundred men,
and controlled two restaurants on the side.

For eight years he ruled the family,
while the old man, ill, huddled near the stove.
Streetwise and intelligent, this uncle
banked millions under aliases
he entrusted to no one, refused to marry
because sharing a life such as his,
he told his mother, was unfair to any woman,
and gave away at least as much money
to brothers, beggars, charities, and friends
as he did to judges and cops.

Eventually the police unearthed the satchel,
but not the money or the triggerman.
The newspapers call this uncle an example
of "the immigrant's dilemma,"
and label him "a modern Robin Hood."

All this means nothing to the family,
who cannot understand why one so kind
should be cut off so young.
To them he remains uncle, son, and brother,
whose name they remember but refuse to say.

3.

Who were you, Uncle? The newspapers
say one thing, the family another.
Did family tradition lead you to the rackets,
some fly speck in your chromosomes
that swarms through me? In another time
would you have followed the life of the mind
toward which your gentle eyes inclined?

Or did you pursue the same pragmatic hopes,
stripped of morality, which drove the old man
from the snows of southern Russia
to the tenements of New York?

Questions addressed to the wind
come back on the wind unanswered,
and the only words anyone remembers
you saying—"If you want something
from someone, kiss his ass.
When he wants something from you,
he'll kiss yours"– tell nothing,
provide only a momentary glimpse of you,
and, ironically, like your life and fortune
and the circumstances of your unsolved death,
by balancing both phrases, rub themselves out.

In time the family accepted your death
as a corrupted New World version
of your biblical namesake's life,
where the angel sent by God arrived too late,
and where you were son and father both—
father to your short-lived youth.
There was also the fear,
an almost palpable foreboding,
that whoever did the killing
would come back to annihilate
brother, nephew, aunt—the entire family,
one by one—like an avenging angel
whose mission no one could comprehend.
As a result, the family agreed
that no one would speak your name
or seek the ones responsible for your death,
hoping that would end it, and it did.

Now you are a picture in a scrapbook—
those brooding eyes, that relentless stare.
And when a nephew or a grandchild
come upon your fading photograph,
you are identified as someone who died young
and left no son to intercede for him.

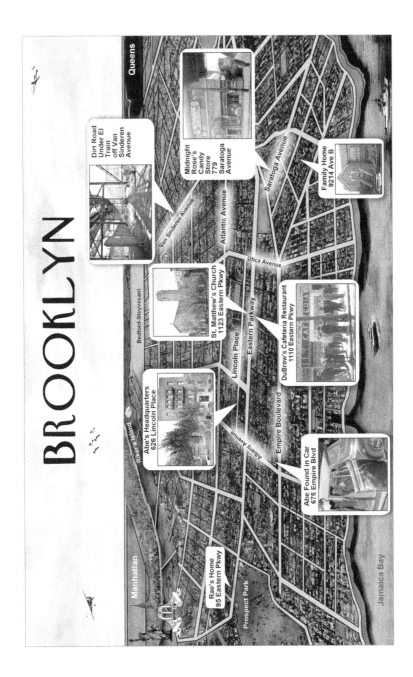

BROOKLYN

Dirt Road Under El Train off Van Sinderen Avenue

Midnight Rose's Candy Store 779 Saratoga Avenue

Family Home 9214 Ave B

Queens

Van Sinderen Avenue

Atlantic Avenue

Saratoga Avenue

Bedford-Stuyvesant

Utica Avenue

St. Matthew's Church 1123 Eastern Pkwy

Eastern Parkway

Lincoln Place

DuBrow's Cafeteria Restaurant 1110 Eastern Pkwy

Rikers Island

Abe's Headquarters 626 Lincoln Place

Albany Avenue

Empire Boulevard

Abe Found in Car 675 Empire Blvd

Manhattan

Rae's Home 95 Eastern Pkwy

Prospect Park

Jamaica Bay

345

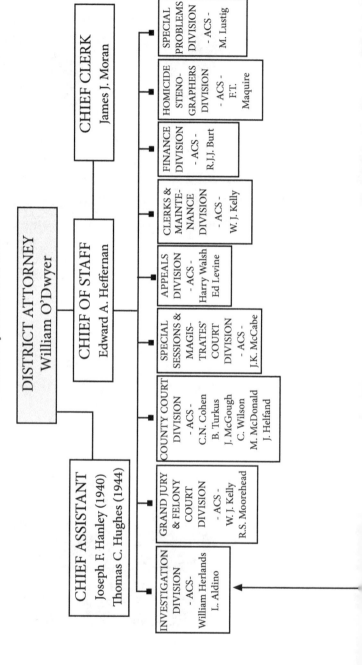

**Organizational Chart of the
Brooklyn District Attorney's Office - Kings County**

Select List of Postions 1941–1945

DISTRICT ATTORNEY
William O'Dwyer

CHIEF CLERK
James J. Moran

CHIEF OF STAFF
Edward A. Heffernan

CHIEF ASSISTANT
Joseph F. Hanley (1940)
Thomas C. Hughes (1944)

SPECIAL PROBLEMS DIVISION
- ACS -
M. Lustig

HOMICIDE STENO-GRAPHERS DIVISION
- ACS -
F.T. Maquire

FINANCE DIVISION
- ACS -
R.J.J. Burt

CLERKS & MAINTE-NANCE DIVISION
- ACS -
W. J. Kelly

APPEALS DIVISION
- ACS -
Harry Walsh
Ed Levine

SPECIAL SESSIONS & MAGIS-TRATES' COURT DIVISION
- ACS -
J.K. McCabe

COUNTY COURT DIVISION
- ACS -
C.N. Cohen
B. Turkus
J. McGough
C. Wilson
M. McDonald
J. Helfand

GRAND JURY & FELONY COURT DIVISION
- ACS -
W. J. Kelly
R.S. Moorehead

INVESTIGATION DIVISION
- ACS-
William Herlands
L. Aldino

Key NYPD Police

POLICE COMMISSIONER
Lewis J. Valentine, 1934–1945
Arthur W. Wallander, 1945–1949

Louis Costuma	Chief Inspector
William T. Reynolds	Deputy Chief Inspector, Brooklyn West (1941)
Michael A. Wall	Deputy Chief Inspector, Brooklyn East (1941)
John J. McGowan	Deputy Chief, Homicide (1936, 1940–46)
Harry Lobdell	Deputy Chief Inspector of Detectives, 11th Division
John J. Ryan	Asst. Chief Inspector
Howard O'Leary	Captain (Abe's investigation under Reynolds)
Abraham Brody	Captain, Coney Island Station (Fox case)
James McNally	Captain (Malinski/Fox cases)
Cuthbert Behan	Lieutenant, Prospect Park Station & Canarsie
Robert Bowe	Detective, Brooklyn Homicide Squad (Beitler Death)
Hyman Levine	Detective, Manhattan (Beitler Death)
Charles Celano	Detective, Homicide Squad (Reles/Malinski cases)
William Cush	Detective (Reles Death)
Frank Sarcona	Detective (Abe's Murder, Druckman Case)
Francis Carney	Patrolman, 10th Division (Raid on Abe's Headquarters)
Edward McGowan	Patrolman, 71st precinct (Beitler Death, Abe's Murder)

DA'S SPECIAL INVESTIGATION SQUAD (1940–1945)

Captain Frank Bals
Lt. Maurice Gaughran

Reles Detail:
Srgt. Elwood Divvers
Det. Victor Robbins
Det. James Boyle
Det. John E. Moran
Det. Harvey McLaughlin
Det. Francesco Tempone

Malinski Case:
Capt. James McNally
Det. James A. Bell, Jr.

SELECT OFFICERS NAMED IN AMEN INVESTIGATION

Chief Harry Lobdell
Charles Jeffrey
Lt. Cuthbert Behan
Robert E. Connor
John E. Kelly
James Sweeney
Francis Carney
Lawrence Bein
Harry McDonald
Patrick Connolly
John Sweeney
Harry McDonald

Sources: Burton Turkus Papers, 1945
Brooklyn Eagle, Dec. 30, 1939

Acknowledgements

Over the many years of investigating and writing this book there have been more people to thank then I can count, but I give my deep love and heartfelt appreciation to the following people:

My dedicated research team—without them this adventure could have never happened and the journey never completed.

Mark Basoa, a great friend who listened to my stories for years, always jumped in to help with humor and new perspectives, and lent his keen police knowledge to every situation.

Eric Sassaman, whose brilliant mind for research techniques was priceless. His love of the subject matter and midnight brainstorming sessions helped me stay enthusiastic.

Maria Saganis, whose gifts are beyond measure. She added a whole new layer to the investigation and endured much physical pain to bring the truth of this story to life.

Amy Scott, who lived with this story and its cast of characters for many years. Her unwavering interest and unending patience, support, and love, during long periods when I never left my computer or countless times I flew off to New York, gave me the foundation needed to complete the family mysteries.

Greg Larson, who spent many months working on the manuscript with me, helping me to dig deeper in order to shape its contents to have greater meaning.

My mother and step-father, Wilma and John Chandler, who have been enormously supportive in countless ways, and spent much of their spare time reading, line editing, and making suggestions to the manuscript.

My sister, Valerie Marcus Ramshur, for hours of xeroxing and research, for always digging her heels in when something was needed, and being a sounding board for my theories.

Many thanks to the archivists whose work is invaluable: Ken Cobb, Commissioner of Records at the New York Municipal Archives, who always took the time to keep searching and answered my endless questions and emails—and to his wonderful staff; Ellen Belcher, Special Collections at the Sealy Library, John Jay College of Criminal Justice for sharing treasures with me; Allyson Malinenko of the Brooklyn Collection at the Brooklyn Public Library for her help researching photos.

I am indebted to the following people who leant their knowledge, expertise, and time:

Julie and Patrick Callahan, Detective Wendell Stratford, Kristen Vaughan, Ellen Poulson, Emery Hudson, Katherine Ramsland, Kevin Baker, Jory Post, Joe Ortiz, Michael Tubis, Sheila Diamond, Deborah Gentile, Jared Ostrov, Susan Mayer, Kaitlin Vaughan, David Adler, Stacy Horn, Mary Planding, Theresa Skovera, Anne Kopilak, Jim Aschbacher, Lisa Jensen, Kirby Scudder, and Max-the-Cat, whose companionship got me through many long nights of writing.

I owe much gratitude to the following people who took the time to read and comment on the manuscript in its early form, giving me their keen perspectives: Jim Eckhart, Steve "Spike" Wong, Paul Kantrowich, George Ow, Jr., Mary Planding, Ron Slack, Clifford Henderson, Kathy Chetkovich, Brian Spencer, Ron Johnson, Jr., Patrick Callahan, and Rob Bielfeldt.

Paul Kantrowich, Liz Meryman, Mark Robinson, Mark Williams, Justine Mercado, Hilary and Patrick Kelly, and Maureen Loftus for their support of the Brooklyn adventures on many levels. And, to all the donors of the video adventure: Martha Macambridge, Carter Wilson, Karen Long, Camryn Manheim, Wilma Chandler, Brian Taylor, Tommy Marquez, Lyle Blake, Greg Larson, Bonnie Ronzio, Marc Luettchau, Donna Gorman, Susan Myer, Jamilah Vittor, Topsy Smalley, and others…you know who you are. Thank you for believing in me and this story.

Special thanks to George Ow, Jr., who makes dreams come true. He has been at almost every important moment in my creative life and made the Brooklyn video adventure a reality—as well as eagerly listening to the stories of Uncle Abe, first from my father and then from me.

Lastly, this book would have never even been a thought if it wasn't for my father, Morton Marcus, and his wonderful stories and constant encouragement. He inspired this journey and the short story that came out of it in 2009. He was my original co-investigator and has guided me through the years—both in this world and the next. Thank you for learning to communicate through Maria…*we were listening.*

Bibliography

Government and Archival Sources

United States. Congress. Senate. Special Committee to Investigate Organized Crime in Interstate Commerce. (1951). *The Kefauver Committee Report on Organized Crime*. New York. 1951.

New York City Department of Records. New York Municipal Archives. Murder Inc. Case Files, 1929–1966. People vs. John Doe. Boxes 6–16.

People vs. John Doe, working file: time chart of events #195.

"Nathan Katz: Information regarding his criminal activities and associates," Captain Frank Bals: Miscellaneous Papers, Murder, Inc. Files, Box 17, Folder 1.

Working file: Michael A. Wall. Box 12 #192. Statement #46817.

People vs. John Doe, Grand Jury Presentment

People vs. John Doe, Newspaper clippings. Box 10 #73.

People vs. John Doe, Police Disciplinary Hearings, 1941. Box 10 #76.

People vs. John Doe, Police Investigation, 1941, 1951. Box 10 #77

People vs. John Doe, Case Files, 1929–1966. Box 10

New York City Department of Records. New York Municipal Archives, Murder Inc. Subject Files, 1906–1959. Box 17.

New York City Department of Records. New York Municipal Archives. Manhattan DA's Papers. Lucky Luciano Trail Materials. 1933–1938??

Extraordinary Grand Jury Subpoenas , Oct 1935–Feb 1936.

Series III: Trial and Related Materials, Box 1, Folders #1–12; Box 6, Folders 54–71.

Series III: Trial and Related Materials, Box 27, Folders #298–311:c Defendant: Marcus, David, witness Pincovitch, Max, Nov. 1935–Dec. 1936.

Burton B. Turkus Papers, Lloyd Sealy Library, Special Collections, John Jay College of Criminal Justice, New York, N. Y.

New York City Department of Records. New York Municipal Archives. Civil Lists, 1938, 1941, 1945.

Kings County Investigation, Report 1938–1942, by John Harlan Amen, Assistant Attorney General in Charge. Albany State Library.

Kings Co., N.Y. Grand Jury. *A Presentment Concerning the Enforcement By the Police Department of the City of New York of the Laws Against Gambling.* April,1942. Presented by John J. Bennett, Jr., Attorney General and John

Harlan Amen, Assistant Attorney General. *Criminal Justice in America.* New York: Arno Press, Reprint Edition. 1974.

Kings Co., N.Y. The People of the State of New York vs. Samuel Kovner, #27059, Brooklyn Law Library.

Office of the Westchester County Clerk. Grantor/Grantee Land Records. Town of Harrison Assessment Report.

Kings County Surrogate's Court. Anna Babchook Estate, 1948–1955. #5256-48

Kings County Clerk's Office. #3917 Gertrude Siegel vs. Laurence Siegel Affidavit. #261008.

Kings County Office of the Medical Examiner. Case Number #3263, File Unit September 24, 1941. Box 90, Shelf 207982, Bush Terminal. City of New York Department of Records.

New York Supreme Court. The People vs. Luciano. New York Association of the Bar Library. Vol 8423

Federal Bureau of Investigations. Abe Reles File. Freedom of Information Act. Bound, print-on-demand. Filiquarian Publishing. LLC.

Franklin D. Roosevelt's Message To Congress Urging The Arming Of American Flag Ships Engaged In Foreign Commerce. October 9, 1941.

Newspapers

Brooklyn Citizen, 1941
Brooklyn Daily Eagle, 1933–1960
Chicago Tribune, 1941–1946
The Daily Mail, Hagerstown, MD, 1941–1946
New York Daily News, 1941–1952
New York Daily Mirror, 1941
New York Herald Tribune, 1941–1946
New York Journal-American, 1941- 1946
New York Post, 1940–1951
New York World-Telegram, 1941–1946
New York Sun, 1941–1943
New York Times, 1930–1968
The Post-Standard, Syracuse, NY, 1946
Trenton Evening Times, 1941

Articles

Phillip Weiss,"George Soros's Right-Wing Twin," *New York Magazine*, July 24, 2005.
<http://nymag.com/nymetro/news/people/features/12353/>
"Murdered By Mistake in His Hour of Triumph," *The Oregonian*, 1942.
"The 'Secret' Tunnel Beneath the 1909 Police Headquarters at 240 Centre Street," <http://www.boweryboogie.com/2015/10/secret-tunnel-beneath-old-police-headquarters-240-centre-street/>

Online Resources

Ancestry.com
Wikipedia: Arthur W. Wallander, Jewish Legion, Kefauver Hearings, Tammany Hall

Peoplefinders.com
https://hatchingcatnyc.com/2013/11/01/pigeons-nypd-air-services-chase/

Dialogues/Interviews

Carol Hecker, 1988, 2002, 2006, 2007, 2009
Leo Hecker, 1988, 2002
Carol Kramer: Correspondence on James Moran, 2016
Abe Kovner: Interview 2007
Willy Marcus, 2007
Selma Malberg, 2008
Susan Mayer, 2008
Ellen Poulsen, 2015
Stanley Rothstein, 2007
Catherine Siegel, 2016
Mickey Sunkin, 2007
Thelma Ward: Interview on Abe Reles, 2015

Books

Block, Alan. *East Side West Side: Organizing Crime in New York 1930–1950*. New Brunswick, NJ: Transaction Publishers, 1983 edition.
Capone, Deirdre Marie. *Uncle Al Capone: The Untold Story From Inside His Family*. Recap Publishing, 2012.
Cohen, Rich. *Tough Jews: Fathers, Sons, and Gangster Dreams*. New York: Simon & Schuster,1998.
Coons, Philip M. *Letters Home: From a World War II Black Panther Artilleryman*. iUniverse, 2012.
Critchley, David. *The Origin of Organized Crime in America. New York: Routledge, 2008.*
Donati, William. *Lucky Luciano: The Rise and Fall of a Mob Boss*. McFarland, 2010.
Downey, Patrick. *Gangster City: The History of the New York Underworld 1900–1935*. Fort Lee. NJ: Barracade Books, 2004.
Elmaleh, Edmund. *The Canary Sang, But Couldn't Fly*. New York: Sterling Publishing, 2009.
Finkelman, Paul, editor. *Encyclopedia of American Civil Liberties*. New York: Routledge, 2013
Fried, Albert. *The Rise and Fall of the Jewish Gangster in America*. New York: Revised Morningside Edition. Columbia University Press, 1993.
Friedman, Bill. *30 Illegal Years To The Strip: The Untold Stories Of The Gangsters Who Built The Early Las Vegas Strip*. CreateSpace Independent Publishing, March 22, 2015.
Friedman, John S., editor. *The Secret Histories: Hidden Truths That Challenged the Past and Changed the World*, New York: Picador, 2005.
Hanson, Neil. Monk Eastman: The Gangster Who Became a War Hero. New York: Alfred A. Knopf, 2010.
Hortis, C. Alexander. *The Mob and the City: The Hidden History of How The Mafia Captured New York*. New York: Prometheus Books, 2014.
Howe, Irving. *World of Our Fathers: The Journey of the Eastern European Jews*

to America and the Life They Found and Made. New York: New York University Press, 30th edition, 2005.

Johnson, Claudia Durst. *Youth Gangs in Literature*. Greenwood Publishing Co., 2004.

Joselit, Jenna Weissman. *Our Gang: Jewish Crime and the New York Jewish Community, 1900–1940*. Bloomington: Indiana University Press, 1983.

Lardner, James, and Thomas Reppetto. *NYPD: A City and Its Police*. New York: Owl Books, 2000.

Marcus, Morton. *Pages From a Scrapbook of Immigrants*. Minneapolis: Coffee House Press Books, 1988.

Marcus, Morton. *Pursuing the Dream Bone*. Quale Press, 2007

Marcus, Morton. *Striking Through The Masks: A Literary Memoir*. Capitola: Capitola Book Company, 2008.

Poulsen, Ellen. *The Case Against Lucky Luciano: New York's Most Sensational Vice Trial*. Clinton Cook Publishing Corp., 2007.

Reppetto, Thomas. *American Mafia: A History of its Rise to Power (1st ed.)*. New York: Henry Holt and Company, 2004.

Reppetto, Thomas. *Shadows Over The White House; The Mafia and the President (1st ed.)*. Enigma Books, 2015.

Rice, E.E. *Murder, Inc.* Zebra Picture Books, 1949.

Rockaway, Robert A. *But He Was Good To His Mother: The Lives And Crimes of Jewish Gangsters*. Jerusalem: Gefen Publishing House, 2000.

Sifakis, Carl. *The Mafia Encyclopedia*. 3rd Edition, Checkmate Books, 2005.

Smith, Richard Norton. *Thomas E. Dewey and His Times*. New York: Simon & Schuster, 1982

Turkis, Burton B., and Sid Feder. *Murder, Inc.: The Story of the Syndicate*. Cambridge: Da Capo Press, Paperback Edition, 2003.

Walsh, George. *Public Enemies: The Mayor, The Mob, and the Crime That Was*. New York: W.W. Norton & Company, 1980.

References

Chapter 1: The Secret Drawer

1. "Neighbors Ignorant of Babchick's Racket," *New York Daily Mirror*, 26 September 1941, p. 29

Chapter 4: The Glamour Girl & The California Kid

1. "Bullets for Breakfast; The Mobster Died at Dawn," *New York Daily News*, September 25, 1941, p. 1, 4

Chapter 6: The Little Professor, Kid Twist & The War For Brownsville

1. Irving Howe. *World of Our Fathers: The Journey of Eastern European Jews to America and the Life They Found and Made* (New York: New York University Press, 1976), p. 170
2. "Racketeer Slain Near Brooklyn Police Station," *New York Herald Tribune*, 25 September 1941, p. 20
3. Alan Block. *East Side West Side: Organizing Crime in New York 1930–1950* (New Brunswick: Transaction Publishers, 1983), p. 223
4. Jenna Weissman Joselit, *Our Gang: Jewish Crime and the New York Jewish Community, 1900–1940* (Bloomington: Indiana University Press, 1983), p. 152
5. Patrick Downey. *Gangster City: The History of the New York Underworld 1900–1935* (Fort Lee: Barracade Books. 2004), p. 237
6. Patrick Downey. *Gangster City: The History of the New York Underworld 1900–1935* (Fort Lee: Barracade Books. 2004), p. 241
7. Albert Fried. *The Rise and Fall of the Jewish Gangster in America.* (New York: Revised Morningside Edition, Columbia University Press. 1993), p. 125
8. "Racketeer Slain in Auto," *New York Herald Tribune.* 25 September, 1941, p. 20
9. "Reles, 11 Face Court In Mayor's Cleanup," *Brooklyn Daily Eagle.* 31 January 1940, p. 2
10. "Reles, Held As Vagrant, Posts $1000," *Brooklyn Daily Eagle*, 29 January 1940, p. 3

11. Turkis & Feder. *Murder, Inc.: The Story of the Syndicate* (Cambridge: Da Capo Press Paperback Edition 2003), p. 332
12. Ibid
13. Author interview with Thelma Ward, 2015.

Chapter 7: The Man Who Would Be King

1. Morton Marcus. *Pursuing the Dream Bone* (Quale Press. 2007), p. 15

Chapter 8: Trail of Blood, Part 1

1. "Amen's Key Figure Slain," *New York Journal-American*, 24 September 1941, p. 1
2. "Bullets for Breakfast: The Mobster Died at Dawn," *New York Daily News*, 25 September 1941, p. 4
3. "Gambler Slain to Seal Lips Amen Hints; Paid 20 Cops," *New York World-Telegram*, 25 September 1941, p. 1
4. Ibid
5. "2 Men Took Bebchick For Ride, His Aid Says," *New York Daily News*, 27 September 1941, p. 1
6. Murray Davis, "Kings' Police 'Take' Put At $500,000. Slaying of Babchick May Hasten Charges," *New York World-Telegram*, 27 September 1941. p. 1
7. Ibid.
8. Ibid.
9. "Amen Declares Break Near in 'Slush' Probe," *Brooklyn Daily Eagle*, 27 September 1941, p. 1
10. "Tipsters Called on for Aid in Solving Bebchick Murder," *Brooklyn Daily Eagle*, 29 September 1941, p. 3
11. "Amen Asks Info on Babchick," *New York Post*, 29 September 1941, p. 2
12. Ibid.
13. "Amen Seizes Brooklyn Court Calendars As He Widens Inquiry Into Corruption," *New York Times*, 3 December 1938, p. 1, 3
14. "Amen Uncovers Wide Graft Data; 2D Jury Ordered," *New York Times*, 7 January 1939, p. 1

Chapter 9: Mystery Road

1. "5 Sentenced in Policy Racket," *New York Herald Tribune*, 10 February, 1942, p. 21

Chapter 10: Trail of Blood–Part 2: Everyone's Going Down

1. Alan Block. *East Side West Side: Organizing Crime in New York 1930–1950* (New Brunswick: Transaction Publishers, 1983), p. 116
2. "Thug Ends life After Wild Dash," *New York Times*, 20 October 1941, p. 25
3. "Guards Demoted In Reles Escape," *New York Times*, 14 November 1941, pgs. 1, 48
4. "Reles' Guards Demoted," By Irving Lieberman, *New York Post*, 13 November 1941, p. 1, 4

5. Franklin D. Roosevelt to Congress, Message from the White House, December 8, 1941

Chapter 12: Trail of Blood, Part 3

1. Kings Co., N.Y. "The People of the State of New York vs. Samuel Kovner," #27059, Brooklyn Law Library.
2. Ibid.
3. "Orders Thug To Name Gambler's Killers," *New York Times*, 12 February 1942, p. 17
4. "Name Bebchick Killers 'or Else' Court Tells Thug," *Brooklyn Daily Eagle*, 12 February 1942, p. 3.
5. Phillip Weiss,"George Soros's Right-Wing Twin," *New York Magazine*, July 24, 2005. <http://nymag.com/nymetro/news/people/features/12353/>
6. Ibid.
7. "3 Convicts' 'Love Life" Financed By State, Malinsky Jury is Told," *Brooklyn Daily Eagle*, 18 June 1946, p. 1, 7.
8. "Singing' Convict Repeats Today at Malinski Trial," *Brooklyn Daily Eagle*, 25 June 1946, p. 1.
9. "Malinski 'Singer' Squawks Frame-up," *Brooklyn Daily Eagle*, 19 June 1946, p. 2.
10. "Admits Urging Pay For State Witness," *New York Times*, 20 June 1946, p. 46.
11. Ibid.

Chapter 13: Brooklyn's Finest

1. "Bullets for Breakfast: The Mobster Died at Dawn," *New York Daily News*, 25 September 1941, pgs. 1, 4
2. Elmaleh, Edward. *The Canary Could Sang But Couldn't Fly. The Fatal Fall of Abe Reles, the Mobster Who Shattered Murder, Inc.'s Code of Silence*, (New York: Union Square Press/Sterling. 2009), p. 76
3. Ibid.
4. Ibid, p. 103
5. <https://en.wikipedia.org/wiki/Tammany_Hall>
6. James P. McCaffrey, "O'Dwyer Accused By a Grand Jury of Laxity in Office," *New York Times*, 30 October 1945, p. 1, 10
7. Block, Alan *East Side West Side: Organizing Crime in New York 1930–1950*, (New Brunswick: Transaction Publishers, 1983), p. 113
8. "Abstract of Bedlock's Jury Presentment," *Brooklyn Daily Eagle*, 21 December 1945, p. 13
9. Norton Mockridge and Robert H. Prall. *The Big Fix*, (New York. Holt. 1954), 112–113
10. Reppetto, Thomas. *American Mafia: A History of Its Rise to Power,* (New York: Holt Paperbacks, Reprint Edition, 2005), 227.
11. Friedman, Bill. *30 Illegal Years To The Strip: The Untold Stories Of The Gangsters Who Built The Early Las Vegas Strip.* (CreateSpace Independent Publishing, March 22, 2015)

12. Norton Mockridge and Robert H. Prall. Ibid
13. Block–Ibid. p. 121
14. "Highlights of a Week of Crime-Busting," *Brooklyn Daily Eagle*, 18 March 1951, p. 8
15. Ibid
16. "O'Dwyer Unnerved in Clash with Probers, Asks Recess," *Brooklyn Daily Eagle*, 19 March 1951, pgs. 1, 9
17. "Excerpts From O'Dwyer's Testimony on 7th Day of Senate Crime Group's Hearings Here," *New York Times*, 21 Mar 1951, p. 28
18. "James J. Moran, 66 is Dead; Jailed in '52 City Kickback Case," *New York Times*, 6 January 1968, p. 29

Chapter 16: Suspicion

1. "Six Crimes Baffle Brooklyn Homicide Squad: Are They What You'd Call Perfect, Insoluble?" *Brooklyn Daily Eagle*, 18 July 1943, p. 4

Chapter 20: Back to the Future

1. "Biography of Morton Marcus." www.mortonmarcus.com, produced by Paula Mahoney for Comcast TV. Originally air date 2005.

Chapter 23: We Know Who You Are and We Saw What You Did

1. Morton Marcus. *Pages From a Scrapbook of Immigrants*, (Minneapolis: Coffee House Press Books. 1988), p. 55

Chapter 26: O Brother, Where Art Thou?

1. Kings County Surrogate's Court. Anna Babchook Estate, 1948–1955. #5256-48. Report of the Special Guardian, November 24, 1953. p. 2
2. Ibid. Correspondence from Hoover to Skolnick, October 27, 1953.
3. Ibid. Report of the Special Guardian, November 24, 1953. p. 6
4. Ibid

Chapter 27: My Cousin Jared

1. Morton Marcus. *Striking Through The Masks: A Literary Memoir.* (Capitola: Capitola Book Company. 2008), p. 26

Chapter 28: New York Noir, Redux

1. Jonathan Lethem. *Motherless Brooklyn*. (New York: Vintage Contemporaries, 2000).

Chapter 33: Winter Is Here & It's 90 Degrees in the Shade

1. Arnold Prince, "Key Man in Brooklyn Gambling Ring Slain; Long Sought By Amen," *New York Daily Mirror*, 25 September 1941, p. 5
2. "Hunt Slayers of Babchick Out of Town," *New York Daily Mirror*, 29 September 1941.

3. New York City Department of Records. New York Municipal Archives. Manhattan DA's Papers. Lucky Luciano Trail Materials. Extraordinary Grand Jury Subpoenas, Oct 1935–Feb 1936.
4. Ibid., Series III: Trial and Related Materials, Box 27, Folders #298–311: Defendant, Marcus, David, witness Pincovitch, Max, Nov. 1935–Dec. 1936.

Chapter 34: Where the Sidewalk Ends

1. James P. McCaffrey, "O'Dwyer Accused By a Grand Jury of Laxity in Office," *New York Times*, 30 October 1945, pgs. 1, 10
2. "James J. Moran, 66, is Dead; Jailed in '52 City Kickback Case," *New York Times*, 6 January 1968, p. 29

Chapter 35: The Departed

1. Marcus, Morton. *Pages From a Scrapbook of Immigrants*, (Minneapolis: Coffee House Press Books. 1988), p. 123

CPSIA information can be obtained
at www.ICGtesting.com
Printed in the USA
LVHW050328230720
661336LV00001B/267

9 780983 343431